Trigger Warnings

Trigger Warnings

TEACHING THROUGH TRAUMA

Edited by

Ian Barnard, Ryan Ashley Caldwell,
Jada Patchigondla, Aneil Rallin,
Morgan Read-Davidson, Ethan Trejo,
and Kristi M. Wilson

Afterword by Anu Aneja

LEVER
PRESS

Lever Press (leverpress.org) is a publisher of pathbreaking scholarship. Supported by a consortium of higher education institutions focused on, and renowned for, excellence in both research and teaching, our press is grounded on three essential commitments: to be a digitally native press, to be a peer-reviewed, open access press that charges no fees to either authors or their institutions, and to be a press aligned with the liberal arts ethos.

The complete manuscript of this work was subjected to a partly closed ("single blind") review process. For more information, please see our Peer Review Commitments and Guidelines at https://www.leverpress.org/peerreview

DOI: https://doi.org/10.3998/mpub.13074989
Print ISBN: 978-1-64315-089-5
Open access ISBN: 978-1-64315-090-1

Library of Congress Control Number: 2025935161

Published in the United States of America by Lever Press, in partnership with Michigan Publishing.

Front cover painting by Sebastián Chillemi. Used by permission of the artist.

Contents

Member Institution Acknowledgments

Lever Press is a collective effort. This work was made possible by the generous support of Lever Press member libraries from the following institutions:

Amherst College
Bard College
Bennington College
Berea College
Boston College
Bowdoin College
Carleton College
Claremont Colleges
Claremont Graduate University
Claremont McKenna College
Colby College
Davidson College
Denison University
DePauw University
Grinnell College
Hamilton College
Hampshire College
Harvey Mudd College
Haverford College
Hollins University
Iowa State University
Keck Graduate Institute
Knox College
Lafayette College
Macalester College
Middlebury College
Norwich University
Pitzer College
Pomona College
Randolph-Macon College
Rollins College
Santa Clara University
Scripps College
Smith College
Swarthmore College
Tilburg University

Trinity University
Union College
University at Buffalo (SUNY)
University of Rhode Island
University of Sheffield
University of Texas at Austin
University of Vermont
Vassar College
Washington and Lee University
Whitman College
Williams College
Yale University

INTRODUCTION

Ian Barnard, Ryan Ashley Caldwell, Jada Patchigondla, Aneil Rallin, Morgan Read-Davidson, Ethan Trejo, and Kristi M. Wilson

The individual histories of both trigger warnings and trauma have evolved rapidly in the overlapping wakes of COVID, mental health crises, attacks on educational institutions in the United States, climate apocalypse, ever-growing economic inequities, and, more promisingly, attempts at political redress and educational equity. At the same time, trigger warnings and trauma have become exponentially more intimately linked in the past few years. But however often the topic of trigger warnings provokes heated discussion, the appeals and alignments of the interlocutors equally as frequently defy neat political binaries. Critiques of trigger warnings come from all sides of the political and pedagogical spectra, and even scholars and practitioners who offer a trauma-informed approach to the topic are not unified in their view of trigger warnings, as this anthology illustrates. These messy cross-cuts make this topic especially timely and especially appealing to us as past, current, and future educators, and especially in light of the "new forms of anxiety, trauma, and disaffection" that students are experiencing (Comstock 697).

We hope that the subtitle of this volume, "teaching through trauma," will be interpreted generously. While many of the chapters attend to teaching in formal educational settings, others speak to the pedagogy, politics, and impact of trigger warnings in culture at large—after all, even popular culture "teaches" in a way. Similarly, "trauma" functions fluidly throughout this volume as a broad category that names psychic and bodily remembrances of various forms of state and interpersonal violence. The many collaborators to this collection carry various usages of "trauma," but are linked by examining the viability of trigger warnings as a pedagogy from which to decrease the afterlives of trauma.

As pedagogical practice, trigger warnings are commonly understood as statements made by instructors that warn students of content that they might find "triggering." Even the naming of this practice is rooted in trauma discourse. Alexis Lothian notes that the term "trigger warning" rose in online fan communities. Yet, the specific naming of the term is shaped by the language of post-traumatic stress and the possibility (hence the call to a "warning") of one who has experienced trauma to be *retraumatized* (Stringer 62). Rebecca Stringer understands the usage of trigger warnings as an equalizing praxis in service of students with trauma backgrounds: trigger warnings "promote equality of access to education because they can allay the substantial disadvantages associated with being triggered" (62). For Stringer, trigger warnings are specifically for these students with trauma, and merely a "courtesy" for others. This may seem like a sort of specialized description that perpetuates the idea that trigger warnings only service a small portion of students. However, the move to connect trigger warnings to trauma understands trauma as omnipresent. Yes, material with particular content may be more triggering to students who have traumatic histories with such content. Yet, when the trauma in question encapsulates various forms of systemic harm, then the trigger warning serves to remind us that such traumas *affect us all*. While we each have individualized histories with these traumas, the trigger warning could work to remind us of the larger injustices we must continually face as subjects living under systems of oppression that imprint trauma upon our bodies and psyche.

The connection between trigger warnings and trauma also lies in the power of language as a world-making practice, in that trigger warnings speak to the ontological capacity of discourse, a discourse that both students and instructors are called to participate in. Much of the discourse and scholarship around trigger warnings center on the role of the student's trauma and the student's responses to triggers. The impetus for labeling content as "triggering" is usually assumed to lie with the instructor—it is supposedly the responsibility of the instructor to be the judge of content and screen material for possible triggers. But instructors themselves also have triggers. As Amy E. Robillard reminds us, neither instructors nor students check their trauma at the door: "What we can see instead is that anybody can be triggered any time, anywhere, when we least expect it. We carry our trauma with us" (330). Student calls for trigger warnings remind us that the classroom is not a utopian space free of the harm of the "real world." Instead, both instructors and students bring their trauma into the classroom space. Thus, trigger warnings can be seen as an intimate pedagogical tool, building a relationship between instructor and student wherein both can openly share their understandings of the traumatic materials. Such an open dialogue works toward constructing the classroom as what Davina Cooper calls an "everyday utopia" (cited in Lothian 751). Rather than imagining some egalitarian utopia that we can gravitate toward, Cooper suggests that we understand everyday life as a utopian praxis. Such a praxis means that "we can try to create and inhabit a world that allows for aesthetic and political disturbance without retraumatizing survivors" (Lothian 751). By living in a way that, while not ignoring systemic (traumatizing) oppression, actively seeks to not reproduce such traumas, we can reframe how we experience our everyday lives and the trauma impressed upon us.

We are intentionally using the idea of trauma loosely in this volume in order to be suggestive rather than definitive, and in this sense are not confining ourselves to clinical definitions of trauma. (For an example of work that focuses more properly on trauma in educational settings, see Stromberg.) We deploy "trauma" as part of an effort to recognize the current epidemic of mental health challenges facing students and others, and how this epidemic has reshaped ideas around trigger warnings. This recognition distinguishes this book from earlier work on trigger warnings precisely because mental health crises have become part of the constellation of post-COVID contexts enabling and shaping trigger warnings and the discourse around them today. The pre-pandemic 2017 anthology, *Trigger Warnings: History, Theory, Context*, edited by Emily J. M. Knox, a scholar and teacher in the field of information sciences, offers us a helpful foundation to build on in this book. The culture and education wars in the United States have escalated exponentially since 2017, especially attacks on Critical Race Theory and LGBTQIA+ identities (topics treated in several of the contributions to this volume), and COVID-19 has clarified and amplified the mental health concerns facing students as well as teachers and staff at educational institutions. Knox and her contributors nevertheless offer important accounts of the history of trigger warnings and useful theoretical frameworks (including articulating connections between trigger warnings and post-traumatic stress disorder (PTSD), and between trigger warnings and trauma) for the new work our contributors undertake in the current volume. While a significant amount of published scholarship has been quite skeptical of trigger warnings (e.g., Halberstam, "Trigger Happy" and "You are Triggering Me"; Hanhardt et al.; Lothian), trigger warnings have also been defended as, for example, ways of privileging trauma and disability in the classroom (e.g., Carter; Daniels; Gerdes, "Trauma"; Rae; and see Morgan Read-Davidson's chapter in this volume). As COVID's ongoing afterlife exacerbates the continuing mental health challenges many young people face (Carillo 25–28), we feel expressly called upon to revisit, update, and augment that earlier generation of trigger warning scholarship.

Despite our commitments to student well-being, we recognize that the topic of trigger warnings is complex, and the dilemmas it poses don't have obvious solutions. (Sophia Greco prompts us in their chapter in this collection to keep in mind that "there is no trigger warnings for this moment," that no trigger warning for "genocide—ethnic cleansing—apartheid" could be sufficient.) Scholars from diverse pedagogical and political perspectives have been critical of the notion of classrooms as "safe spaces" (see, e.g., hooks), and social justice-focused teachers have been as critical of what gets conventionally constituted as a "trigger warning" (e.g., Grayson, and Aneil Rallin's chapter in this volume) as have critics of critical race theory and DEI (diversity, equity, and inclusion) work. Indeed, as the seven co-editors of this volume, we don't necessarily all share the values or endorse the views presented in each of the chapters that follow. The goal of this anthology, then, is not to advocate for or against trigger warnings—certainly, in this volume Dave Morris is no fan of trigger warnings, and Kevin Moore is at least conflicted about them. Nor is our goal to create a list of injunctions about trigger warnings. Rather, we hope to provide a space for us, our contributors, and our readers, especially those who are teachers and students, to deepen and complicate our understandings of trigger warnings.

Moore reminds us that trigger warnings didn't originate in academia. However, although not all the chapters in this volume directly address teaching, unsurprisingly, all of the contributors are teachers or students in some capacity, a demographic tilt that speaks to the lopsided attention that the topic of trigger warnings has generated around sites of pedagogy in the United States. Why are teachers so caught up in debates about trigger warnings? Why has the classroom become an especially contested space to demand or refuse trigger warnings when they could equally be applied to other spaces that exhibit potentially triggering discourse? After all, California's Official State Theater, the Pasadena Playhouse, mounted an acclaimed production of Stephen Sondheim's *A Little Night Music* in 2023 with nary a trigger warning in sight about the show's explicit treatment of suicidal ideation. Ditto for *Les Misérables*, promoted as "the world's most popular musical," and still touring across the United States with no trigger warnings about suicide, rape, and child exploitation, even though its official website includes a "content advisory" about fog, haze, moving lights, sound effects, live flame, and gunshots. And films, plays, books, operas, novels, and scholarly articles frequently address and represent suicide and rape without providing trigger warnings and with little backlash for failing to do so. In fact, as recently as October 2023 Ian McKellen called the prospect of trigger warnings for theater productions "ludicrous" (Sherwood).

But while it's true that, up to now, extra-classroom spaces haven't had quite the same degree of investment in trigger warnings, this landscape, too, is changing, a topic addressed in Pauline Menchavez's chapter in this volume. As a case in point, see Stephanie R. Larson's 2021 essay on "The Rhetoricity of Fat Stigma" in *Rhetoric Society Quarterly* that begins with the following "content warning": "This essay includes descriptions of lived experiences with eating disorders, particularly anorexia nervosa." Or see the *Journal of Multimodal Rhetoric*'s Fall 2022 special issue on "Carework and Writing During COVID": it includes a "Content Warnings: Parental death, gun violence, medical gaslighting." And, of course, care-focused social media users have been providing their followers with trigger warnings for a long time. Even so, trigger warnings in these arenas haven't become as visible a discussion point as they have in educational contexts, and it's telling that *Rhetoric Society Quarterly* and the *Journal of Multimodal Rhetoric* use the phrase "content warning" rather than "trigger warning," given that content warnings in some form or another have long been a staple, however contested, of US culture, and have often been supported by the very conservatives who are regularly skeptical of trigger warnings in the classroom (though, as we mentioned above, positions in the trigger warnings wars do defy traditional political binaries). Television programs and films in the United States are rated according to their supposed suitability for viewers by age and given content advisories, and news outlets routinely preface news stories with warnings about flash photography and potentially disturbing content—for example, the BBC websites prefaced a 2023 story about Japan "redefining rape" with an italicized "*Warning: this article contains details that some readers may find distressing*" (Wong and Shiraishi). Some kind of "content warning," then, is becoming more ubiquitous across a range of institutions, platforms, and discourses.

How are or aren't "content warnings" different from "trigger warnings" (a topic addressed in Whitney Lew James's chapter in this volume), and why have the two types of warnings spurred such different discourses around them? Might there be a question of individual blame in claiming something to be a "trigger warning" as opposed to a "content warning?" A content warning might be a sort of keyword guide to the material that the cultural artifact in question tackles, so consumers have a choice of whether to willingly consume the text. Indeed, there is additionally a sort of naturalization to this content, as it generates a discourse of *this is what the piece just happens to be about, take it or leave it.* In rebranding content descriptors into trigger warnings, the discourse potentially becomes one of individual blame wherein a weaker consumer seemingly comes in contact with the text ready to be triggered. Yet, this framework, too, naturalizes harmful content and additionally appears to put the blame for the perpetuation of harm onto the consumer. There is an enforced sense of "You've been warned, why are you still upset?" Perhaps the care ethos associated with pedagogy, together with the construction of Generation Z "snowflakes"[1] have fueled the opposing battle lines when it comes to classroom trigger warnings? Might classroom contexts of power relations and the relatively young ages of average students exacerbate student vulnerability, thus increasing the demand for pedagogical trigger warnings compared to other sites of social and cultural exchange and production (say operas or scholarly articles)?

* * * * *

This anthology started life as a workshop session organized by the co-editors at the annual convention of the National Council of Teachers of English, to which teachers across institution types and levels and from diverse geographical spaces brought their seemingly countless questions, concerns, anxieties, stories, and pieces of advice about trigger warnings:

- How do new and experienced instructors navigate the tension between facilitating safe spaces for students while also challenging students intellectually (and otherwise) in increasingly politicized classroom settings?
- How can trigger warnings be used to empower or support students and facilitate anti-racist, queer, anticolonial, and other social justice-oriented pedagogies?
- How can we think through the changing historical and cultural contexts of triggers? How do power differentials (among students, between students and faculty) impact the ways trigger warnings can and do get deployed?
- What are the stakes for contingent faculty versus tenured faculty?
- What role do students have in giving trigger warnings in the classroom?
- What can teachers and students learn about trigger warnings through engaging with each other?
- Who decides what a trigger is?

- Trigger warning discourse has tended to focus on student needs and demands, but what about teachers, especially teachers from historically marginalized communities?
- And what about the divergent and sometimes conflicting demands and needs of diverse student constituencies?

The urgency of the questions at this workshop and the hunger for discussion among teachers and others on the topic of trigger warnings helped us to quickly recognize the need for this volume. Many, but not all, of the above questions are addressed by the diverse array of contributors who have written chapters in this anthology. We recognize that strategies, best practices, and consequences for trigger warnings in educational settings are necessarily region-particular (see Paolena Comouche's chapter in this volume) and determined by specific student demographics and instructor positionality, as well as educational institution level and type. And while the debates around trigger warnings have taken a particular shape in the United States, we are also interested in finding out how these debates have or haven't taken shape outside the United States, and how scholars, teachers, students, cultural workers, and others outside the United States view the US debates about trigger warnings. We thus hope that our discussions will also invite conversations about the usage of trigger warnings in non-US or global contexts. In any case, the US focus of this book seems particularly pertinent now: not only does trigger warnings discourse have a particularly fractured history in the United States, but recent and current political reckonings and culture wars in the United States, the latter especially around education, and sometimes directly about trigger warnings (see Rosman), give an added urgency to these discussions of political struggle, student agency, educational equity, and care networks.

As multigenerational scholars, teachers, and students in the humanities and social sciences, we co-editors have inevitably brought our own varied disciplinary, interdisciplinary, and anti-disciplinary perspectives and trainings to bear on this book. These include our interests in questions of representation, a particular attention to the fields of rhetoric and composition, fields to which all of us co-editors have varying degrees of connection, and interdisciplinary histories and political dispositions that demand our attention to questions around teacher safety and equity, student agency, and pedagogies of social justice.

We are especially excited about the variety of forms and genres that the contributions to this collection take: long and short teaching narratives, student perspectives, manifestos, memoirs, vignettes, autoethnographies, reflections, case studies, theory, history, personal essays, research articles. Not only does this diversity create a more varied engagement experience for readers, but it also allows for a wider variety of voices to be heard and for the articulation of experiences that might not be well accommodated by traditional scholarly essays. Over the past few decades, scholarship in the humanities, social sciences, and education has become increasingly wary of the privileging of a narrow strain of academic discourse and a constrained understanding of evidentiary acceptability, given the voices, communities, and experiences that these privilegings and understandings perforce silence/make invisible/marginalize/demonize. Diversity of discursive typologies, then, is as much a political and social imperative as it is a matter of readerly and writerly pleasure.

Trigger Warnings: Teaching Through Trauma is theoretically informed but attentive to praxis, as can be seen by chapters that attend to the ideological underpinnings and pedagogical dispositions of assumptions about trigger warnings and those that offer heuristics for practical classroom implementation. This book, of course, could have been organized in a number of ways, but while the section divisions are somewhat (inevitably) arbitrary, they nevertheless enable us to highlight particular strains in trigger warning scholarship, to curate conversations among linked chapters, and to indicate the range of trigger warning coverage we want this collection to point toward. For example, the already large Part II, Pedagogical Practices, could easily have been supplemented with other pedagogically focused chapters, but we are especially interested in drawing attention to some of the political arguments around trigger warnings in the classroom that speak specifically to activist politics and marginalized subjectivities—hence the separate section on Queer/Feminist/Anti-Racist Interventions. And while these queer/feminist/anti-racist interventions certainly qualify as "political," we hope to gesture toward a larger political field outside the classroom in the Political Predicaments section. And so on. Thus, we've resisted the temptation to provide an in-depth layout of each section, as is typical of edited collections, but instead ask readers to recognize that the overlaps speak to the broad, often intersecting, discursive realms that trigger warnings are currently situated in. In this case, overlap isn't a bad thing. And in any case, we invite readers to remix as you see fit!

We don't know if trigger warnings are here to stay, but whatever their specific future, they have instigated important debates inside and outside the academy about the relationship between learning and discomfort, and about duties of care, social justice, and cultural norms. These debates will have lasting impacts on our political, social, and pedagogical imaginaries and practices.

NOTE

1 See Kleiber and Gerdes, *Sensitive* for critiques of this construction, and Ryan Ashley Caldwell's and Sophia Greco's chapters in this anthology.

WORKS CITED

Carillo, Ellen C. *The Hidden Inequities in Labor-Based Contract Grading*. Utah State UP, 2021.

Carter, Angela M. "Teaching With Trauma: Disability Pedagogy, Feminism, and the Trigger Warnings Debate." *Disability Studies Quarterly*, vol. 35, no. 2, 2015.

Comstock, Edward. "Toward a New Neurobiology of Writing: Plasticity and the Feeling of Failure." *College Composition and Communication*, vol. 74, no. 4, 2023, pp. 695–730.

Daniels, Brandy. "Trigger Warnings, Trauma, and a Politics of 'Thick Life': On Halberstam's 'You Are Triggering Me' and Povinelli's *Empire of Love*." *Women in Theology*, 14 July 2014.

Gerdes, Kendall. *Sensitive Rhetorics: Academic Freedom and Campus Activism*. U of Pittsburgh P, 2024.

Gerdes, Kendall. "Trauma, Trigger Warnings, and the Rhetoric of Sensitivity." *Rhetoric Society Quarterly*, vol. 49, no. 1, 2019, pp. 3–24.

Grayson, Mara Lee. "Who is it Really for? Trigger Warnings and the Maintenance of the Racial Status Quo." *College Composition and Communication*, vol. 73, no. 4, June 2022, pp. 692–721.

Halberstam, Jack. "Trigger Happy: From Content Warning to Censorship." *Signs*, vol. 42, no. 2, Winter 2017, pp. 535–42.

Halberstam, Jack. "You Are Triggering Me!: The Neo-Liberal Rhetoric of Harm, Danger, and Trauma." *Bully Bloggers*, 5 July 2014.

Hanhardt, Christina B., et al. "Beyond Trigger Warnings: Safety, Securitization, and Queer Left Critique." *Social Text*, no. 145, Dec. 2020, pp. 49–76.

hooks, bell. "Conflict." *Teaching Critical Thinking: Practical Wisdom*. Routledge, 2010, pp. 85–90.

Journal of Multimodal Rhetorics, The. Special issue on Carework and Writing During COVID: Part II. Vol. 7, no. 1, Fall 2022.

Kleiber, Anna. "On the Epistemology of Trigger Warnings, or Why the Coddling Argument Against Trigger Warnings is Misguided." *Feminist Philosophy Quarterly,* vol. 7, no. 4, 2021.

Knox, Emily J. M., ed. *Trigger Warnings: History, Theory, Context.* Rowman, 2017.

Larson, Stephanie R. "The Rhetoricity of Fat Stigma: Mental Disability, Pain, and Anorexia Nervosa." *Rhetoric Society Quarterly*, vol. 51, no. 5, Fall 2021, pp. 392–406.

Lothian, Alexis. "Choose not to Warn: Trigger Warnings and Content Notes From Fan Culture to Feminist Pedagogy." *Feminist Studies*, vol. 42, no. 3, 2016, pp. 743–56.

Rae, Logan. "Refocusing the Debate on Trigger Warnings: Privilege, Trauma, and Disability in the Classroom." *First Amendment Studies*, vol. 50, no. 2, 2016, pp. 95–102.

Robillard, Amy E. "Confronting the Real: The Trigger Warning Debate and the Rhetorical Space of the Classroom." *Pedagogy: Critical Approaches to Teaching Literature, Language, Composition, and Culture*, vol. 20, no. 2, 2020, pp. 327–347.

Rosman, Katherine. "Should College Come With Trigger Warnings? At Cornell, It's a 'Hard No.'" *New York Times*, 12 April 2023.

Sherwood, Harriet. "'It's Ludicrous': Ian McKellen Sparks Debate Over Trigger Warnings in Theatre." *The Guardian*, 2 October 2023.

Stringer, Rebecca. "Reflection from the Field: Trigger Warnings in University Teaching." *Women's Studies Journal*, vol. 30, no. 2, Dec. 2016, pp. 62–66.

Stromberg, Ernest, ed. *Trauma-Informed Pedagogy in Higher Education: A Faculty Guide for Teaching and Learning*. Routledge, 2023.

Wong, Tessa, and Sakiko Shiraishi. "Why is Japan Redefining Rape?" *BBC News*, 6 June 2023.

PART ONE

INSTITUTIONAL CONTEXTS

CHAPTER ONE

TRIGGER WARNINGS, INTERSECTIONS, AND PEDAGOGICAL OSCILLATIONS

Kristi M. Wilson

> *The classroom ultimately stands as a site where theory meets practice, and as such as a place where our material realities meet our theoretical ambitions. Thus, nothing less than a fully integrated and collaborative feminist disability approach to trauma in the classroom will be sufficient for supporting all our students.*
>
> Angela Carter

> *Because they are not limited to the natural (biological) sphere but participate in the creative dimension as well...[people] can intervene in reality in order to change it. Inheriting acquired experience, creating and re-creating, integrating themselves into their context, responding to its challenges, objectifying themselves, discerning, transcending...*
>
> Paolo Freire

TRAUMA, TRIGGER WARNINGS, AND THE PANDEMIC

In his now well-known post for *Bully Bloggers*, "You are Triggering Me!: the Neoliberal Rhetoric of Harm, Danger, and Trauma," Jack Halberstam suggests that a "neoliberal rhetoric of individual pain," often underscores a rush to offer trigger warnings at every turn...obscuring "the violent sources of social inequity." Moreover, he refers to the relatively recent push for trigger warnings as "the reemergence of a [1980s 'weepy,' 'anti-fun,' definitely not intersectional] rhetoric of harm and trauma," citing examples from Monty Python's 1979 film *The Life of Brian* (banned in some cities when it was released) to make his point.

The *Bully Bloggers* post calls to mind the fine line between excessive content warnings and censorship, a dangerous gray-zone not lost on me as I reflect, along with other academics, upon recent pedagogical struggles between faculty, administrators, and students on college campuses, and upon ongoing criticisms across the nation that have resulted in the censoring of queer and critical race theory (CRT) curricula.

In this essay, I consider the topic of trigger warnings in the context of intersectional student activist and advocacy struggles for disability rights that impacted a small liberal arts campus between the pre- and post-lockdown years of the COVID-19 pandemic. I consider trigger warnings from the perspective of a composition and rhetoric faculty member and from the perspective of an ally of student activists. I bring interdisciplinary scholarly perspectives on systems of power (David Harvey, Nancy Fraser, Angela Carter, Naomi Klein, and Byung-Chul Han) into dialogue with student voices to analyze the effectiveness of trigger warnings in all their complexities during a period of time best described as the "Coronavirus window."[1]

In the years just before the COVID-19 pandemic, members of the SWDCC student group (Students With Disabilities Chronic Conditions) launched a critique of what they saw as our community's inability to adequately deal with mental health crises and disability issues on campus. Their demands would be formalized six months into the pandemic in an open letter to the campus community at large emailed on August 26, 2020. Among other things, the letter emphasized what the SWDCC members felt to be the inherently ableist nature of academia:

> We are tired emotionally, physically, and mentally. We are trying to survive and thrive in this pandemic just as much as you are, but we particularly have needs that were never met pre-pandemic and are still not being met during the pandemic. Disability isn't included in academia, then again

academia is inherently ableist, but even in places that promote "global citizenship and equality" its existence beyond a disability services office is hard to find. There's a whole field called Disability Studies, which has subcategories like deaf studies and mad studies, but hardly any higher education institutions have classes dedicated to anything relating to disability. Trust me, we've looked. ("Letter to Admin.")

Trigger warnings played an important role in the SWDCC list of demands and, as a faculty member whose responsibilities included delivering student-centered education, I felt an urgency to revisit my classroom practices. The students advocated for faculty to: "Require trigger warnings...on text and material that has things like r*pe, assault, abuse, death, violence, racism, homophobia, transphobia, etc....," adding:

> WE ARE NOT SAYING TO CENSOR ANYTHING. WE ARE NOT TAKING AWAY ANYONE'S FREE SPEECH OR EDITING CLASSIC WORKS. We are simply asking to have trigger warnings prior to engaging with these materials so we can be better prepared and choose how to engage with these things. Topics that are triggering can be debilitating physically, mentally, and emotionally for students so how would the student be able to engage within a classroom that allows for this to happen? How would they be able to continue in the discussion or class activities when they might be reliving trauma right next to you?

The prolonged pandemic lockdown resulted in a gray-zone for faculty and students alike. Students (40% of whom were international students) were sent off campus and went, along with the rest of us, into survival mode. Student activist and advocacy communities could no longer gather in person, leading to a lapse in momentum.

"THE MAIN COURSE IS US"

Most faculty on our campus did not return to live teaching in the fall of 2022 and when they returned, many felt exhausted and distressed from a year of managing the pandemic lockdown (which included a variety of forms of care-work and possibly grieving) while delivering "smart," platform-based education. Rhetoric and composition faculty (most of whom had expressed support for the student activists) faced a uniquely challenging re-entry to live teaching. Upon returning to campus, we were surprised by an emailed announcement that our writing program would undergo an unanticipated, rapid restructuring, in spite of the fact that we had only recently begun a year-long self-study. Adding to this stress and confusion was more unexpected and perplexing news: the only queer faculty of color in our program and on our campus would be subjected to a disciplinary hearing and was up for potential dismissal from the university on charges of using course materials that were "triggering," and that constituted "deviant pornography."[2]

Thus, in the fall of 2022, Jack Halberstam's warnings about the potential dangers trigger warnings could pose to queer communities was at the top of my mind. And Naomi Klein's prediction that Coronavirus Capitalism would undermine democratic processes, rebrand, and restructure behind closed doors, had never felt more relevant ("Coronavirus Capitalism"). While faculty were struggling to survive and keep students engaged online amid a sea of fear and screen fatigue, the Coronavirus window proved to be an opportunity to chip away at "shared governance"; a set of practices Klein calls an "inconvenient public engagement in the designing of critical institutions and public spaces" ("How Big Tech Plans to Profit From the Pandemic").

Understanding neoliberal power dynamics takes on an even greater urgency for academics negotiating the use of trigger warnings in their pedagogical practices in the era of COVID-19. Institutionalized precarity, hyper-surveillance, increased authoritarianism, top-down policy making, the growth of digital capitalism (‟"Big Data"), an amnestic drive toward "progress," and intensified overexploitation of labor (Harvey 2007) are just a few of the characteristics of neoliberal power. Pandemics (like wars) offer a unique opportunity for institutions (and States, for that matter) to strengthen themselves in an absence of shared governance, as most collective energy is focused on survival. Naomi Klein calls the heightened neoliberalism that would take advantage of the pandemic as a window of opportunity to outrun public/democratic pushback against institutions "Coronavirus Capitalism" ("How Big Tech Plans to Profit From the Pandemic"). Nancy Fraser refers to a similar set of dynamics as "Cannibal

Capitalism": "an institutionalized feeding frenzy – in which the main course is us" (xiv).

In the post-lockdown COVID landscape, Angela Carter's brand of feminist disabilities studies pedagogy allows for the nuanced analysis of systems of power and oppression and helps me to think about my own ongoing oscillations around trigger warnings. Carter is critical of the American Association of University Professors (AAUP)'s 2014 report on trigger warnings, in which trigger warnings are framed as a threat to academic freedom and understood as infantilizing students and anti-intellectual.[3] Rather, Carter suggests that in its statement on trigger warnings, the AAUP "misunderstands what trauma is. Being triggered is re-experiencing trauma in an embodied way (a fully embodied shift that goes beyond cognitive control). It is not the same thing as being made to feel uncomfortable. Being triggered is being disabled" (Carter). As a faculty member who has not experienced the level of embodied trauma that Carter has, I am starkly aware that treatment and support for trauma is outside of my expertise wheelhouse and, as Peter Alilunas suggests, perhaps best addressed in the realm of institutional policies and accommodations (in *Synoptique* 285). And yet, our students had been warning us for years that formal policies and accommodations were insufficient:

> Teachers need to be advocates for students with disabilities and chronic conditions first, not only advocates when Disability Services validates the disabled student experience. We need to trust that we are the expert on our own lives and want our educational experience to be as best as possible, accommodations are not ways to "be lazy," it's a way for us to survive academia which is inherently ableist. ("Letter to Admin")

During the pandemic lockdown, in part as an attempt to respond to student claims that academia is inherently ableist and as a way of educating myself further about disabilities and chronic conditions, I designed an online composition and rhetoric course which explored intersections between disability studies and writing. When I returned to live teaching the following semester, I had developed an interdisciplinary upper-division rhetoric and composition course which considered the intersections between gender science, and empire, and which included an emphasis on disability. These rhetoric and composition courses became student-centered learning labs in which I and my students explored and experienced some of what Angela Carter frames as the contradictions of gender, disability, and institutional power. Such contradictions required a level of what Paolo Freire referred to as critical optimism, a strong sense of social responsibility and engagement in the notion of transformation.[4]

By fall 2022, for the first time in over two decades, I found myself considering some of the materials on my syllabi and feeling especially nervous about the potential for certain films I was planning to screen in an upcoming Writing About Film course to be triggering for students. Some of the texts in my courses dealt with topics such as medical racism, sexual violence, reproductive rights, forced sterilization, and intersexuality, among other topics. And up until the publication of the SWDCC open letter, I did not include trigger warnings on my syllabi because, as someone who works extensively with documentary and feminist film and media (in my rhetoric and composition classes as well as my film classes), I prioritized the unanticipated element of filmmaking as an especially powerful and meaningful rhetorical strategy.[5]

I had a student in my Writing About Film class (Student A) who asked for trigger warnings on all potentially sensitive materials. My experience with this student proved to be a pivotal moment in my pedagogy, as I began to think more seriously about the challenges inherent in establishing safe pedagogical spaces in which to show representations of, to process, and to talk about trauma; how best to do so in the context of a university whose e-surveys, virtual desktops, digital platforms and assessment protocols might be said to comprise a digital panopticon (Han). Such a digital panopticon, according to Han, would position forms of knowledge that are not easily quantifiable as secretive, foreign, other; as impediments to "unbounded communication," and as such, threats to the compulsion toward quantifiable transparency. Or, as Miguel Benasayg suggests in *The Tyranny of Algorithms*: "Anything in the territory [of pure abstraction] (the reality of bodies, of ecosystems...) that resists attempts at modeling thus becomes, in the world of digital models, 'noise in the system'" (23).

Thus, in the fearful confluence of the return to live teaching during a pandemic, the imminent restructuring of our program, and the despair that many faculty felt over our colleague's pending disciplinary hearing,

I thought about materials I had screened in the past and wondered if they would be too provocative to use in the present. Take, for example, the Argentine film *XXY* (directed by Lucía Puenzo, 2007), whose plot revolves around an intersex teenager whose parents are being pressured by a well-known surgeon to coerce their child into following medical protocols that will lead to their transition to a female. The film paired well with my course themes and readings, especially those around the topic of intersexuality, gender, the medical industrial complex, and the history of Dr. John Money's sexology work at Johns Hopkins University. The film includes a sexually explicit sex scene between two teenagers in which consent is intentionally vague. If I had given this scene a trigger warning using the words "sexual assault," it would not have been true to the film's intentionally complex depiction of desire and sexuality, and it might have conditioned the way others in the class experienced the film. I did not quite know how to create a trigger warning that would not simultaneously judge its depiction of intersexuality as dangerous, problematic, or predatory. Any trigger warning of this sort might render my syllabus complicit with "the violent sources of social inequity" (Halberstam) by working against the film's redemptive depiction of its protagonist's decision to remain intersex and reject the binary options offered to them.

I had similar concerns over French filmmaker Catherine Breillat's film, *A Ma Soeur!* (2001), which features full frontal nudity, explicit sex scenes between a minor and an adult, and a shocking, surprise violent scene that prompts audiences to consider their own ideas about rape, sexual assault, desire, violence, and sex acts. I feared that a host of films I had screened in previous years could be interpreted as traumatizing. An award-winning film that I frequently screen in class, Ari Folman's 2008 animated documentary about Israel's 1982 invasion of Lebanon, *Waltz With Bashir*, is entirely animated until the final scene which features VHS footage from a massacre. Theo Kohler's thoughts about the paradoxical potential for trigger warnings to strengthen a university's disciplinary policies rang accurate:

> In many ways, trigger warnings are a powerful student-led critique of traditional pedagogy—yet we cannot ignore the ways they now converge in the neoliberal, managerial university.... From this perspective, student

> demands may actually empower the university as an institution, strengthening it as an apparatus for surveillance and disciplinary-bureaucratic policies, contra the very people who teach them.

Compelled by the SWDCC open letter to our campus community, faculty began to consider how to best incorporate trigger warnings into course texts, and classroom discussions. I created trigger warnings for my readings and films using topic-specific language like "content related to violence at abortion clinics," "discussion of sexual abuse in prisons," "theoretical discussions of sex work," etc. I also included readings on the topic of trigger warnings and informal response spaces in which students could share their thoughts. While it felt gratifying to feel as if I were responding to one of the key SWDCC demands—that faculty be advocates for students with disabilities and chronic conditions—I did so with a sense of unease. The trigger warnings did not add the sense of classroom safety I was hoping for.

My trigger warnings felt like compromises at best...

Student A let me know that they would have to leave the classroom and take breaks from time to time, when material was triggering. The class dynamic grew more complicated when we watched media clips in class and, afterward, a visibly shaken Student A would receive supportive hugs and consolation from other students. I felt responsible for a certain level of suffering. Despite my trigger warnings, a lot of the materials I had selected seemed to be making students suffer. And yet, grief was a feature of many of the course materials and of the course theme, in general. I kept thinking about the complex discussion of trigger warnings in the SWDCC list of demands:

> Trigger warnings are important for reasons far beyond accessibility and creating a safe environment. We deal with traumatic and draining content often...with no plans for after-care or how students might feel about these topics... Teachers, faculty, and everyone else need to do better. We cannot simply talk about systems of domination every day without thinking about how do I provide some hope to these students after? ("Letter to Admin")

WRITING TRAUMA

I typically assign informal writing assignments each day in my writing and rhetoric classes. These consist of discussion forum free-writes about anything going on in class or in the reading for the day. When I look back over Student A's discussion forum posts, I notice that they wanted to challenge themself to write about difficult topics like female genital mutilation, while remaining, as they wrote, "objective."

After one class in which Student A seemed particularly upset, I asked what else I could do to make the learning environment more comfortable for them. The student told me that they felt ignored by faculty, despite asking for trigger warnings repeatedly, and that faculty should provide more detailed trigger warnings more often. For example, Student A requested that I provide detailed trigger warnings for media, down to minute and second markers in videos, and that I should provide more detail about what would be shown. When I mentioned using certain texts from feminist and/or queer directors that feature emotionally provocative scenes, they responded that, in their opinion, many faculty were arrogant and dismissive of students' feelings; that the act of prioritizing course materials over students' mental well-being was self-serving. I took their concerns to heart and thought about Alilunas's contention that "professors should absolutely not, even inadvertently, use our power as teachers to spring things on students, or to have a paternalistic attitude that subtly or unintentionally sends the message that 'we know what's best for you even if it hurts'" (in *Synoptique* 285).

I could see that my student was truly upset, and I felt bad being part of a situation that was potentially triggering. That said, I hesitated to cut materials from the class because other students found them important, and I did, as well. I continued to have conversations with Student A throughout the semester but in the end, I can't say that either of us felt satisfied with the pedagogical adjustments I had attempted.

In a subsequent course, I embedded the topic of trigger warnings into some of the course assignments and overall design. For example, I spent a lot of time up front unpacking the politically conservative, racist, ideological history of the Hollywood Hays Code, which gave rise to the ratings system (a warning system that is built into the viewing experience of most media). I also started the course by giving students a prompt about trigger warnings and asking them to reflect upon how they felt about them. We read Halberstam's post for *Bully Bloggers*, which presented a perspective most students had not considered. Halberstam points out that content warnings have grown in parallel with calls for increased attention to students with disabilities (especially invisible disabilities) and, as I have suggested, this has been the case on our campus, as well. For my part, I did not want to reproduce trauma for students who might have invisible disabilities like post-traumatic stress disorder (PTSD), but I also wanted to avoid extensively pre-censoring materials. Certain forms of rhetoric (especially visual rhetoric) rely on the unexpected. Halberstam suggests that a jump to pre-censor is reductive and at risk of over-simplifying "complex discourses on trauma readily available as a consequence of decades of work on memory, political violence and abuse."

Student responses to the trigger warnings reading and prompt were varied. One student suggested:

> I think trigger warnings are important, and that there can be different levels of them. Most people who argue against them refer to the removal of the element of surprise or how it could spoil the film. However, there can be general trigger warnings (sort of content warnings? Not quite sure on the difference) that emphasize the triggering content that would be in the film. I've also seen time stamp trigger warnings, which could be helpful for those who'd like to watch but have the chance to skip over as they please. I don't think TWs hurt those who don't see them as necessary, but they could help those who do. I prefer the general form of trigger warnings, just so I know what to prepare myself for mentally.

Another offered a personal story about being censored by a teacher in grade school and concluded:

> So, what does this all have to do with the article? I think one of the article's main points is that trigger warnings and cancel culture are not the best ways to deal with issues that we are trying to understand and re-conceptualize, like racism or violence. Rather than telling people what

> not to do through tyrannical policies, we should be trying to lay out the problems in a way that people can understand them and then offer solutions or alternatives (when possible). In addition, I do not think setting rules on fiction is ever a good idea.

A third student pondered the nature of criteria for trigger warnings and claimed that "making a criterion for trigger warning is extremely hard and will never be completed." Peter Alilunas suggests that the type of neutral learning environment promised by trigger warnings is itself a fallacy:

> it's basically the definition of cis hetero white privilege for me to suggest that I could even be capable of building some neutral learning environment where we don't have to account for actual lived experiences, which are unquestionably and disproportionately unfair, and even fatal, for many people. To stick blindly to the mythology that the classroom is free from those systemic power imbalances will only result in being complicit in perpetuating them. (in *Synoptique* 285)

THE MYTHOLOGY OF THE CLASSROOM: REFLECTIONS...

I still offer trigger warnings when I teach certain films in my film and media courses, but I opt not to provide down-to-the-minute-and-second, detailed content warnings. I (along with other faculty on my campus) have also adopted a consent policy on my syllabi that places a certain level of responsibility on students to think seriously about the course materials and invites them to advocate for the types of trigger warnings that might be helpful to them before we get started with the course. In this sense, I take inspiration from Carter's work to understand trauma and disabilities as personal, political, and relational and to structure her classroom as a space of "collective reimagining."

One year later, I am still thinking about these experiences and reimagining my own oscillations around trigger warnings. If, as Carter suggests, the classroom is a space in which material realities overlap with theoretical ambitions, faculty could frame trauma as disability and thus, along with students, reimagine what education can look like. But, as Thomas Waugh suggests, administrative support of such embodied reimaginings is crucial for faculty (in *Synoptique* 278). As institutions of higher education in the United States become increasingly neoliberal in governance structure, the kinks, rough edges, and quantifiably elusive nature of queer, feminist, Indigenous or interdisciplinary theoretical positionalities are in danger of being reduced to "ideology" or worse, to being liquidated from curricula entirely due to a lethal combination of hierarchical academic politics, political fear, and the ongoing pursuit of uncontroversial deliverable "data" packaged as objectivity but embroiled in assessment eroticism (Han). In such a context, official language around universal values combined with ableist praxis often clash with diverse embodiments. Dean Spade points out that academic administrative systems are guilty of "distributing life chances and promoting certain ways of life at the expense of others, all while operating under legal regimes that declare universal equality" (in Carter 103). Carter draws upon the experience of a trigger:

> to call for solidarity between individuals typically understood as mentally disabled and communities who have experienced racial and post-colonial traumas. In doing so, I am purposely expanding the category of neurodivergence to include people who may never receive a medical diagnosis, or clinical recognition as such. This is an overtly political move toward an intersectional approach to trauma and disability...to draw attention to the intersecting forces of white supremacy and ableism.

Thus, trigger warnings can and should be understood from an ecological perspective with multiple intersecting points of potential trauma: students' lived experiences, the classroom, faculty members' lived experiences, administrative support systems, disability rights. If, as one of my students suggested, a list of trigger warnings will never be completed, perhaps faculty should follow Carter's lead and pursue a path of classroom solidarity rooted in expansive thinking around disabilities and an intersectional praxis. To oscillate in a neoliberal educational ecology is to give the vast topic of trigger warnings the nuance it deserves.

NOTES

1 I am excited to have the opportunity to consider a pedagogical and political topic such as trigger warnings during the pandemic years. This work coincides with other pandemic-related scholarship I have recently collaborated on. See Crowder-Taraborrelli, Scott, and Wilson.

2 https://www.thefire.org/news/california-writing-professor-investigated-after-admin-calls-works-black-brown-queer-authors.

3 https://www.aaup.org/report/trigger-warnings

4 See Freire 11.

5 That said, as Thomas Waugh reminds us, prioritizing the surprise element in the cinematic experience might be overrated. Spoilers, created by publicity industry and widely used to promote films in film trailers, often expose unexpected plot elements (in *Synoptique* 287).

WORKS CITED

AAUP Statement on Trigger Warnings. 2014, https://www.aaup.org/report/trigger-warnings.

Alilunas, Peter, Ummni Khan, Laura Helen Marks, Thomas Waugh, and Kyler Chittick. "Porn and/as Pedagogy, Sexual Representation in the Classroom: A Curated Roundtable Discussion." *Synoptique*, vol. 9, no. 2, 2021, pp. 269–94.

Benasayag, Miguel. *The Tyranny of Algorithms*. Europa Editions UK, 2021.

Carter, Angela M. "Teaching With Trauma: Disability Pedagogy, Feminism, and the Trigger Warnings Debate." *Disability Studies Quarterly*, vol. 35, no. 2, 2015.

Crowder-Taraborrelli, Tomás, Alexander Scott, and Kristi M. Wilson. "COVID-19 Coronavirus: Pandemic Politics in Latin America." *Latin American Perspectives,* vol. 50, no. 4, 2023, pp. 4–17.

FIRE. "California Writing Professor Investigated After Admin Calls Works by Black, Brown, Queer Authors 'Triggering,' 'Deviant Pornography.'" 11 May 2022, https://www.thefire.org/news/california-writing-professor-investigated-after-admin-calls-works-black-brown-queer-authors.

Fraser, Nancy. *Cannibal Capitalism: How our System is Devouring Democracy, Care, and the Planet – and What We Can Do About It*. Verso Books, 2022.

Freire, Paulo. *Education for Critical Consciousness*. Bloomsbury Publishing, 2013.

Gómez-Barris, Macarena. *The Extractive Zone: Social Ecologies and Decolonial Perspectives*. Duke UP, 2017.

Halberstam, Jack. "You Are Triggering Me!: The Neo-Liberal Rhetoric of Harm, Danger, and Trauma." *Bully Bloggers*, 5 July 2014.

Han, Byung-Chul. *Psychopolitics: Neoliberalism and new Technologies of Power.* Verso Books, 2017.

Harvey, David. *A Brief History of Neoliberalism*. Oxford UP, 2007.

Klein, Naomi. "Coronavirus Capitalism and How to Beat It." *The Intercept*, 16 March 2020.

Klein, Naomi. "How Big Tech Plans to Profit from the Pandemic." *The Guardian*, 13 May 2020.

Kohler Theo. "Trigger Warnings: A Feminist Theory of Trauma Versus the Neoliberal University." *Overland,* 27 September 2016.

Students With Disabilities and Chronic Conditions (SWDCC). "Letter to Admin, Faculty, and the Entire Soka Community on Disability Justice, Demands, And Giving Disabled Students at SUA More Than Disability Services As Our Support." 26 August 2020, https://d1fdloi71mui9q.cloudfront.net/JIBvqRGFQM2GcgOgDSMc_-SWDCC%20Demands%20and%20Plans%20of% 20Action.pdf.

CHAPTER TWO

WHAT WERE TRIGGER WARNINGS? NEW FORMS OF KNOWING AND THE USE OF THE CLASSROOM

Kelli Fuery

When I asked students[1] about their thoughts on trigger warnings in a number of classes in spring 2023, I was looking to discover their views and experiences regarding the efficacy and validity of such warnings when used in a classroom setting. Over the course of three separate hour-long discussions, a number of shared conclusions emerged: 1) The trigger warning is no longer an unfamiliar event within higher education, either as phenomenon or pedagogical tool. Despite having been first introduced into education lingo circa 2012, via an online guide (http://new.oberlin.edu/office/equity-concerns/sexual-offense-resource-guide/prevention-support-education/support-resources-for-faculty.dot) produced at Oberlin College (Halberstam) that advised faculty "there may be about 2 to 3 students in the class who have experienced some form of sexualized violence," my students concurred that the trigger warning has transitioned into low-impact disclaimer, losing much of its meaningful consciousness-raising potential. 2) The students further shared their views that the trigger warning has seemingly passed into general awareness in university settings and syllabi, and continues to be closely associated with the potential of related repetition of traumatic response experience to predominantly visual material.

3) Further, students remarked that more recently, less and less positive comments about trigger warnings have circulated, suggesting that the rhetoric calling for trigger warnings may have lost its sting. Following critiques, such as those offered by Jack Halberstam, it does seem that trigger warnings have fallen out of popular discourse, only to be replaced by another new fear of what is not known: AI. The logic behind the trigger warning is consistently defined by its relationship to the past, a temporality that is prefigured by the "warning" and the foreclosure of alternative reflective response. Its apparent purpose is to offer the opportunity to avoid whatever might be triggering, not to engage with it or think about why the material might be triggering in the first place. In this way trigger warnings can be viewed as actively facilitating the temptation of not-knowing, what psychoanalyst Wilfred Bion defined as an emptying of connections within everyday experience that offer us meaning or which create growth in emotional experience. He writes, if not-knowing is a state that is facilitated, "the way is therefore prepared for a severe arrest of development" ("Second Thoughts" 107). This arrested development is very much linked to traumatic response, as trauma is a rupture of our ability to think and feel emotional experience coherently and creatively.

In some ways the trigger warning, if left as a form of not-knowing, shares a similar threatening sensibility to the current fear of future technology[2] and my interest in this chapter is to consider what has happened to trigger warnings so that we might rethink the ways in which a classroom can be used to embrace unthought experiences in productive and creative ways. Have trigger warnings already become a reductive part of well-intended classroom instruction, or might there be something more to be gained by considering an evolution of their function, one that moves trigger warnings from disclaimers to possible new forms of knowing? Whatever the function of trigger warnings is, or has become, it is the student experience, and the question of whether or not warnings have worked for them, and *continue* to work, that is at the forefront of my concerns here.[3]

The students I spoke with in these spring classes were very forthcoming in their responses, with the most repeated experience across all classes being that trigger warnings are used as a synonym for "brace for impact," or as an invitation to leave the room if they felt uncomfortable about content (primarily film or television), or to signal the possibility of encountering a sensitive topic (such as rape, racism, or graphic violence). Overall, student comments showed their thinking on trigger warnings: when used as "brace for impact," the warning ultimately removed the responsibility from both the professor and the class from working through the material and its triggering capacity; when left as a disclaimer, there was no follow-up or later contextualization about the triggering material or why it might evoke triggered responses in an individual or group setting. More concerningly, students commented on feeling awkward if they chose to leave a classroom, as it publicly outed their trauma which would have preferably remained private. Two sophisticated statements in particular stood out from the group discussions: 1) "things I need trigger warnings for aren't normally the content they are given for," and 2) "the word itself ('trigger') has become its own phenomenon," indicating that students are very aware of the deeply complicated relationship that exists between the use of trigger warnings and the use of a classroom, and more significantly, they understand that triggers are not dependent solely on the presence of material. Rather, triggers were seen to be generative—they can be caught (following Teresa Brennan's "transmission of affect" argument) as much as they may lie latent in either individuals or groups. It became evident from discussion that classroom experience was equally impactful (not positively so) when conversations were left unspoken, not followed up, and especially when difficult responses were not properly worked through. However, in all of the three informal classroom discussions, it was clear that the connection between trigger warnings and content material remains at the forefront of student understanding.

Halberstam has referred to the trigger warning as a:

> structure of paternalistic normativity...[that] presumes and to a certain extent produces putative viewers or listeners who *want to know* what is to come in class or online because they fear their reaction to such material and wish either to *mentally prepare to engage with it or to avoid it altogether*.

> The trigger warning, in other words, believes in a student or viewer who is unstable and damaged and could at any moment *collapse into crisis*. (536–37, my emphasis)

Halberstam's comments, particularly the phrases I have emphasized, relate to the underlying premise of the two student statements that I see as an acknowledgment of the role the trigger warning has in one's desire to know and not-know. His comments also help me consider how trigger warnings might evolve as part of the use of the classroom; that is, how they can play a role in facilitating new ways of knowing. Halberstam is not a fan, stating "we must oppose the trigger warning" (541), but I don't think it is the trigger warning itself that is his primary issue, rather it is the lack of sustained and close analysis of responses (what are thought/felt and not-thought) that emerge from class experience which Halberstam is concerned with. Given that trigger warnings are so closely linked with the belief that explicit material is likely to evoke traumatic response (or more accurately a return of traumatic response to stimulating material), I want to explore the potential transformative thinking trigger warnings could lead to through two contemporary psychoanalytic thinkers, D. W. Winnicott and Wilfred Bion, and in particular their respective works "The Use of an Object and Relating through Identifications" (Winnicott 86–94) and "A Theory on Thinking" (Bion, "Second Thoughts" 110–19).

Winnicott was a pediatrician who became a psychoanalyst and helped found the British School of Psychoanalysis, also known as object-relations psychoanalysis or the Independent Group. The "use" of an object, as Winnicott termed it, is specifically focused on one's capacity to create (or think with)—that is, "the making of interpretations, and not about interpretations as such" (Winnicott 86). How one develops and establishes a capacity to use objects, and significantly where that capacity is thwarted or absent, is the project. In this case, the capacity to use the trigger warning would not be determined by content (the "what") but instead, the "why" (investigating the experience—either to embrace, modify or avoid the material altogether). Bion, an object-relations psychoanalyst, is often introduced as "revolutionary," due to his theory of thinking which proposed a reversal of dream-thought, where one uses the sensory data of everyday life to create (or not) a psychical structure (alpha function) to think/dream emotional experience. As Antonio Ferro succinctly puts it: "What is revolutionary in Bion's thought lies in its having postulated the existence of a continual day-dreaming which constantly alphabetizes all the sensoriality (and obscurity) that pervades us, building a chain which leads from alpha elements to pictograms, to waking dream thought, and to the perennial construction of an unconscious" (Ferro xv). Here, Bion's ideas help to understand the critical importance of what it means to develop a capacity to tolerate frustration, or put another way, to tolerate experiences that might trigger us. For the purposes of this argument, I locate the classroom as an object of use and examine the purpose and role of trigger warnings as a mechanism for creating "safe spaces," that might permit a group to think difficult emotional experiences so that mental growth, or new forms of knowing, might occur. The aim being to situate trigger warnings as properly successful only if they act as markers of whether or not the classroom has succeeded in establishing a safe space and, most significantly, the capacity to create through student object-use.

In order for a classroom to become an effective safe space (perhaps it is better to call this an authentic safe space), it helps to regard it as an object and, as such, all that exists within that space, what goes into creating that intersubjective area of experience, falls under the auspices of "object." This includes students, the instructor, architecture, material furniture, audio-visual texts and equipment, etc. As a result, trigger warnings work as just one part of how a classroom is used as an object, and therefore take on many different functions in maintaining the way in which a safe classroom is used as an object by instructor and student alike. The examination of "use," then, is very much attendant to the student's point of view, because it is how the student uses, or rather develops a capacity to use the classroom (or indeed the instructor) that determines the construction and viability of a safe space. Trigger warnings, as a particle of this use, might function better if regarded as indicators of how successful (or not) a safe space has been established collaboratively as part of a classroom's group dynamic. Instead of leaving the warning as a disclaimer, or "brace for impact," the subject of triggering is better served by viewing it as an intentional act, so that emotional responses to material and context can be properly unpicked with tolerance, modification, and avoidance of the relevant material being given equal time and space for consideration in a safe space.

A classroom that is a safe space can never be a classroom that behaves itself in terms of the good or the positive. This is a sanitized space, not a safe space. A safe space, psychoanalytically speaking, is one that permits and facilitates destruction of an object, whether that be subject, weekly topic, text, thought or, ideally, all four. Most importantly, this space should aim to ensure the survival of the destroyed object. The space of the classroom, when considered in this light, works as a political temporality that depends on the capacity for the instructor and student group to work effectively within a growth mindset. The ability, or willingness, to be confronted with and closely engage with ethically demanding and morally complex material, and to be able to hold different perspectives without the need to colonize one over the other is evidence of a growth mindset.

Winnicott's notion—the destruction of an object—is very confusing. There is always a risk to the magic of an idea when one attempts to simplify its concept, and yet it is best to clarify how to take up or engage with Winnicott's idea of the use of an object. Thomas Ogden regards this as one of Winnicott's most difficult and yet important pieces of writing, saying that it is only through developing one's own answers or response to Winnicott's proposition, reflecting on their "experience of reading" will one encounter what is being argued: "it has to be experienced" ("Destruction Reconceived" 1244). At this point, the link between the classroom as an object to be used, and Winnicott's psychoanalytic theory of object-use should be emerging—they cannot be prescribed but rather as effective, authentic and safe classroom spaces arise, each must be facilitated and directed. In other words, they must be experienced in real time and no classroom will be the same, even between weeks, or potentially, throughout the class time itself.

The psychoanalytic term "object-use" refers to a well-developed capacity to think with objects (people, places, things, etc.) outside the self, to the point that such objects can help lead to emotional and mental growth. This includes objects that threaten, scare or have the potential to suspend, or arrest us. The use of an object refers "to mature object-relatedness in which the subject lives in the outside world of 'shared reality,' and experiences objects as genuinely external to himself. This reversal causes the reader to loosen his grip on what he thought he knew and to open himself to not knowing" ("Destruction Reconceived" 1245). The ability to open oneself to not knowing and bear this existential threat is the first step in what Bion would view as tolerating frustrating experience, and therefore is an indicator of mental and emotional growth. In his article "A Theory of Thinking," he writes that the "[i]nability to tolerate frustration can obstruct the development of thoughts and a capacity to think...If frustration can be tolerated the mating of conception and realizations whether negative or positive initiates procedures necessary to learning by experience" ("Second Thoughts" 113–14). Do trigger warnings, if left as disclaimers, damage this very precious opportunity to learn from experience? If students leave the class, are they able to loosen their grip on what they thought they knew? Do they immediately annihilate the possibility of opening themselves up to not knowing?

As I try to understand what Winnicott means by the befuddling "subject destroys the object" (90), I return to Bion's work *Learning from Experience* (which for those readers familiar with Bion's writing might seem laughable—to search for lucidity in Bion over Winnicott!) where he writes of destruction in terms of one's "concern for truth" ("Seven Servants" 11). Bion is attempting to outline a new theory of emotional experience, one that is tied much more to thoughts that are "in search of a thinker" ("Second Thoughts" 166); that is, how one processes sensory data from everyday life that is too overwhelming to be easily processed. Bion is interested in what one does if emotional experience is unable to be transformed and turned into thoughts that can be dreamed. "To learn from experience alpha-function must operate on the awareness of the emotional experience; alpha-elements are produced from the impressions of the experience; these are thus made storable and available for dream thoughts and unconscious waking thinking" ("Seven Servants" 8). If an emotion is too strong or violent to the psyche, it can block or thwart this transformation resulting in splitting parts of the self. It is not necessary to dive deeper into Bionian theory here (Fuery), suffice to say that destruction is necessary in order to unmake and remake external objects (and therefore our relationship to them) so that the block or hurdle can be overcome or negotiated, permitting everyday sensory data to be transformed into dream-thoughts, developing one's capacity to create. Ogden also says he "genuinely" doesn't know what Winnicott means but arrives at the conclusion that in becoming destroyed, one encounters an experience of themselves (or perhaps we might say part of their self) that has been destroyed, "*in the course of the movement from object-relating to object-usage*" ("Destruction Reconceived" 1247). Put another way, this might be the sensibility of being confronted with some part of our self that we know has been destroyed and which has not yet had the opportunity to be rethought, remade or reintegrated as parts of the self—what is often understood as trauma. For Winnicott, and Bion in particular, this difficult work cannot be done without another mind. By encountering this feeling of "becoming destroyed," Ogden notes that Winnicott is signaling the shift into an intermediate position, a space that permits the possibility of remaking a sense of self through a different relationship to a world of objects.

Returning to the subject at hand, existing imaginations of "safe spaces" that precede a classroom (ones that offer trigger warnings solely as disclaimers) must be destroyed in order for a classroom to be unmade and remade, to permit students (and indeed instructors) to loosen their grip on what they think they know and to open themselves to not knowing. Instead of prescribing a trigger warning over specific content, as a "structure of paternalistic normativity" that Halberstam identifies, setting time aside for discussion on what experiences resulted as triggered responses reroutes facilitation of not-knowing, allowing student experience to lead a concern for truth and new forms of knowing. I would like to share a teaching anecdote that exemplifies my own experience on what I understand to have been an occurrence of the safe space classroom surviving as a "destroyed object" (that is an unmaking and remaking of the classroom space).

I begin my upper-division British Film and Television class with a comparative analysis of Bruce Robinson's *Withnail & I* (1987) and Chris Morris's *Four Lions* (2010). Ignoring all previous experience and knowing just how treacherous it is to screen your film darlings to students, I plowed ahead. The purpose of this film pairing was to suggest a possible historical mapping of culture across the foundational psychical model of humor. The lofty ambition of the claim was that in response to social and political oppression, British cinema has used humor to both resist and repeal conservative thought. This is, of course, not specific to British cinema, but humor remains a critical model to think about myths of coherence and unity within experiences of nationhood and it offers students another way to think about identification within visual culture. What a group finds funny is not solely individual; it is deeply linked to group thinking and experience. By requesting a comparative analysis between two films produced twenty-three years apart, my aim was to encourage the class to think about how they might use such films to determine meaning regarding British Culture and its own sense of identity. (There were three models in total, the other two being class and horror.)

Bion writes: "The whole point about looking at a group is that it changes the field of study to include phenomena that cannot be studied outside the group. Outside the group as a field of study, their activity is not manifest. The group, in the sense of a collection of people in a room, adds nothing to the individual or the aggregate of individuals – it merely reveals something that is not otherwise visible" ("Experiences in Groups and Other Papers" 134). Therefore, the project was not to determine whether or not the films themselves were funny, but how the class group responded to the humor in both films as each uses humor purposefully as a mechanism to break with and through repressive thinking (sexuality and racism, respectively). *Withnail & I* and *Four Lions* rally against a dominant Hollywood sense of humor but they equally showcase Britain's evolving attitudes on what is and is not to be regarded as funny, principally in their efforts to resist homogeneous constructions of identity. For the purposes of this chapter, I am only focusing on *Withnail & I* as this is the film that received the most attention and resistance within the class.

Withnail & I is set in 1969, a transitional time in Britain where public homosexual behavior had recently shifted from illegality to being heavily penalized. Ostensibly, the film follows two out of work actors, Withnail (Richard E. Grant) and Marwood (Paul McGann) who leave London for a weekend in England's Lake District, to get away and regain fresh perspective on their dire situation, before returning and ultimately parting ways. At the end of the film, Marwood successfully lands the lead role in R. C. Sherriff's play *Journey's End*,[4] but Withnail is left behind, bereft and alone. The film's themes of class, sexuality, privilege, and masculinity are tightly woven and its witty dialogue, what Kevin Jackson refers to as "yob baroque" (26) is partly the reason for its cult status. The film is ranked #29 on the British Film Institute (BFI) List 100 Best British Films and remains a firm favorite in fan circles. Withnail and Marwood arrive at Uncle Monty's country house, Crow Crag (borrowed for the weekend), only to be frightened in the middle of the night by the unexpected arrival of Uncle Monty himself. "Monty, you terrible cunt!" It becomes very clear over the course of their stay that Monty is sexually interested in Marwood. The scene in the kitchen, where Marwood is helping to prepare dinner is both suggestive and socially provocative. Marwood says, "I can't find the rosemary" and Monty is only too willing to help. Monty reaches his arms around Marwood (Figure 1)—displaying a proximity of male bodies that at the time of the film's distribution, would have remained contentious.[5]

Not to be dissuaded, Monty continues his pursuit of Marwood, appearing in his room one evening: "Boy, I know you're not asleep boy, but he [Withnail] is. I've been into his room. He won't hear a thing." Marwood, very nervously asks what Monty wants. Monty has been misinformed, as Withnail has told him that Marwood is a closeted gay man, a "toilet trader" unable to come to terms with his sexuality. Withnail has lied, saying Marwood is in love with him, while Withnail is unable to reciprocate. While the scene is initially framed as terrifying for Marwood,

Figure 1. Still from *Withnail & I* (Robinson). Uncle Monty (Richard Griffiths) reaches suggestively around Marwood (Paul McGann) to find the rosemary.

who is highly fearful of Monty's advances, watching it closely discloses an entirely different agenda. Once the audience understands that Monty has been fed the lie that Marwood is closeted, full of "problems," we learn a little more of Monty's motivation: "You mustn't blame yourself. I know how you feel and how difficult it is. And that is why you mustn't hold back, let it ruin your youth as I nearly did over Eric. It is like a tide. Give in to it, boy. Go with it. It is society's crime not ours." While terribly forward and deaf to Marwood's protestations, Monty believes by being clear about his intentions and desires—something that should be possible for all free humans—he believes he is helping Marwood to come out, not hide away (as a "toilet trader") living with shame and guilt. Marwood counters Withnail's deception by telling Monty that it is actually Withnail who is in love with Marwood and the one who is unable "to accept what he is." This changes Monty's perspective *immediately*, who says "Oh my dear boy, if I'd known that, I would have never attempted to come between you." Monty departs under the cloak of night, leaving a letter expressing his sincere apology. This is the scene that arrested the class's thinking.

A year after the film's release, Margaret Thatcher's Section 28 legislation (1988–2003) came into effect, prohibiting any intentional promotion of homosexuality: "teaching in any maintained school of the acceptability of homosexuality as a pretended family relationship," or publication of "material with the intention of promoting homosexuality." After I gave this context, students reviewed their initial reaction to the film, which had been initially very dismissive. The bedroom scene with Monty and Marwood was read as an attempted rape scene (see William's Letterboxd review below) and in first discussions the class's thinking on the film was very split. Instead of offering a trigger warning for either film, I wanted students to feel their responses to the films' comedy and determine how humor is interpreted across culture and time periods. The class had resisted *Withnail & I* (a resistance that interestingly did not occur with *Four Lions*—the humor concerning Islamophobia was read as the film intended) dismissing any potentiality as its starting point—and I used this opportunity to discover why that resistance emerged, to try to determine what was the reason behind the triggered responses. After all, there is no rape, attempted or otherwise in the film. Monty certainly comes on strong to Marwood wanting to have sex with him, but Marwood clearly says no, which Monty hears and immediately retracts. He even apologizes in person and again in a letter. Rapists don't do that.

This means at one level, the class has to confront its own omnipotence, that is, the fragile reality of subjective opinion versus potential and actual external realities (including other perspectives). Ogden uses the term "magical thinking" as a way of labeling this form of not-thinking. For him, magical thinking refers "to thinking that relies on omnipotent fantasy to create a psychic reality that the individual experiences as 'more real' than external reality" ("On Three Forms of Thinking" 319). This enables one to see things as they (unconsciously) wish them to be rather than how they actually are or might be for others. ("Wish" here is a tricky word—I am using it in the proper psychoanalytic sense, which is that the thought is formed entirely within the psychotic part of the personality, that is within the limit of one's own world, ignorant of all else.) Ogden continues, "magical thinking subverts the opportunity to learn from one's lived experience with real external objects" ("On Three Forms of Thinking" 319) and the task for me in this situation as professor was to move the class from this position of not-knowing, to one where the group was able to let go of what they didn't know and learn from the experience of the classroom. Put another way, students began to use the classroom as an object to unmake and remake their thinking. To illustrate, I have quoted one student's Letterboxd review at length and conclude with a brief analysis.

> The whole part of Monty's attempted rape and Withnail not only dismissing Marwood's distress but fully enabling his uncle's aqctions [*sic*] is the kind of story thread that seems genetically engineered to fuck with me. This is fully my bias. I'm horrified by loss of control, and the thought of being alone with someone you thought was your friend selling you to his predatory uncle for, what, booze? Turns my stomach. That's just me though. Maybe it won't bother you. But this part really blinded me when I saw this yesterday and I thought I should give it another try now that I knew what was in store. Also have a much different view of it in light of what Bruce Robinson had to endure from Franco Zeffirelli. I feel like a real jerk for thinking the film of "not sharing my anger."

> The second time around I noticed a lot more rapport between Marwood and Withnail, and I didn't feel as much that Withnail was just sitting around and putting Marwood in line with danger. The scene in the small pub feels key in this regard; just two blokes versus the world. I also felt the class conflict more strongly. Withnail's living with Marwood in a filthy London apartment but his uncle's loaded, betraying the safety of his friend for access to free money. Basic analysis I'm doing right now, but it's making the movie click.
>
> (William's Letterboxd review[6])

I loved William's response to the film, how he moved from a position of magical thinking to one that was able to let go of what was thought known and knowable: "*genetically engineered to fuck with me*," "*This is fully my bias. I'm horrified by the loss of control*," "*That's just me though*," "*this part really blinded me*." William moved to a position of opening himself up to an awareness of another's shared reality: "*Maybe it won't bother you*"; to a new form of knowing, "*I thought I should give it another try*," "*I feel like a real jerk for thinking the film of 'not sharing my anger.*'" Instead of William's psychic reality dominating external reality, he was able to reflect on his reaction, why it occurred as part of his own "bias" and break free from the stronghold of omnipotence. Through his reflection, a new relationship to the film—based on the classroom experience—served to create a new form of knowing. Had a trigger warning been given for the bedroom scene, it is unlikely that his reflective response would have yielded the transformation in thought precisely because the warning would reify the scene as being one that is "engineered" to fuck with people. The transformative thinking evident in William's review demonstrates not simply a change in one student's attitude over one particular film, but indeed, it illustrates how necessary it is to take time to deconstruct triggered responses via class discussion. This then serves to structure spectator reflexivity (what Jacques Rancière has otherwise called the emancipation of the spectator) to any future encounter with a film that initially provokes magical thinking. It is never my intention to have students adopt the very same opinion of a film that I have (that ship has long sailed!), rather the objective is to see them reflect and alter their thinking so that it creates new, open thinking and an ability to use the classroom as an object. Triggers can be valuable if incorporated into reflective group discussion but not if they are prescriptive or foreshadow student experience.

Winnicott reflected on his own interpretations concerning patient analysis, stating "how much deep change I have prevented or delayed in patients [with his own] need to interpret" (86). His solution was to wait and allow the patient to arrive at their own "understanding creatively" so that their capacity to use objects—that is, to think with them—is not impeded and they are able to both feel and know what their emotional experience is. If likened to the use of the classroom, students who are given a trigger warning are immediately directed to determine content as triggering, thereby removing any possibility of self-determination or thought on what it is that is triggering. In this way there is an unconscious collusion between instructor and student to prevent the classroom from encountering and tolerating difficult emotional experiences so that it might be worked through. It shuts down different perspectives and limits understanding, and worse, it denies the opportunity for students and instructors to experience reality outside omnipotent control. Of course, there are interpretations that a classroom instructor has to make, to provide guidance, accuracy of material and also to manage the group dynamic (and indeed, the instructor must also possess enough protomental maturity). But this is part of how a capacity to create, or use an object, is facilitated. "This capacity cannot be said to be inborn, nor can its development in an individual be taken for granted. The development of a capacity to use an object is another example of the maturational process as something that depends on a facilitating environment" (Winnicott 89). The classroom is for the student and interpretations of trigger warnings or related material must be placed in as full a context as possible so that students can use the entire classroom and its objects (instructor, material, other students) in order to create and develop new forms of knowing. The good-enough instructor will also be able to recognize inability to use the classroom in this way (even their own) and this is part of what trigger warnings must attend to.

The inability to use an object, if recognized, can serve as a "teachable moment," where students encounter something outside their omnipotence and begin to either see it for the reality that it is in its own state, or reject it. It is this moment of experience, this object-use, that Winnicott regards as destruction of the object. Destruction used in this context has a positive connotation, because what is being "destroyed" (the object) might also survive, and the survival of the object is what leads to a shared reality; that is, student awareness that there is a world full of other people, with their own thoughts that are not able to be controlled, which they can think with and mentally grow with. Put more simply, a student learns from experience when they are able to move from an omnipotent position (the dominance of their own point of view) to the mature position of recognizing and accepting an external other perspective that may or may not relate to their own situation or inner world. It is very important to emphasize the innovative way in which Winnicott is using the word "destruction" here—as for him, there is "no anger in the destruction of the object" to which he refers (93). What is being destroyed is the subject's eager control over the object and this is why it is important for creativity that the object survives.

Trigger warnings given as disclaimers and without proper, comprehensive group discussion serve as incredibly blunt instruments to deal with complex situations. As universal blanket warnings, they are ill-equipped to provide enough room for the diversity and variety of cultural nuance or historical sensitivities. What of material that intentionally seeks to trigger an audience as much as possible for political reasons? Take Pier Paolo Pasolini's *Saló*, or *120 Days of Sodom* (or indeed any of his films), Catherine Breillat's *À ma soeur!*, Georges Bataille's *Story of the Eye*, or Beyoncé's *Formation.* The explicit content in these creative works is intentionally triggering, seeking to challenge and counter fascist, patriarchal, and supremacist systems of thought respectively. To warn against them will disrupt the political agenda of the work or worse, rob the classroom of the potential experience to uncover more productive discussions about how to work with difficult and emotionally complex situations.[7] Unless we provide classrooms that students feel comfortable destroying and remaking, we are not effectively facilitating their capacity to create new forms of knowing—for them as well as ourselves.

NOTES

1 Fifty-eight Chapman University undergraduate students (61% female; 39% male; over 30% identified as LGBTQIA and around 3% identified as non-White, either Islander, Asian American, or Other) from film and media studies as well as the interdisciplinary minor Creative and Cultural Industries (CCI) were polled. CCI students represented the widest cross-section of the university campus, coming from business, computer science, performing arts, and humanities disciplines. All students said they had encountered trigger warnings in either their syllabi or classroom settings. Other students volunteered that they had used them in sorority recruitment (but interestingly no students commented about use in fraternity recruitment).

2 It is beyond the scope of this chapter, but the rise in generative AI technology use in student papers signals a very clear form of not-knowing; that is, a fear or inability to tolerate frustration which results in an absence of creative and productive thinking.

3 I should state from the outset that I do not offer trigger warnings about content in my classes per se. Instead, I offer a broader discussion that warns against the vacuity of trigger warnings if not properly considered or managed in a group setting, which I suppose is a trigger warning in and of itself. I outline that if trigger warnings are to be associated with traumatic response, it is not possible for me to predetermine what might cause the trigger. Like Marnie (Tippi Hedren) in Alfred Hitchcock's *Marnie*, whose traumatic response occurs when she sees either the color red or hears thunder and lightning, a film might emphasize a color (like the color yellow in Wes Anderson's *Fantastic Mr. Fox*) or weather pattern (e.g. *Twister*, de Bont)—but in no way could I be sure this would incite traumatic response in a class audience, or indeed what experience it was linked to for individual students.

4 R. C. Sherriff's *Journey's End* is a play that recounts an officer's experiences within World War I, where homosexuality is not explicit yet drives much of the play's intermeshed relationships.

5 As noted, homosexual acts were illegal in Britain prior to the 1967 Sexual Offences Act.

6 William has given his consent for his review to be quoted and has participated in the discussion of this paper. I would like to also thank Cole and Sophia for their contributions.

7 Of course, the counter argument here is films such as *Triumph of the Will* (Riefenstahl) or *The Birth of the Nation* (Griffith) are better served if their political agendas *are* disrupted, where trigger warnings can be used to

reframe reception of such films in ways that intentionally oppose their purported aim(s). In this way, trigger warnings may serve as a crucial part of the creating of "new forms of knowledge" in classroom spaces.

WORKS CITED

À ma soeur!/Fat Girl. Directed by Catherine Breillat. Arte France Cinéma, CB Films, Flach Film, Immagine & Cinema, Urania Pictures, 2001.

Bataille, Georges. *The Story of the Eye* (*L'histoire de l'oeil*). Translated by Joachim Neugroschel. Urizen Books, 1978.

Beyoncé. "Formation." *Lemonade*, Parkwood Entertainment, 2016, www.beyonce.com/album/lemonade-visual-album/.

Bion, Wilfred R. *Experiences in Groups and Other Papers*. Basic Books, Inc, 1959.

Bion, Wilfred R. *Second Thoughts: Selected Papers on Psycho-Analysis*. William Heinemann Medical Books Ltd, 1967.

Bion, Wilfred R. *Seven Servants: Four Works by Wilfred Bion*. Jason Aronson, Inc., 1977.

Birth of the Nation, The. Directed by D.W. Griffith, David W. Griffith Corp, Epoch Producing Corporation, 1915.

Brennan, Teresa. *The Transmission of Affect*. Cornell University Press, 2004.

Fantastic Mr. Fox. Directed by Wes Anderson, Twentieth Century Fox, 2009.

Ferro, Antonino. Foreword. *The Post-Bionian Field Theory of Antonino Ferro*, by Howard Levine (ed.), Routledge, 2022, pp. xv–xviii.

Four Lions. Directed by Chris Morris, Film4 Productions, Wild Bunch and Warp Films, 2010.

Fuery, Kelli. *Wilfred Bion, Thinking and Emotional Experience with Moving Images: Being Embedded*. Routledge, 2019.

Halberstam, Jack. "Trigger Happy: From Content Warning to Censorship." *Signs: Journal of Women in Culture and Society*, vol. 42, no. 2, 2017, pp. 535–42.

Jackson, Kevin. *Withnail & I*. BFI Film Classics. Bloomsbury Publishing, 2022.

Marnie. Directed by Alfred Hitchcock, performances by Tippi Hedren, Pierre-François Caille, Universal Pictures, 1964.

Ogden, Thomas. "On Three Forms of Thinking: Magical Thinking, Dream Thinking, and Transformative Thinking." *The Psychoanalytic Quarterly*, vol. 78, no. 2, 2010, pp. 317–47.

Ogden, Thomas. "Destruction Reconceived: On Winnicott's The Use of an Object and Relating through Identifications." *The International Journal of Psychoanalysis*, vol. 97, 2016, pp. 1243–62.

Salò, or the 120 Days of Sodom / Salò o le 120 giornate di Sodoma. Directed by Pier Paolo Pasolini. United Artists, 1975.

Sherriff, R.C. *Journey's End*. Penguin, 1983.

Triumph of the Will/Triumph des Willens. Directed by Leni Riefenstahl, Leni Riefenstahl-Produktion – Reichspropagandaleitung der NSDAP, 1935.

Twister. Directed by Jan de Bont, Warner Bros., 1996.

Winnicott, Donald W. *Playing and Reality*. Routledge, 1999.

Withnail & I. Directed by Bruce Robinson, performances by Paul McGann, Richard E. Grant, Richard Griffiths, Cineplex Odeon Films and Handmade Films, 1987.

CHAPTER THREE

painful (hopeful) ruminations

Sophia Greco

> *What are the words you do not yet have? What do you need to say? What are the tyrannies you swallow day by day and attempt to make your own, until you will sicken and die of them, still in silence?*
>
> Audre Lorde

There are many words I do not yet have. What do I need to say? My writing on this subject leads me into the topic of grief.

Writing about trigger warnings is writing around trauma—
writing around trauma is writing around violence—
is writing around relationships—
is writing around healing—
is writing around grief.

What kind of grief? Mainly: grief over how our cultural practices around trauma sever us from each other, individualizing and compartmentalizing our pain. I struggle to write in the way I struggle to connect with others around my own wounds—wounds I sometimes ignore, or forget, or hide. I struggle to write in the same way I can't quite seem to figure out where my fragmented thoughts belong—*if* they belong. I struggle to write, especially when it starts seeming like I write alone, in isolation from my writing community.

At first, I struggle to write through fear—and then, I even struggle to identify that fear. Is it fear that my words might be inadequate, will misrepresent my own experiences? Fear that my writing will be misinterpreted? Fear that, in fact, I might have nothing worthwhile to say or contribute to this conversation? Is it fear because, as Lorde describes, "the transformation of silence into language and action is an act of self-revelation and that always seems fraught with danger?"

Or: is it fear that my writing will force me to contend with painful memories that have largely gone untouched until now? Fear that my writing will not reach or connect with others in the ways I am so painfully desperate for? Fear that the topic of trigger warnings is too polarized within the sphere of public discussion, far too polarized to allow for nuance as I messily write through my memories, my confusion, my questioning?

I know that in part, this fear stems from the fact that writing into the void feels markedly unsafe. Mariame Kaba says: "You cannot have safety without strong, empathic relationships with others" (98). Without writing in conversation with those I trust and have relationships with, I write aimlessly, awkwardly, guardedly. I start, stop, start again, find myself in another ditch or dead end. My ideas are stuck, cyclical, tangled, going nowhere. The more I write the more I feel alone. The more I feel alone, the more my writing spirals, wandering into new and old paths.

To write is a process; to write is to process. I keep writing. Sometimes alone; sometimes in conversation. To write alone is to think, to make sense, to respond to my own "needs for language and definition" (Lorde). To write in tandem with others is to respond, to exchange ideas, to share space. To be a political writer, as Cherríe Moraga says, is to be the ultimate optimist, to reject our cultural tendencies toward a privatism "which renders us politically useless."

I struggle to write on this subject. While struggling to write, I am baffled to find myself teeming with fear. As I continue to write, I discover that beneath the fear, I am, maybe, more so just brimming with grief.

+

Against my best efforts, I triggered myself while writing this piece...

It happens. It happens quickly, unexpectedly, while sifting through old writings in the hopes that they might dislodge something in this stuck process of writing. I'd forgotten that some of my old writings documented pain, loneliness, shame. What is this—an accidental archive of abandoned memories?

It happens like this: looking through the countless text files I have authored in my years of owning a personal computing device (a phone, a computer, access to the internet in any form), I am quickly overwhelmed. See, there are so many files—fits and starts in story-form, fleeting thoughts jotted down in the anonymous rush of a crowded commute, detailed affections that sometimes felt like the only respite-escape-joy in my world. I am overwhelmed because there is a literal torrent, a rush of file after file after file, and as I wander through a note app, an email account, this archive of pained adolescence, I am reminded of how deep my love for writing runs, yes, my own personal history of turning to the page, of typing furiously and endlessly when the words finally come. I am reminded that this is what I periodically did when I found myself in a powerless space, a place that felt like it couldn't possibly get lonelier; a place that, very occasionally, I might revisit, but which never quite hits the same terrible note it once did.

yeah.
in the depths of low lows, i managed
to write.
my tether
my anchor
my outlet?

I imagine that the way to move through this flood of memory and grief is to be rooted; to be seen and held and loved as we wade and weather through the water. To be tethered through rain and storm; and eventually, for this pain to be a scar I can wear visibly, rather than a mark left on internal tissue. Without roots, without an anchor, without the grounding force of those who understand and forgive and perceive you wholly in your pain and your worst—there is no moving through. It is too hard to bear this alone.

I feel it like it lives in my bones: we, as living beings, are not made to do this alone.

+

I carry this idea with me, the idea that we carry a base need for company; a part of us that necessitates being together to be well. It's an idea that breathes life and purpose and momentum into stubborn hope, contrasts gloom with stark relief; it informs my teaching, guides my slow drafting of pedagogical blueprints. It's a risk that we take with intention, with a willingness to resist; the risk to hold and be held; the risk to see what aches can be shared, until some weight might lift.

+

Something keeps bothering me.

I'm trying to bring it out of my head, to bring it into words. If I think of trigger warnings as road signage, or traffic signals, I think they tend to read something like this: "Tread carefully—if need be, take care of yourself instead of proceeding down this road." The thing is, is that taking care of yourself? It's expected to happen alone. Contained and private; dealt with individually, never collectively. There is no signage that is meant for the group, and there is no warning for others that urges us to take care of each other because this may be too hard to bear alone. We are made into hyper-independent, compartmentalizing units. This individualized pain *is* that tyranny, the one we swallow and attempt to make our own. A tyranny we swallow, until it swells, until we choke.

If safety necessitates healthy, strong relationships, the routines and procedures we've built around trigger warnings are anything but relational. The classroom is a space we are asked to take risks in, a space where we are challenged and at times, made uncomfortable, but it is rarely a space where we are taught what to do with that discomfort, how to wrestle and share the risk of vulnerability. If, as bell hooks says, "we rather think of safety as knowing how to cope in situations of risk," then how do participants in the classroom learn to cope with situations of risk?

I often feel untethered, lost at sea, unprepared for those situations of risk. I feel especially unprepared to support others through those moments of risk. It is dangerous to go alone; but we do not acknowledge, nor do we reconvene, nor do we address any wounds torn open in the room. We do not compose new narratives around that hurt. Instead, we leave elephants in the room, we sit idly and numb to their presence, and then we move on; refusing to contend with our routine apart-ness.

+

By arguing for or against trigger warnings, I wonder if we risk ignoring the more insidious problem at hand. I sense that we dehumanize pain, that by isolating our pain we support the larger lethal forces at work, and that we sever ourselves from our relational nature by not assuming the shared responsibility that comes with shared space.

bell hooks says:

> Students stated quite openly and honestly that reading the literature in the context of class discussion was making them feel pain. [...] Later, we discussed the way in which all their comments implied that to experience pain is bad, an indication that something is wrong. We talked about changing how we perceive pain, about our society's approach to pain, considering the possibility that this pain could be a constructive sign of growth.

I imagine that part of our society's approach to pain makes it so that socially accepted practices of collective grief are only sanctioned in certain moments—death, namely. What if we changed our approach to pain? What would come of a classroom full of students that did not flinch in the face of a peer who dares to reveal their hurt?

I sense there is a possibility there; for the trigger warning to form a framework, a conversation, a shared responsibility, a glimpse of what mutual care could be. A question, a process of questioning. Maybe it's possible to bridge the divide, to reject compulsory expectations of dividing-compartmentalizing-distancing in our learning spaces. To bring in our baggage, rather than to leave it at the door. Maybe all it takes is willing participants and an invitation to subvert.

+

As a teacher, I worry. Am I equipped to handle the responsibility of teaching, of the title "teacher"? I am fearful; I hardly know my own triggers, let alone how to facilitate a classroom full of students with power to heal and hurt. Can I help bring them together? Can I help them hold each other? Is that even a reasonable hope? Especially now, in times like these?

> I am filled with this worry.
> And I am stuck with this question: what preparation—training, experience, or otherwise—would adequately prepare me to best hold these delicate spaces together?
> I worry, I worry, and I wonder, thinking of my own fragile adolescent self.

+

It is mid-October when a teacher informs us during a faculty meeting that he is triggered by war.

I hardly understand it. I *don't* understand it—the urge to individualize this trigger. What does he mean? Are we not all triggered? I certainly think we *should* be. War—genocide—ethnic cleansing—apartheid. It is triggering. It is traumatic. It is traumatic to witness. It feels only human to feel shaken by the abundant evidence, footage and testimony so undeniably present we can see, and hear, and know it all.

There is no trigger warning for this moment. We are all under a moral obligation to bear witness. To bear it is difficult. It *should* be difficult. After all, this is living pain, and suffering, and importantly, resistance that we stand as witness to. When we hold that pain in our heads, our hearts, our bodies, our hands—remember, that our hands bear responsibility—when we hold this fragile thing, when we speak of these horrible acts, when we name it for what it is, we reject the lethal forces that would otherwise have us isolated, apathetic, unfeeling.

To say that one is triggered by war is a vast understatement. The implication that war does not, should not trigger us all? It unsettles me, disturbs me.

In the weeks (months) that follow, I am even more unsettled to see how so many of my colleagues seem unaffected, how willing, even eager they are to go on "as normal." A few, like me, seem to be losing sleep, but the rhythm of our schedules, our curriculum, our teaching goes undisturbed. There is little acknowledgment of "news in the Middle East," as though this news is a regional issue and not a mass killing and displacement we are directly implicated in, one that our very own paychecks fund, one sanctioned by the country we live and work in.

Don't we have a responsibility to teach to the moment?

I go to work. I'm sick to my stomach every day. I am triggered. I am ashamed. Faculty are asked to refrain from sharing "personal, political, and religious beliefs with students." Setting aside the immense irony in this ask—an ask that contradicts many other asks made of us, as well as the day-to-day reality of what it means to teach, an inherently political act—who do we protect, by avoiding this topic? Whose interests do we serve by preserving the status quo, by "keeping the peace"? In the grand scheme of things, our vocation is rendered meaningless when such basic acknowledgment of Palestinian humanity is denied.

I am triggered.
Shouldn't we all be?

+

Written by Carmen Berríos in a letter to her husband Luis Urzúa, one of the thirty-three Chilean men trapped when a mine in Copiapó caves in, this poem reads:

Generous, simple, suffering miner
drinking from the wounded innards of the Earth
looking without seeing with your tired eyes.
I say miner and I say your name

miner of coal, of dust, of minerals
your hands wizened by early winters
that know the shovel, the carved rock, and the pick. (Tobar)

I am reading this poem and I am thinking about how we grieve processes of literal extraction. How do we grieve for the deep wounds inflicted on this earth's wounded innards? I am thinking about the consequences of extraction on earth and air and water, and the disasters these extractions eventually give way to when they inevitably collapse like the San José mine.

I am thinking of how capital is extracted. Extracted as knowledge; extracted from bodies. The shovel as the co-opting of Black, Indigenous, and immigrant practices, the carved rock rebranded anew into mainstream environmentalisms that ignore root causes, and the pick as the ideological and literal weapons that continue to gouge and scar.

Are we grieving when we breathe ashy air, when we drink dirty water, when we can no longer grow things out of soil stripped bare? I think that soon, our grief may eat us alive no matter how hard we try to turn away from it. I am thinking that the more we ignore our grief, the more it will consume us.

+

The grief we experience is all tied up. As agents of empire, our relationships to grief, loss, and life are broken.

+

I write, and as I write, I pick at a raw wound. Or—maybe I'm not picking, but more so cleaning intentionally despite the sting, so that my wounded inner flesh can heal well over time. Does it really matter in the end? After all, "The ruptures do not always leave visible marks. The wounds heal, then rupture again. The wounds do not heal completely" (Rallin).

+

Perhaps it is here that my writing and observation lead me: maybe the trigger warning itself is a symptom, a limb extended from the festering wound that is our generational? cultural? collective? trauma. Our cultural condition is a societal, multigenerational trauma that cuts deep, a trauma that runs clean through to the brittle bone of our fractured communities, an ongoing trauma, a trauma that you can trace through history, memory, family.

A trauma that we can sometimes treat topically with the trigger warning. A trauma we are slowly uncovering, discovering together; a trauma that we barely cope with by stepping away when it's too much to bear because it is ALWAYS too much to bear, let alone bear alone. Again—we are not made to bear it alone.

Perhaps if we were to start with the trigger. Perhaps if it were an invitation, an offer and a risk we collectively own.

WORKS CITED

hooks, bell. *Teaching Critical Thinking.* Routledge, 2010.

Kaba, Mariame. *We Do This 'Til We Free Us.* Haymarket Books, 2021.

Lorde, Audre. "The Transformation of Silence into Language and Action." *The Cancer Diaries,* Spinsters Ink, 1980, pp. 18–23.

Moraga, Cherríe, and Gloria Anzaldúa, eds. *This Bridge Called My Back: Writings by Radical Women of Color.* SUNY P, 2015.

Rallin, Aneil. *Dreads and Open Mouths: Living/Teaching/Writing Queerly.* Litwin Books, 2019.

Tobar, Hector. *Deep Down Dark: The Untold Stories of 33 Men Buried in a Chilean Mine and the Miracle That Set Them Free.* Picador, 2015.

PART TWO

PEDAGOGICAL PRACTICES

CHAPTER FOUR

COMPOSITION VS. CREATIVE WRITING

A First-Year Instructor's Reflection on the Use of Trigger Warnings in the Classroom

Megan Friess

In the realm of education, the dynamics of teaching and learning are in constant flux, influenced by a multitude of factors ranging from pedagogical practices to the demographics of the students in a classroom. As an instructor of introductory composition courses at Cypress Community College and creative writing at the Orange County School of the Arts, a public charter high school, I have found myself at the intersection of two distinct educational landscapes. The 2022–2023 school year was my first year of teaching after earning dual master's degrees in English and Creative Writing and I was excited and eager to enter the classroom as an educator. As the spring 2023 semester progressed, the similarities and differences between my two groups of students, and how I approached them as their instructor, sparked my interest and prompted me to go deeper in my exploration of specific pedagogical strategies, notably the use of trigger warnings. This teaching reflection explores the contrasting awareness and approaches to trigger warnings among my college and high school students, shedding light on the nuanced ways in which these warnings are perceived and integrated into the classroom experience by both students and instructor.

Working my way through my master's program and first experiences teaching, I did not know much about trigger warnings. In my traditional English literature classes, I had not encountered warnings before about content such as sexual assault, self-harm, racism, or the like. The place that I first started to see these warnings was online—social media, reading fanfiction, and popular blogs. There would be a little note at the top or before I clicked a link pointing out that there was content that could be disturbing to people. I didn't think too much of these notes beyond taking note of their existence. I had not suffered such personal trauma and, while I empathize with people who had, would not suffer mentally or emotionally from engaging with the content. Discussions of the use of trigger warnings in the classroom came to my attention during my master's program when I decided to focus on gaining teaching experience. My opinion was not a strong one at the time. The use of trigger warnings seemed like a nice idea—warning students about triggering content—but the topic tended to be dominated by the sense that trigger warnings were just another product of a "snowflake" generation. (I personally dislike that term.) There were plenty of opinions that trigger warnings were overused: that everything had to be warned about, that this was "babying" people, and that it led to an unwillingness or inability to engage with critical or challenging material.

During my first year of teaching at Cypress College, I did not use specific trigger warnings for material that I gave in class. I now question if being a new professor inadvertently contributed to an excess of caution on my part when selecting learning material that had the potential to inspire thought-provoking discussions among my students. It is also worth noting that none of my students broached the subject of trigger warnings during this course, even tangentially. This lack of initiative on their part has prompted me to consider whether my initial approach may have, unintentionally, restrained open conversations about challenging topics. But this line of thinking only really came into being after I started teaching at the Orange County School of the Arts and encountered students who would openly, and even enthusiastically at times, talk about such topics.

In my creative writing class with high school students, the idea of trigger or content warnings for readers is not a new concept. I wonder if being introduced to the concept of trigger warnings has empowered my high school students to not only analyze the work they create, but also the work they consume, more critically. It seems like trigger warnings could be an empowering agent for my young students. In the class on Crime Fiction that I taught in the spring of 2023, where the reading material includes stories by Agatha Christie and Sir Arthur Conan Doyle, I provided a class-wide trigger warning in my syllabus for themes such as violence, murder, and racist or sexist depictions of people. While that prompted class discussions around those specific topics, I found that the students operated independently of any instruction when deciding whether to apply trigger warnings to their own creative writing work. As they began to turn in stories, I noticed that at the top of the first page of some of them, there would be a note telling potential readers that the story contained potentially triggering concepts. One example of a trigger warning note was this: "WAIT MS.FRIESS I would like to give you a heads up that it is kinda dark topic (IPV) Okay that all I want to say you can read it now if want" (Nunez 3). My student wanted to make sure that I knew before I read her short story that there would be a depiction of intimate partner violence. While the story did not go into explicit detail, the "off-screen" violence was central to the plot of the story and the female character's decision to leave an abusive relationship. A challenging topic for a high schooler to read and write about, yet my students were willing to engage with such topics in their own writing.

After finishing out the school year, and my first year as an instructor, I reflected on things that went well in my classes and things that I wanted to improve on. I did this with particular attention to the idea of increasing equity and accessibility in my classroom and content. And that was when I really started to contemplate the differences in the use of trigger warnings between my two demographics of students. I acknowledged that I could have done a better job of bringing the topic up in my college composition classroom as a discussion point or even thought to use more challenging readings for my course instead of playing it so safe. But I also wondered what made the differences in awareness and use of trigger warnings between high school creative writers and college composition students so varied.

My college students, in contrast to my high school students, span various stages of life. I wonder if, since the discussion around trigger warnings in academia is relatively new, their age or other demographic factors that differ from my high school students might be responsible for their potential lack of knowledge or discussion about trigger warnings. I also ponder about how I can modify my teaching practice to think more deeply about trigger warnings in both educational contexts. As a still-new educator, it is intriguing to see not only the influence of my pedagogy on my students but also their influence on my thinking as I define my role as a teacher.

In order to take that step and to also figure out my own personal feelings in regard to the broad and complicated concept of trigger warnings, I turned to others. In the classic move of teachers everywhere, I have looked around to see what other teachers are doing in their classrooms and then borrow and adapt their activities and strategies to fit my own teaching. The first place I ended up when doing some deeper looking into trigger warnings in the classroom was the "Inclusive Teaching" pages of the University of Michigan's website. The site is clearly geared toward those looking for ways to make their classrooms more inclusive and equitable. One resource they had was an aptly named PDF, "An Introduction to Content Warnings and Trigger Warnings." This source deepened my understanding of trigger warnings. It started with how they define the motivation behind the use of trigger warnings: "The motive behind including content warnings in classes is based on the simple recognition that our students are people with lives, histories, and struggles that we are not privy to, and cannot always understand. And those lives, histories, and struggles do not stop existing when class starts" (pabdoo 3).

When reflecting on my experiences and the resources that other teachers have created on this topic, it becomes clear that trigger warnings possess the capacity to fulfill multiple purposes in the classroom. These warnings can be interpreted as a form of empathy on the part of educators, signifying an understanding of the diverse backgrounds and sensitivities that students bring to the learning space. By incorporating trigger warnings, instructors are proactively acknowledging the potential emotional and psychological impact of certain content and displaying a willingness to tailor their teaching methods to accommodate individual needs. This practice aligns with the broader pedagogical principle of inclusivity, wherein students' emotional well-being is held in high regard alongside their cognitive growth.

However, as with any pedagogical tool, there exists a necessity to maintain a delicate equilibrium. While trigger warnings can be instrumental in fostering a safe and supportive learning environment, there is an intrinsic danger that an excessive reliance on such warnings might accidentally impede the intellectual exploration that education inherently involves. If taken to an extreme, trigger warnings could inadvertently evolve into a form of censorship, potentially deterring educators and students from engaging with material that challenges preconceived notions or prompts uncomfortable yet enlightening discussions. The University of Waterloo's Centre for Teaching Excellence makes the good point that

> [t]rigger warnings do not mean that students can exempt themselves from completing parts of the coursework. Ideally, a student who is genuinely concerned about being re-traumatized by forthcoming course content would privately inform the instructor of this concern. The instructor would then accommodate the student by proposing alternative content or an alternative learning activity, as with an accommodation necessitated by a learning disability or physical disability. ("Trigger Warnings")

Treating students as arbiters of their own mental well-being when interacting with challenging course content seems like a good step to take within my own classroom. Trigger warnings can be the practical application of that step. However, that does not mean that I, as the teacher, need to bow to any mention of discomfort or to change my curriculum in a way that lessens the content. Instead, I can treat this in the same flexible but equitable way that I try to accommodate my students with documented physical or mental disabilities. I agree that my goal is to

> help [my] students understand the difference between emotional trauma and intellectual discomfort: the former is harmful, as is triggering it in the wrong context (such as in a classroom rather than in therapy);

> the latter is fundamental to a university education—it means our ideas are being challenged as we struggle to resolve cognitive dissonance. ("Trigger Warnings")

Consequently, a crucial aspect of effective teaching lies in striking a balance between providing thoughtful warnings and cultivating a space wherein the exchange of ideas can flourish.

Navigating this equilibrium can be particularly nuanced in different educational settings. In the realm of higher education, such as a college or university, students often span a wide spectrum of age groups, life experiences, and maturity levels. This diversity of perspectives can significantly influence how trigger warnings are perceived and received. For community college students who are generally at a more advanced stage of personal development than high school students, discussions spurred by trigger warnings can lead to intellectually stimulating dialogues that enrich the learning experience. This demographic's broader exposure to a variety of ideas and experiences might equip them with a more comprehensive toolkit for digesting challenging content. However, there is no guarantee that they have encountered the concept of trigger warnings before. If the instructor wants to use trigger warnings for material they provide or to prompt discussion around the topic of them in general, they may need to introduce their students to what trigger warnings are and how they are employed in the wider world.

In contrast, the context shifts when considering trigger warnings in a high school environment. High school students are frequently younger and may possess a narrower range of life experiences to draw from. As a result, the potential emotional impact of certain subjects might be more pronounced. Consequently, trigger warnings within a high school setting may carry a weightier significance, enabling instructors to delicately introduce difficult material while providing students with the emotional preparation necessary for its absorption. In essence, the age and relative life inexperience of high school students could make trigger warnings a more potent facilitator of meaningful learning, offering a structure through which these students can engage with complex topics at their own pace.

Within my creative writing classroom, these high schoolers might be ahead of the curve due to their immersion in the vast sea of creative writing and, therefore, have encountered the use of trigger warnings more often than the average high school or even college composition student. In my experience, trigger warnings will often appear in, or be applied to, creative writing or online forms of writing (such as fanfiction and blogs), the realms my high school students are operating in. My guess is that they have a much higher level of exposure to others using trigger warnings and have emulated that—and as such, a cycle of trigger warning use begins.

The familiarity of my high schoolers with trigger warnings and difficult content, however, does not mean that I, as their instructor, should ignore the fact that these students are still young and could benefit from my facilitating their introduction to the materials that I provide in my specific courses. When providing the material in which I would potentially apply a trigger warning to, I can also craft or adapt activities meant to help my students engage with the subject matter at an age-appropriate level. The University of Waterloo's Centre for Teaching Excellence has a couple of examples such as "Try to 'scaffold' a disturbing topic to students... Whenever possible, allow students to progress through upsetting material at their own pace...[and] [p]rovide captions when using video materials: some content is easier to watch while reading captions than while listening to the audio" ("Trigger Warnings"). Even if students are not dealing with any mental health issues or trauma, these kinds of activities can help all students to be introduced to difficult material that will stretch their critical thinking capabilities and knowledge of the world.

In summation, a simple Google search of trigger warnings will give you a lot of results on both sides of the debate—helpful to harmful—but where I have landed for my teaching practice is somewhere in the middle. The earliest form of content or trigger warning that I can think of actually comes from TV news—a news anchor will begin a story and, before showcasing images or video, say something along the lines of "Viewers should be advised that this may be disturbing." I think that is a good way for me to think about trigger warnings going forward for my classroom. While I may not know everything that could be "triggering" to an individual, I can make broader statements about the content that I present to my students and ask them to engage with. This enables them to potentially prepare themselves for hard content and discussions or make the personal choice to discuss alternative assignments or reading with me. Additionally, the activities that I ask my students to participate in around these materials can also be created for or adapted to each group of students—college or high school—depending on the material and the individual classroom of students.

Trigger warnings, when thoughtfully integrated into pedagogical practices, offer a multifaceted tool that reflects educators' commitment to empathy and inclusivity. While they can undoubtedly foster a supportive atmosphere, the careful balance between their application and potential pitfalls must be upheld. Furthermore, this equilibrium varies between educational contexts, with college students benefiting from the intellectual discourse they can ignite, while high school students may rely on them to navigate emotionally charged subjects. Ultimately, the efficacy of trigger warnings hinges on their ability to encourage exploration without sacrificing the pursuit of knowledge and understanding.

WORKS CITED

Nunez, Emily. "Tick-Tock." 14 Dec. 2023. Madwoman in the Attic, Orange County School of the Arts, student paper.

pabdoo. "An Introduction to Content and Trigger Warnings." *Equitable Teaching*, University of Michigan, https://sites.lsa.umich.edu/equitable-teaching/an-introduction-to-content-warnings-and-trigger-warnings.

"Trigger Warnings." *Centre for Teaching Excellence*, University of Waterloo, https://uwaterloo.ca/centre-for-teaching-excellence/catalogs/tip-sheets/content-warnings.

CHAPTER FIVE

TRIGGER WARNINGS IN THE CLASSROOM

An Examination of Student and Faculty Views

Rhyan Warmerdam

INTRODUCTION

This Institutional Review Board-approved research study consists of two parts: 1) a survey administered to students and 2) faculty interviews. The purpose of this research study is to evaluate student and faculty preferences on the topic of trigger warnings in educational classroom settings. Using the data collected, this study presents options for reconciling student and faculty needs.

Key research questions:

- Is there a way to fulfill student desires around trigger warnings while taking into account the needs and capabilities of the faculty?
- Which topics do students hope to see trigger warnings around?
- What kinds of practices have varying faculty members already implemented around trigger warnings?

- What makes for a successful classroom policy around trigger warnings?
- Are student desires for trigger warnings incompatible with the faculty's ability to implement them?

This project highlights the variety of ways that faculty have chosen to navigate trigger warnings in tandem with student desires, creating a more cohesive picture of the dynamic behind the complicated topic. This will provide teacher-practitioners with a better understanding of their options when it comes to designing a safe classroom.

Many thanks to Dr. Quaylan Allen for making this project possible, as well as all the faculty in the Integrated Educational Studies Department at Chapman University for allowing me to administer the survey in their classrooms—without which this project would not have been possible. I am incredibly grateful. Thank you.

METHODS

The student survey was administered to n=200 students in the Attallah College of Education at Chapman University, a private university in Southern California. The sample size of this survey is within a fair–good range, thus rendering these results statistically significant (Batterton and Hale 34). Eligible students in the study were eighteen years or older and either an education major, minor, or were enrolled in an education class. Participants were recruited during the first or last ten minutes of an education class.

The survey consists of:

- Six "yes, no, or neutral" questions.
    a. Have you ever felt triggered by class content while in class?
    b. Do you believe that receiving trigger warnings before viewing sensitive content would help mitigate stress to potentially triggering content?
    c. Do trigger warnings help you feel better prepared to watch/discuss sensitive content?

d. Do you think that universities should require all instructors to issue trigger warnings before sensitive content comes up in their classes?
e. Do you think that universities should require all students to issue trigger warnings before presenting any research with sensitive content to their peers in class?
f. In general, do you like it when teachers include trigger warnings in the classroom?

- Nine questions formatted as a Likert scale for topics students might hope to see trigger warnings around:
  Format example:

  > "A trigger warning issued for _____ is 1) Not at all necessary, 2) Slightly necessary, 3) Somewhat necessary, 4) Very necessary, 5) Absolutely necessary"

  The nine topics:
  a) Sexual assault
  b) Child abuse
  c) Violent/catastrophic trauma
  d) Suicide
  e) Self-harm
  f) Sexual orientation/gender identity
  g) Racial issues
  h) Sexism
  i) Substance abuse
- Three free response questions.

Students were not required to answer every single question, as stated in the consent form. The topics listed in the Likert scale are all topics listed in Boysen et al.'s study. Boysen et al.'s study was an examination of psychology student views, whereas this study is of education student views.

The faculty interviews consisted of five faculty from the Attallah College of Education at Chapman University. Because of the low quantity of these responses, the results should not be generalized to all faculty but instead offer a snapshot of faculty policies. Each interview lasted thirty minutes. The faculty interview questions were:

1. What are your thoughts on trigger warnings in the classroom?
2. Are there any situations in which you think it could be beneficial for instructors to administer trigger warnings? If so, what are they?
3. Do you have any reservations about including trigger warnings in the classroom? If so, what are they?
4. Do you have any personal experience or anecdotes about trigger warnings in the classroom that you would be open to sharing?
5. As a faculty member, would you feel comfortable or uncomfortable if the university required trigger warnings to be issued before sensitive content?
6. Do you have any final closing comments you would like to share on the topic of trigger warnings in the classroom?

The five faculty in the Attallah College of Education were selected to be interviewed on a voluntary basis. Faculty received a $5 gift card for their participation. Faculty will be referred to as Professor A, B, C, D, and E to maintain anonymity.

RESULTS

Survey results (n=200):

- Six "yes, no, or neutral questions:"
    - 45.64% of student respondents say that they have been triggered by class content
    - 79.08% of student respondents believe that receiving a trigger warning before viewing sensitive content would help mitigate stress to potentially triggering content
    - 73.98% of student respondents say that trigger warnings help them feel better prepared to watch/discuss sensitive content
    - 88.27% of student respondents believe that universities should require all instructors to issue trigger warnings before sensitive content comes up in their classes

- 82.65% of student respondents believe that universities should require all students to issue trigger warnings before presenting any research with sensitive content to their peers in class
- 1.56% of students do not like it when teachers include trigger warnings in the classroom in general; 98.44% of students like it or feel neutral when teachers include trigger warnings in the classroom (69.27% like it, 29.17% feel neutral)

- Nine Likert scale topic questions:
  a Sexual assault:
    - Not at all necessary: 0.53%
    - Slightly necessary: 3.16%
    - Somewhat necessary: 7.89%
    - Very necessary: 24.74%
    - Absolutely necessary: 63.68%
      - Very necessary + Absolutely necessary = 88.42%
      - Not at all necessary + Slightly necessary = 3.69%

  b Child abuse
    - Not at all necessary: 0.53%
    - Slightly necessary: 2.11%
    - Somewhat necessary: 11.58%
    - Very necessary: 22.63%
    - Absolutely necessary: 63.16%
      - Very necessary + Absolutely necessary = 85.79%
      - Not at all necessary + Slightly necessary = 2.64%

  c Violent/catastrophic trauma:
    - Not at all necessary: 0%
    - Slightly necessary: 4.21%
    - Somewhat necessary: 15.79%
    - Very necessary: 31.58%
    - Absolutely necessary: 48.42%
      - Very necessary + Absolutely necessary = 80%
      - Not at all necessary + Slightly necessary = 4.21%

  d Suicide:
    - Not at all necessary: 0.53%
    - Slightly necessary: 2.63%
    - Somewhat necessary: 7.37%

- Very necessary: 25.26%
- Absolutely necessary: 64.21%
  - Very necessary + Absolutely necessary = 89.47%
  - Not at all necessary + Slightly necessary = 3.16%

e Self-harm:
- Not at all necessary: 0.53%
- Slightly necessary: 3.17%
- Somewhat necessary: 7.94%
- Very necessary: 26.46%
- Absolutely necessary: 61.90%
  - Very necessary + Absolutely necessary = 88.36%
  - Not at all necessary + Slightly necessary = 3.70%

f Sexual orientation/gender identity:
- Not at all necessary: 20.74%
- Slightly necessary: 12.77%
- Somewhat necessary: 32.98%
- Very necessary: 18.09%
- Absolutely necessary: 15.43%
  - Very necessary + Absolutely necessary = 33.52%
  - Not at all necessary + Slightly necessary = 33.51%

g Racial issues:
- Not at all necessary: 7.94%
- Slightly necessary: 11.11%
- Somewhat necessary: 33.33%
- Very necessary: 28.57%
- Absolutely necessary: 19.05%
  - Very necessary + Absolutely necessary = 47.62%
  - Not at all necessary + Slightly necessary = 19.05%

h Sexism:
- Not at all necessary: 16.40%
- Slightly necessary: 14.81%
- Somewhat necessary: 38.62%
- Very necessary: 15.87%
- Absolutely necessary: 14.29%
  - Very necessary + Absolutely necessary = 30.16%
  - Not at all necessary + Slightly necessary = 31.21%

- i Substance abuse:
  - ■ Not at all necessary: 1.59%
  - ■ Slightly necessary: 11.11%
  - ■ Somewhat necessary: 29.10%
  - ■ Very necessary: 25.93%
  - ■ Absolutely necessary: 32.28%
    - Very necessary + Absolutely necessary = 58.21%
    - Not at all necessary + Slightly necessary = 12.70%
- Free response questions:
  - o Results presented in the discussion section
- Faculty interview:
  - o Results presented in the discussion section

DISCUSSION PART 1: STUDENT SURVEY

While only 45.64% of student respondents report having been triggered by class content, almost double the percentage of students (88.27%) believe that faculty should be required to implement trigger warnings. This suggests that although not all students are triggered in class, the majority of students still appreciate the use of trigger warnings even if it does not directly apply to them.

- Q2 – Have you ever felt triggered by class content while in class?
  - o Yes: 44.95%
  - o No: 55.05%
- Q3 – In general, do you like it when teachers include trigger warnings in the classroom?
  - o Yes: 69.07%
  - o No: 1.55%
  - o Neutral: 29.38%

Most student respondents believe that students should be required to put trigger warnings on their research/presentations (82.65%) as well as faculty (88.27%). There is only a small 5.62-point difference; therefore, students seem to care that their peers include trigger warnings as well as the professors.

In the student survey, the number one topic that the highest percentage of students deemed “absolutely necessary” to warrant a trigger warning is suicide (64.21%) followed closely by sexual assault (63.68%) and child abuse (63.16%). The highest combined percentage of “absolutely necessary” and “very necessary” responses were: 1) suicide (89.47%) 2), sexual assault (88.42%), and 3) self-harm (88.36%).

The topics with the highest percentage of “not at all necessary” responses are: 1) sexual orientation/gender identity (20.74%), 2) sexism (16.40%), and 3) racial issues (7.40%). The topics with the highest combined percentage of “not at all necessary” and “slightly necessary” responses are in order: 1) sexual orientation/gender identity (33.51%), 2) sexism (31.21%), and 3) racial issues (19.05%).

A possible reason for the low percentage of racial issues could be due to the demographics of the response pool; respondents may not have personal experience with these identities, which might affect their needs to have trigger warnings on the topic. According to the publicly available and most recent 2023 demographics on the Chapman University website, Chapman’s undergraduate population is 46.8% White, 2.2% Black, 16.0% Asian, and 18.1% Hispanic/Latino (“Student Headcount”). The high percentage of white students might account for a low rating for racial issues.

As of 2023, Chapman’s undergraduate population apparently consists of 4778 female students and 3090 male students. Six students are “nonbinary or unknown” (“Student Headcount”). Because “nonbinary and unknown” are grouped together as a third category (the statistic is extremely low, only 6 out of the total 7874), this statistic is therefore inaccurate in depicting the gender identity of Chapman University students. Therefore, the low response rating for the sexual orientation/gender identity question is unclear.

Interestingly, a very small percentage of respondents said that it is “not at all necessary” to include a trigger warning for substance abuse: only 1.59% of respondents. Substance abuse is not always a topic brought up when discussing triggering, yet student ratings describe substance abuse as an important topic to administer a trigger warning for: 32.28% believed that a trigger warning for substance abuse is “absolutely necessary.” For reference, 48.42% of students believe that a trigger warning for violent/catastrophic trauma is “absolutely necessary.” There is only a 16.14-point difference between those two topics. Therefore, substance abuse is a topic worth considering when administering trigger warnings.

DISCUSSION PART 2: FACULTY INTERVIEWS AND STUDENT FREE RESPONSE IN CONVERSATION

Possible Benefits of Trigger Warnings

A student in the free response section reports, "I have had various professors that are intent on providing trigger warnings before speaking on a triggering topic. This creates a safe comfortable environment where students don't feel on edge that a specific topic will be touched on." Laguardia describes one benefit of trigger warnings, that it, "acknowledges the reality of trauma and possible triggers, suggests that the professor does not think less of people who must confront these challenges, and encourages fellow students to follow suit" (898).

A systematic review of literature on trigger warnings discovered that "trigger warnings contribute to inclusive practices by improving accessibility, engagement, and support for all students, as well as those who have experienced trauma-specific mental health challenges (Byron, 2017)" (Bryce et al. 2889). On average, most students seem to agree. In the free response portion of the survey, a student reports, "Any time a trigger warning is provided it makes me feel more comfortable in the space because it makes me feel as though the professor and peers are understanding of how the content can be difficult." Another student articulates, "As someone who has severe PTSD, it is helpful to be able to know when triggering content is coming so I can step out or use coping skills."

However, this systematic literary review also concluded that "if employed in isolation or in a tokenistic way, as a disingenuous gesture of trauma awareness, trigger warnings can be harmful to students, potentially inflaming existing stressors and exacerbating maladaptive behaviors" (Bryce et al. 2892). This indicates that it is not only a trigger warning that creates an effect, but also the intention with which it is given and how it is used.

In the interview portion of the study, Professor A believes that trigger warnings are useful "to give people the opportunity to say, I know that that's going to be really hard for me to sit through, so I'm going to remove myself from the situation because I don't feel capable of being in the environment, at least right now, where this is being talked about in this way." Professor E has a similar mentality as Professor A, encouraging students to advocate for themselves when discussing weighty topics: "I think students need to be able to say, I'm just not okay with this discussion right now." But Professor B wonders, "Are they going to be able to advocate for themselves? Has anyone taught them to do that?"

Avoidance

One often-cited argument against trigger warnings is the worry that students will use a trigger warning as an excuse to skip class or miss content. The faculty interviewed had varying thoughts on the topic.

Professor A is not concerned about students skipping class using trigger warnings as an excuse, stating that, "With education, I think in general, education is something where you get out of it what you put into it." Professor A notes the particularity of this discussion to higher education, explaining that, "They are paying to be here. So, if they do not want to be there, then that's a different conversation than maybe at like the high school level or the middle school level."

Other professors feel differently. Professor B says, "I have set up norms in my classroom where they could then say, like, I'm really having a hard time with this, and I need a minute, and they can step out and then return. That's okay. But what's not okay is for you to just step out and say, I don't want to participate in this at all." Professor B wants to make sure all students receive the opportunity to learn and don't simply leave when things get uncomfortable because that is where learning happens: "Sometimes we have to put them in situations where they really have to confront biases, and that's super uncomfortable...but what's an appropriate amount of discomfort? And what are you uncomfortable about?"

Professor B wants to ensure that students don't "just hide behind these trigger warnings and say, I'm not going to do that, and it's handled, I don't have to think about it anymore." Professor C also wonders, "What are the lessons that are not learned if the student leaves the classroom?"

When it comes to avoidance, Professor C worries that "By giving a lot of these trigger warnings, we might be not allowing students the opportunity to productively deal with like, their trauma or troubling events or, like developing strategies to kind of like self-regulate."

But interestingly, a 2021 study by Kimble et al. discovered that receiving a trigger warning did not increase the avoidant response when subjected to triggering material. A 2023 study by Bridgland also presented results that "trigger warnings did not seem to increase the avoidance of warned-of material" ("Meta-Analysis"). Similarly, a 2021 study by Bruce et al. found that students did not avoid content even when given a trigger warning. All of these studies present a very low rate of avoidance when it comes to the implementation of trigger warnings. The results of both of these studies, "perhaps relieves some concern that trigger warning-related avoidance would mean incomplete homework or missing class" (Bruce et al. 5476). This is supported by the interview section of this study. Both Professor C and Professor D have not had students refuse to come to class. Professor C says, "I actually haven't had students opt out. And this is my fourth year in higher ed." Professor D reiterates, "nobody has ever said I don't want to come."

While research demonstrates that trigger warnings do not seem to increase avoidance behavior, numerous studies have warned of a "nocebo effect." A nocebo effect can be defined as "negative expectancies in which students appraise upcoming material as more threatening than if the warning was absent (e.g., a nocebo effect)" (Bruce and Roberts 485). Vatz also brings up the nocebo effect as a major concern when implementing trigger warnings: "the use of trigger warnings to ward off students' suffering disturbing reactions to stimuli may serve as a self-fulfilling prophesy in which students who are socialized to look for discomfort may experience it by virtue of that anticipation" (55). Bruce's 2023 study titled "Students' Psychophysiological Reactivity to Trigger Warnings" found that "trigger warnings appear to create a nocebo-like effect." Another study found that "the warnings did create a negative anticipatory phase" (Bridgland et al., "Expecting the Worst" 614). This appears to be a significant drawback of trigger warnings.

The idea behind the nocebo effect is what Professor B refers to with their concern that "saying I'm worried that you can't handle this sends an implicit message that they can't handle this." Because research does suggest validity to the nocebo effect, this effect should be taken into consideration when deciding how often to use trigger warnings in the classroom.

Too Sensitive?

Another concern that a few professors bring up is that students might be too sensitive. Professor B worries that giving trigger warnings might encourage "frailty" and "treating students like, I know that you can't handle this." Professor D also says, "This generation, it's been called the snowflake generation. A snowflake means you're delicate, and you melt really easily." Professor C also expresses that, "I would I fear and kind of maybe foresee that we're coddling them too much right? Or they're too sensitive."

Is this generation really so sensitive? Or are they simply more aware of their emotions? Perhaps, the students in this generation simply have the language to describe their emotions. Based on their personal experiences in the free response section of the study, triggered students seem to exhibit very visceral reactions to content being presented. A student expresses that, "A teacher showed a clip of a woman being assaulted with no trigger warning and I ended up having a flashback in class and had to leave." Another student says, "When talking about or showing sexual assault in a movie I was given no warning and had to mask my PTSD response in the back of the classroom until it was over. I was given no warning and I freaked out more than when I had prepared to have that response." A third student says, "A teacher was talking about a triggering subject in class without warning and I had an anxiety attack because of it." A fourth student communicates that "my classes never use trigger warnings and it usually dysregulates me." These students are all describing very involuntary reactions to content, using terminology like "PTSD," "anxiety," "flashback," and "dysregulation"—all terms that indicate psychological awareness, terms that are often used in clinical offices. These terms are becoming more prevalent in our language at this point in time, perhaps contributing to student awareness of what exactly these responses are.

Lockhart suggests, "It has been said—repeatedly—that the current generation of college students cannot handle the real world, and that trigger warnings have contributed to this incapacity. I suggest instead that it is the world that cannot handle today's college students" (68–69). In a 2019 article titled "Trauma, Trigger Warnings, and the Rhetoric of Sensitivity," Kendall Gerdes quotes Sara Ahmed's assertion that "'[t]he moral panic over trigger warnings often evokes this figure...of the over-sensitive student who is not attuned to the difficulty and discomfort of learning, as if to say: if we let your sensitivities become law, we lose our freedom' (262)" (Gerdes 19). Gerdes's argument "flips the claim" (Gerdes 19) and instead argues that "Sensitive students are attuned precisely to the difficulty and discomfort of learning (and are looking for ways to face it)" (19). Sensitivity doesn't necessarily have to mean an unwillingness to deal with content; instead, it can represent and address the reality of dealing with difficult content. Gerdes promotes "a more sensitive rhetoric" (20) that would "seek out ways of teaching and persuading that equip students with the rhetorical resources to respond" (20). This mirrors what Professor B wondered earlier: "Are they going to be able to advocate for themselves? Has anyone taught them to do that?"

Creating a Safe Environment

Professor B firmly believes, "More effective than any trigger warning is the establishment of a safe, intellectually and emotionally safe relationship, between the instructor and the student, whether you use a trigger warning or not." Indeed, "When students are assured of both their physical and emotional safety, they can more fully engage in classroom discussions, thus promoting a more academically rigorous environment" (Byron 123). Byron explains a difference between "Creating safe, though not necessarily comfortable spaces" that allow "students to express a broader range of viewpoints and the security needed to freely engage with academic material" (124). Creating a safe environment to have difficult discussions can actually improve learning.

Additionally, Professor A reveals the possibility that "the content itself might not be triggering, but the way that peers or a professor of the classroom community have responded to it may be the trigger." Professor

A has learned that a content warning doesn't help if class discussions are not held carefully: "It was important to have a content warning, but also guidelines around how that conversation was going to be had." Nolan and Roberts explain that "warnings are not a silver bullet for navigating contentious subjects and emotional responses in professional learning, nor should they act as substitutes for wellbeing support" (8).

Professor D does not give trigger warnings but intentionally works very hard to create a safe environment: "When we work through pain, we grow. I always say that I am here if you want to talk."

Timing

Many students express a desire to be warned far enough in advance about potentially triggering content, rather than directly before it will be presented. A student says, "The more time in between the warning and the topic the better." Another student says, "I think it's beneficial when told in advance rather than right before the potentially triggering material is presented." Another student says, "If a trigger warning is not given far in advance, the student might not have time to prepare themselves for what they are about to be discussing." Another student says, "Often they are not used correctly. I have experienced the teacher or peers just saying 'trigger warning' without revealing the content of the warning or giving students the chance to step out of the room. There is not much warning when the class doesn't take a pause to leave." Laguardia explains that if violent/traumatic content is presented in advance, "the potentially affected student has an opportunity to prepare to address the situation. Students may fortify themselves emotionally...rather than being accidentally, biologically, and uncontrollably removed from class activities" (897).

Professor A gives plenty of time before administering a trigger warning, actually allowing students permission to take the class off if a particular topic is going to be too much: "I think it's good for people to have advance notice and also to not have to remove themselves in the heat of the moment when you just heard this. It's probably best practice to have some time to consider before you even show up." The amount of time that students are given to make a decision is one consideration to make when using trigger warnings. Professor B worries, "If someone gets up in the middle of class, is that drawing everyone's attention to that student?" Warning students far enough in advance could potentially combat this fear.

Rather than giving trigger warnings throughout the semester, Professor D gives one big one at the beginning:

> I just kind of lay it all out. I say that the issues are in the syllabus and they're in the course outline. So I'm going to tell you right now, that's what's happening. So if this is not a good semester for you to take the course, if you've recently experienced something traumatic, and one of these topics is going to trigger it, why don't you think about taking it next semester? Or when you feel like you can handle it.

Professor D explains, "I don't give trigger warnings every class. I just can't. Because some people are triggered by things that I would have never guessed."

How Often to Use Trigger Warnings?

If trigger warnings are used too frequently when not needed, Professor C worries, "I fear that they may get watered down because you use it too much." Students also emphasize the importance of not overusing them all the time: "I think sometimes they're necessary because certain topics are very triggering, but I also believe the use of trigger warnings can get out of hand in the terms of like it's not really necessary but some might put one just in case." Another student says, "I think it helps you understand the content better and take care of yourself, but we need to be mindful of when their use gets out of hand." A third student said, "I think they're good if they're used correctly but in general I think they're overused, taking away the importance of them."

One student actually provided a possible solution to overuse: "I think they're helpful but I also think we should have a list of topics that are reserved for trigger warnings so that they're taken seriously." As analyzed in the first portion of the discussion, students expressed the highest desire for trigger warnings around the topics of suicide, sexual assault, child abuse, and self-harm. The students rated their preferences on topics on a five-point Likert scale from "not at all necessary" to "absolutely necessary." Refer to this section for more specific topic preferences.

Professor C explains that the term "trigger warning" itself specifically might contribute to their overuse: "How can I be more intentional, maybe using another term besides trigger warning, right? Or explaining it." A student agrees, saying, "I feel like the word trigger warning itself adds more stress than it should for most people."

In Bruce et al.'s 2021 study, researchers found that "the trigger warning phrase condition created more arousal than the PG-13 and control conditions" (5475). In other words, the phrase "trigger warning" itself created higher rates of stress than having no warning. This study showed that using the specific phrase "trigger warning" is particularly likely to have a nocebo effect and therefore should be used intentionally.

One solution to decreasing this anticipatory anxiety and the stress that comes with the phrase itself is to avoid using the words "trigger warning" every time and instead use an alternative method of explaining that sensitive content will be covered. Laguardia presents the word "content notification" (899) as a possible substitution.

Possible Solutions (by Each Professor)

Professor A: When in doubt, Professor A chooses to give a trigger warning around potentially troubling topics: "I think I tend to err on the side of caution of safety and making students feel comfortable." Professor A listens to student desires around trigger warnings on a class-by-class basis, having conversations with individual students when needed as well: "I think it helps, if possible, to be able to have personalized discussions with students about their preferences and kind of what they need from you to feel safe."

Professor B: Professor B isn't a huge fan of trigger warnings in general, rarely using them, instead emphasizing the importance of creating a positive relationship between faculty and student: "Whether you use a trigger warning or not, if I have a student who trusts me, they're going to be able to say, I need to step out. And I'm going to be able to say, all right, you know, we'll circle back in a minute. But if that relationship does not exist, then a trigger warning or no is not going to be helpful." Professor B strongly believes that it is important to challenge students: "my theory of learning is that learning is actually really uncomfortable," a value that results in a less-frequent implementation of trigger warnings.

Professor C: Professor C works hard to set up classroom norms to create a safe environment: "I'm very intentional about the culture and the community that I create. I begin a lot of the conversation at the beginning of semester, setting classroom norms, community norms. I ask students, what are some of the expectations that you have of yourself, of your peers, and of me as your instructor?" Professor C finds that this creates an environment that is more conducive to safe discussions. Professor C plans ahead about which topics might warrant a trigger warning. "I review my syllabus and my content, and figure out, okay, do I need to do more trigger warnings? Were these necessary? Setting it up in the beginning of the semester, I think that that's a lot of the crux of my own approach to them." Professor C does utilize trigger warnings, but chooses to give them selectively only on topics that they believe truly necessitate such a warning.

Professor D: Professor D does not utilize trigger warnings at all, instead choosing to focus on how to support students through difficult conversations: "How do we prepare you so that you can cope with all of that?" Professor D wants to support students through dealing with their triggers, rather than just leaving the class and dealing with it on their own: "Wouldn't it be better for us to talk about these topics here in a safe place at a university before you go into the real world?" When classes discuss tough topics together, Professor D believes that once students learn that "they are not in the world alone, you know? Once people start knowing that they're free. And then they talk about things. And the groups, they become very close, you know, because we're sharing experiences that are tough sometimes."

Professor E: Like Professor A, Professor E believes, "When in doubt, I always try to be as upfront as possible." Professor E has a policy that "it's just always best to be upfront with what's going on and knowing that everybody could be in a season where something's difficult." Professor E utilizes trigger warnings in their classroom as a means of transparency, ensuring that students are not taken off guard about what will be discussed in class that day. Professor E gives trigger warnings fairly frequently because "we just don't know where everyone is coming from in the classroom." Professor E hopes that students check in with themselves frequently and will take care of themselves however they need: "we're very big on mental health in all of my classes, and if they need to take some time for themselves, that's absolutely acceptable."

While all of the instructors interviewed have different approaches to using trigger warnings, all of their approaches demonstrate genuine intentions to support the growth and well-being of their students.

CONCLUSION

There is no one correct way to utilize trigger warnings. Student survey results reveal that students tend to prefer classrooms that use trigger warnings. However, best practices around trigger warnings will vary based on instructor and classroom setting. This study has presented a multitude of options for designing a safe classroom space. Instructors have different methods for using trigger warnings largely based on their own differing theories of learning and learning outcomes. What is most important is maintaining student engagement and safety while supporting learning, whether that involves explicit trigger warnings or not.

WORKS CITED

Batterton, Katherine A., and Kimberly N. Hale. "The Likert Scale What It Is and How To Use It." *Phalanx*, vol. 50, no. 2, 2017, pp. 32–39.

Boysen, Guy A., et al. "Trigger Warnings in Psychology Classes: What Do Students Think?" *Scholarship of Teaching and Learning in Psychology*, vol. 4, no. 2, June 2018, pp. 69–80.

Bridgland, Victoria M. E., et al. "A Meta-Analysis of the Efficacy of Trigger Warnings, Content Warnings, and Content Notes." *Clinical Psychological Science*, vol. 12, no. 4, Aug. 2023, pp. 751–71.

Bridgland, Victoria M. E., et al. "Expecting the Worst: Investigating the Effects of Trigger Warnings on Reactions to Ambiguously Themed Photos." *Journal of Experimental Psychology: Applied*, vol. 25, no. 4, Dec. 2019, pp. 602–17.

Bruce, Madeline J., et al. "Students' Psychophysiological Reactivity to Trigger Warnings." *Current Psychology*, vol. 42, no. 7, Mar. 2023, pp. 5470–79.

Bruce, Madeline J., and Dawn C. Roberts. "Trigger Warnings in Context: The Role of Institutional Betrayal in the Trigger Warning Debate." *College Student Journal*, vol. 54, no. 4, Dec. 2020, pp. 484–90.

Bryce, India, et al. "Pulling the Trigger: A Systematic Literature Review of Trigger Warnings as a Strategy for Reducing Traumatization in Higher Education." *Trauma, Violence, & Abuse*, vol. 24, no. 4, Oct. 2023, pp. 2882–94.

Byron, Katie. "From Infantilizing to World Making: Safe Spaces and Trigger Warnings on Campus." *Family Relations*, vol. 66, no. 1, Feb. 2017, pp. 116–25.

Gerdes, Kendall. "Trauma, Trigger Warnings, and the Rhetoric of Sensitivity." *Rhetoric Society Quarterly*, vol. 49, no. 1, Jan. 2019, pp. 3–24.

Kimble, Matthew, et al. "Student Reactions to Traumatic Material in Literature: Implications for Trigger Warnings." *PLOS ONE*, vol. 16, no. 3, Mar. 2021, pp. 1–18.

Laguardia, Francesca, et al. "Trigger Warnings: From Panic to Data." *Journal of Legal Education*, vol. 66, no. 4, June 2017, pp. 882–903.

Lockhart, Eleanor Amaranth. "Why Trigger Warnings Are Beneficial, Perhaps Even Necessary." *First Amendment Studies*, vol. 50, no. 2, Oct. 2016, pp. 59–69.

Nolan, Helen Anne, and Lesley Roberts. "Trigger Warnings as Tools for Learning-Theorising an Evolving Cultural Concept." *Medical Education*, vol. 58, no. 2, Aug. 2023, pp. 185–95.

"Student Headcount: Institutional Datamart: Chapman University." Chapman University, https://webfarm.chapman.edu/datamart-reports/student-headcount.asp?r=e.

Vatz, Richard E. "The Academically Destructive Nature of Trigger Warnings." *First Amendment Studies*, vol. 50, no. 2, Oct. 2016, pp. 51–58.

CHAPTER SIX

TRIGGER WARNINGS, WOKENESS, AND CRT

Containment Rhetoric and the Straw (Wo)Man Student

Wendy Hayden

As I prepared to submit a proposal for this collection, my Saturday morning reading of *The Washington Post* included an editorial in which the Editorial Board opined on the dangers of trigger warnings, praising a university for "pushing back on censorious students. Finally." The example used? Not someone "upset" about hearing a stance they disagree with or a word they were offended by, but an incident where a Cornell student proposed trigger warnings after witnessing a classmate's reaction to a graphic rape scene in a book they were reading.

The same week, I streamed a movie called *The Fallout* whose characters dealt with the aftermath of a school shooting. It was preceded by a message that explained the movie contained content that may be traumatizing for some viewers. No one calls such a warning censorship.

On my first day teaching a course on feminist rhetorics in fall 2013, I assigned each student to follow a feminist blog for the semester. Giving an overview of terms they might encounter in the feminist blogosphere,

I explained to them what trigger warnings were, a common practice in feminist blogs at the time to warn readers of a graphic description of rape. Impromptu, I added a trigger warning by pointing out that feminist discussion of rape culture rhetoric is clearly marked on the syllabus, and they were welcome to leave the room if needed. A few years later, I came to question this choice. I was using trigger warnings in their original context in feminist blogs: as an ethics of care for readers with eating disorders or post-traumatic stress disorder (PTSD) from a sexual assault. This was two years before trigger warnings "triggered" a lamenting of the "Coddling of the American Mind" (Lukianoff and Haidt). Before feminists began to say that "We've Gone Too Far With Trigger Warnings" and characterized them as a feminist form of virtue signaling (Filipovic). Before the right and the left used trigger warnings as a defining characteristic of "the imaginary college student" (Hsu) who doesn't want to hear stances they disagree with. Before the critics themselves were triggered by simply seeing—not reading—a book by a Black author.

Scholarship in rhetoric and composition on the trigger warning examines how it can be used as a tool for empathy and accessibility (Robillard; Gerdes; Orem and Simpkins), much like the example from Cornell deemed "censorious" by *The Washington Post*. I have also examined the trigger warning in the context of feminist blogs as constitutive rhetoric rather than censorship (Hayden). In this chapter, instead of arguing the merits or dangers of trigger warnings as a practice, I analyze the use of the trigger warning as a line of argument or signifier used against those who call out injustice. The trigger warning joins the rhetoric of free speech, wokeness, political correctness, cancel culture, and critical race theory (CRT) as a signifier weaponized by both the right and the left to delegitimize the concerns of a generation of students—as well as higher education itself.

FREE SPEECH AND THE RHETORIC OF FREE SPEECH

Once "The Coddling of the American Mind" brought terms like trigger warnings and microaggressions into public consciousness, they came to describe a group seen as threatening, the college students and "social justice warriors" (SJW) who employed these terms to call attention to injustice. Thus, trigger warnings, wokeness, and CRT became a form of containment rhetoric. Containment rhetoric, as discussed by Poirot, Smith, and Anderson, attempts to rein in challenges to those with power by characterizing a group as different and their behaviors as threatening. It defines two sets of values, with one set of values a threat to the other. It may shape public understanding of certain groups, in this case, college students. For example, "woke" has been co-opted and its meaning changed "from a virtue signal to a dog whistle" (Rose). Labeling something as woke as a form of containment rhetoric means it can be rejected as extremism, political correctness, or sensitivity, much like the trigger warning. Of course, not all critics of trigger warnings are using the term as containment rhetoric. They could simply disagree with the practice, as is represented in this collection. This chapter, then, groups trigger warnings not as a practice but as one of the recent components of a specific rhetoric of containment.

Since this containment rhetoric identifies a specific threat to what they define as "free speech," I refer to those employing the terms as containment rhetoric as free speech warriors (FSW). Just as they use SJWs to deride those with progressive views, FSWs characterize those who see difference of opinion or protests as threats to free speech. Specifically, they imagine a free speech "crisis" that is taking away the voices of white men (see Beauchamp; Thrasher; Malik). Rather than framing the trigger warning within the debate on free speech on college campuses, we might view the trigger warning as part of a rhetoric of free speech on campus: That is, while critics see the trigger warning as an example of how free speech is restricted on college campuses, we might also see these critics' rhetoric of free speech—where free speech is defined as a guaranteed platform to say anything, anywhere, without consequences—as containment rhetoric to dismiss and delegitimize criticisms.

FSWs who use trigger warnings as a line of argument construct a public threatened by wokeness and political correctness. This public is constructed as reasonable people threatened with being canceled in contrast to the young college student who is coddled and sheltered from ideas. Trigger warning rhetoric would have us believe that colleges were taking away the rights to free speech on campus to pacify the students. That students are resisting ideas which make them uncomfortable. That students and professors are not "open-minded." That is how to contain the feminist/student/racial justice threat: define them as unreasonable and close-minded. Michelle Smith points out, "Containment rhetoric neutralizes the threat of the imagined group—often by circulating its tropes and images to more public, powerful venues—and implicitly defines the group as peripheral to the larger public" (128).

Trigger warnings and wokeness are two terms that transformed from a set of values often indicating empathy to rhetorical frameworks or metaphors employed by the right and the left against those threatening the status quo by calling out privilege or injustice. These terms as frameworks simultaneously define college students as needing protection and as groups the outside world needs protection from. The SJWs are weak and easily offended; at the same time they are threatening and dictating what others say and do. Contradictorily, the critics who use trigger warnings as containment rhetoric use a rhetoric of protection (against sexuality, indoctrination) as they disdain a rhetoric of protection (against violence, for example). Trigger warnings as a framework also allows calls for anti-racism to be deemed "too sensitive" or dismissed as "political correctness." Whether SJWs are seen as coddled or threatening, the purpose is accomplished: both definitions serve as rhetorical tools of containment—often to the same audience.

A RESEARCH EXERCISE

To further analyze how the trigger warning is used as a line of argument, I will share two examples discussed in Greg Lukianoff's essay "Trigger Warnings: A Gun to the Head of Academia" included in a volume called *Unsafe Space: The Crisis of Free Speech on Campus*. Lukianoff is the president of the Foundation for Individual Rights and Expression (FIRE). My research on this essay became a lesson in primary source research for my classes.

Reading Lukianoff's essay, I came across an example of an incident involving my beloved show *Firefly*. Lukianoff didn't elaborate on the case but cited it in his bibliography. I looked for the source, prepared to be outraged at an attack on the best space cowboy show ever. His bibliography cites a piece in the 2012 issue of FIRE's newsletter. The title of the piece is "How '*Firefly*' Fans Saved Free Speech on Campus" (Kissel). My lesson asked students whether this would be a good source to read for information on this incident. For example, I didn't look up the source as I wanted to read a primary source first, without the argument from FIRE. Trying a Google search for "Firefly college campus," I got hits such as "College Campus Police Save Students from Threat of *Firefly* Poster" from *The A.V. Club* (O'Neal), referring to an incident at the University of Wisconsin-Stout, where campus police removed a *Firefly* poster from a theater professor's office door, because it referred to violence. Other sites frequented by sci-fi fans headlined the story with similar snarky and humorous titles indicating the source's stance. I planned to read these articles, but still wanted a primary source for information on the incident. Another Google search netted more articles from FIRE and several articles from the *Huffington Post*, *U.S. News*, the *Daily Caller*, and other publications—all written by Lukianoff ("Censoring Joss Whedon's Firefly"; "College Changes Course"; "Don't Create New Avenues"; "*Firefly*, Free speech"; "Browncoats—1, Alliance—0"; "Neil Gaiman and Fans of Sci-fi Classic Firefly"). Other articles referring to the incident, such as those on the *A.V. Club* (O'Neal), *Wired* (Weldon), and sites for sci-fi fans (Sloan), cite Lukianoff as their only source about the incident. A few articles link to the emails between the professor and campus police and administration, but those links go to FIRE's website where they have posted the emails. Still more articles on other sites turned out to be written by others from FIRE or those citing FIRE as their only source. My searches didn't produce a primary source or even a news article about the incident, so I did an image search.

Figure 2 shows a poster of Captain Malcolm Reynolds (played by Nathan Fillion), guns in holsters, with a quote: "You don't know me, son, so let me explain this to you once. If I ever kill you, you'll be awake. You'll be facing me. And you'll be armed." It's what the Captain said to another character who was scared the Captain would kill him in his sleep. That part of the exchange is not on the poster to contextualize it.

I was prepared to be outraged as a *Firefly* fan and a free speech fan, but looking at the poster, it occurred to me: would the poster be considered appropriate for the workplace? Even more so in a school, given the

Figure 2. *Firefly* Poster

actual gun violence in schools? Is it a firing offense? Or an illegal act? No. But perhaps an issue of appropriateness rather than censorship. When the first poster was removed, the professor replaced it with a poster on fascism, seen in Figure 3, picturing a stick figure drawing of a police officer beating someone with a bat saying "Warning: Fascism can cause blunt trauma and/or violent death. Keep fascism away from children and pets," which Lukianoff describes as a "poster in which he mocked the college for its heavy-handedness" in his *Huffington Post* piece (and other articles). The university asked for its removal as well, because of its violent message.

Figure 3. Fascism Poster

Lukianoff quotes a statement by the administration after they decided the professor could keep the posters up where they say their intention was not censorship but concern about violent messages ("College Changes Course"). Today's college students not only grew up with active shooter drills but possibly a zero-tolerance policy by their schools on potential threats or violent words or imagery. For example, what if a teenager had displayed these posters in their high school lockers? Perhaps these are posters that any workplace would ask an employee to take down, without accusations of censorship.

This reference made me curious about other sources in Lukianoff's trigger warning chapter in *Unsafe Spaces*. Are there other incidents cited that seem like colleges and college students being silly, unreasonable, and censorious, but that, when finding the primary source, may not seem all that egregious?

My second example is a reference Lukianoff makes to an incident at Wellesley College in 2014. Here is how Lukianoff refers to the incident:

> In February 2014, students at Wellesley College were outraged when an artist placed a statue of a man sleepwalking in his underwear on campus. There is nothing overtly sexual or threatening about the statue, which was erected as part of a sculpture exhibit. If anything, the sleepwalker seems vulnerable: his eyes are closed, he is unaware of his surroundings and he is barely dressed. Despite this, students called it "a source of apprehension, fear, and triggering thoughts regarding sexual assault for many members of our campus community" in a *Change.org* petition seeking its removal.
>
> One of the most powerful aspects of art is its capacity to provoke thought and debate, often by raising some hackles. Yet Zoe Magid, who started the petition, asserted that artwork that makes people uncomfortable has no place at Wellesley: "We really feel that if a piece of art makes students feel unsafe, that steps over a line." Make sure to note how *unsafe* is used in this context. (61)

Well this sounded like an example of how unreasonable the students are. Why would they call a statue triggering? This time, Lukianoff cites the petition as a primary source. Right away I noticed a slight difference in his telling of the incident and the title of the cited petition on his bibliography. Lukianoff says the petition calls for the statue's removal, or at least that's how I read it. But the petition title is "Move the 'Sleepwalker' Inside the Davis Museum," which is still on campus. So it is more relocating than removing. Following Lukianoff's provided URL didn't work, but I found the Change.org petition through a Google search. The petition isn't calling for the statue's removal from campus but asking it be placed in a different area of the campus, such as with the rest of the exhibit. Still, one might wonder why a statue is threatening. It's a marble bust, right?

That's no stone statue (Figure 4). And there's nothing around it to indicate it is part of an exhibit at the Davis Museum. It's not in front of the Davis Museum. Nothing to indicate that it is a statue. The petition

Figure 4. *Sleepwalker* Statue

includes the statement of the Director of the Davis Museum (Lisa Fischman) at the time:

> Art has an extraordinary power to evoke personal response, and to elicit the unexpected. We placed the Sleepwalker on the roadside just beyond the Davis to connect the exhibition—within the museum—to the campus world beyond. I love the idea of art escaping the museum and muddling the line between what we expect to be inside (art) and what we expect to be outside (life). I watched from the 5th floor windows today (intermittently, over several hours) as students stopped to interact playfully with the sculpture. They took selfies with him, snapping pics with their phones, and gathering to look at this new figure on the Wellesley landscape—even as the snow fell.
>
> Matelli's Sleepwalker—considered up close—is a man in deep sleep. Arms outstretched, eyes closed, he appears vulnerable and unaware against the snowy backdrop of the space around him. He is not naked. He is profoundly passive. He is inert, as sculpture. But he does inspire narrative. He appears to have drifted away from wherever he belongs and one wonders why; one wonders also how he has gotten so lost, so off course. He is a figure of pathos, and one that warrants measured consideration… Art provokes dialogue, and discourse is the core of education. In that spirit, I am enormously glad to have your response.

I imagined myself walking past this statue at night, not knowing it was a statue. I might jump or gasp before realizing it was a statue. Someone else might scream and run away rather than seeing it up close to identify it as a statue. Someone else might call the police thinking it was a person in distress. Yet, headlines about the incident connect these students' concerns with the "Coddling" rhetoric, such as *Time* magazine's piece headlined "Man Up, Wellesley: You're a Generation of Sheltered Children," for which the URL reads "wellesleys-boogeyman-wears-tighty-whities." The museum director's rhetoric similarly patronizes a group of seemingly censorious students who don't understand art and its purpose. It also indicates the kind of rhetoric Robillard describes, drawing a distinction between inside and outside, or the campus and the "real world." In this distinction, students will never be ready for the "real world" if they are so easily triggered or offended. Much of the coverage, even the *Time* piece with its provocative title, acknowledge the statue is creepy. Yet, it is cited as another example of student entitlement and trigger warnings run amok.

From this exercise, students might compare primary and secondary sources by clicking through links. Who is citing what? Are the emails from the campus police primary sources if they are edited and reposted by FIRE? Are there any pieces that don't cite FIRE as a source of news about the incident (rather than reporting or analyzing FIRE's criticism)? Whether the students agree with FIRE or not, they can start to question the narrative and perhaps identify some of the patterns in the rhetoric of the FSWs. Something that seems like a silly incident when described (what's wrong with a statue, why are these students so coddled?) might instead provoke questions about who is doing the reporting. Is it someone on campus at the time? This is exactly what occurred the first time I tried the lesson. Like with the "Coddling" article, which some students always find more credible than its criticisms which they deem "biased," students initially accepted Lukianoff's argument. But once they saw the statue, they empathized with the students. Perhaps the two incidents are an overreaction. Or perhaps taking down a poster in the workplace or moving a statue to its exhibit is not that unreasonable. But I think it's more important to look at how they are being reported, what sources are used, and what their rhetoric might imply.

A CLOSER LOOK

Turning from this research exercise to an information literacy or rhetorical analysis lesson, we might look deeper at the rhetoric used to trivialize the students' concerns. Let's look back at Lukianoff's description of the statue: "There is nothing overtly sexual or threatening about the statue, which was erected as part of a sculpture exhibit. If anything, the sleepwalker seems vulnerable: his eyes are closed, he is unaware of his surroundings and he is barely dressed" (61). A barely dressed man unaware of his surroundings never posed a threat to anyone, of course. Similarly, the museum director downplays any fear by emphasizing, "Matelli's Sleepwalker—considered up close—is a man in deep sleep. Arms outstretched, eyes closed, he appears vulnerable and unaware against the snowy backdrop of the space around him. He is not naked. He is profoundly passive." Both descriptions portray the figure as vulnerable and passive—a victim—a popular method by FSWs to define who gets to be a victim. Fischman goes on to describe how her five-floors up view showed students taking selfies with the statue, one would assume in the daytime since she could see them and where passersby might do a double-take but maybe not see it as threatening. Both Lukianoff and Fischman emphasize the snow, painting a safe and innocent scene. There are kids having fun in the snow with the statue. It reinforces the innocence of the sleepwalking man. With their descriptions, their rhetoric implies the humorless feminists and college students cannot possibly understand art. Note how Lukianoff, in introducing a quotation from a student who discusses how the statue may make some students feel "unsafe," instead uses the term "uncomfortable." The demanding students who want comfort and safety are a popular characterization of the entitled generation by FSWs. *Time* magazine's headline is joined by other headlines mocking students afraid of inanimate objects or men's underwear, such as "Statue of Underdressed Man Terrorizes Wellesley College" (Lange), where the writer explains, "The museum's director, Lisa Fischman, is patiently helping these students to trust their eyes. While she did not suggest that confused parties buddy-up with an art history student or test out their visual abilities on a television set first, she did work to clarify some questions that people had about the sculpture." Other headlines do note the life-likeness and creepiness of the work ("Put Some Pants On!").

The petition clarifies that not all students would find the statue triggering and urges care for those who do. But Alter, writing for *Time*, decides what they really need: "Survivors need community support and lots of therapy to move forward, but not Soviet-level censorship." She hits the highlights of the containment rhetoric of the FSWs: survivors of trauma are not helped by a trigger warning and it further victimizes them; any denouncing or "outrage" is censorship, and all censorship is Soviet-level; students are "offended" and "quibbling"; and we cannot expect the whole world to accommodate survivors of trauma, as she says, "But let's go back to the underwear zombie. If 'The Sleepwalker' is a sexual assault 'trigger,' then so is every Jockey ad, most men at the beach, and a poster of Mark Wahlberg I have hanging over my bed. Unfortunately, we live in a world where we sometimes see guys in their underwear. Believe me,

I wish it weren't so" (Alter). But that poster of Mark Wahlberg cannot (presumably) be mistaken for a flesh-and-blood Mark Wahlberg in the bedroom. And finally, she admonishes what feminists and SJWs should be concentrating on: "solving real-world problems, like the fact that one in three American women live in poverty or on the brink of it" (Alter). This is also a common technique used against feminists: belittle their concerns by telling them there is something more serious requiring their attention. However, a similar technique shows up in a common comment on *The Washington Post* editorial: why were they writing an article denouncing trigger warnings as censorship when Florida and schools throughout the country were banning books?

And there it is. The rhetoric used to justify the banning of books is more explicit containment rhetoric: banning books contains the threat of racial justice or LGBT acceptance. Any book by a Black person is CRT, which makes white people the victims. Any reference to acceptance is "grooming." We see how the very same containment rhetoric that denounces censorship is used to promote it. Apparently censorship is only censorship when it is certain groups of people being censored.

THE TRIGGER WARNING AS CONTAINMENT RHETORIC

The containment rhetoric used to dismiss these incidents isn't just a disagreement or difference of opinion, as FSWs might claim. And its effects go beyond the classroom. That same rhetoric might be used against sexual assault or sexual harassment victims, for example, implying that accusations are overreactions or deciding who is the victim, as the common practice of "himpathy" for "victims" of sexual assault allegations (Cheung). Another result is that any legitimate concerns college students have, from removing the name of a Confederate general from a school building to student loan debt, can be dismissed as woke and entitled. Emphasizing the passivity of the statue turns the statue into the victim. If a statue can be a victim. But the same rhetoric, emphasizing powerlessness, is used by the FSWs who make themselves the victims of political correctness.

I no longer assign students to follow a feminist blog—as many no longer exist—so I might not use the term trigger warning in noting where discussion of feminist critiques of rape culture rhetoric is clearly marked on the syllabus. Or at least not until they have done the research exercise that makes them question what different people mean when they use the term trigger warning.

WORKS CITED

Alter, Charlotte. "Man Up, Wellesley: You're a Generation of Sheltered Children." *Time*, 6 Feb. 2014.

Anderson, Karrin Vasby. "'Rhymes with Rich': 'Bitch' as a Tool of Containment in Contemporary American Politics." *Rhetoric and Public Affairs*, vol. 2, no. 4, 1999, pp. 599–623.

Beauchamp, Zack. "The 'Free Speech Debate' Isn't Really About Free Speech." *Vox*, 22 July 2020.

Cheung, Kylie. "'Himpathy' Is Making Colleges Suspicious of Women Students Who Report Sexual Assault." *Jezebel*, 6 Sept. 2023.

Editorial Board. "These Universities are Pushing Back on Censorious Students. Finally." *The Washington Post*, 29 April 2023.

Filipovic, Jill. "We've Gone Too Far With Trigger Warnings." *The Guardian*, 5 March 2014.

Fischman, Lisa. "Decision Maker Response: Lisa Fischman's Response to 'Move the Sleepwalker Inside the Davis Museum.'" *Change.org*, 4 Feb. 2014.

Gerdes, Kendall. "Trauma, Trigger Warnings, and the Rhetoric of Sensitivity." *Rhetoric Society Quarterly*, vol. 49, no. 1, 2019, pp. 3–24.

Hayden, Wendy. "From *Lucifer* to *Jezebel*: Invitational Rhetoric, Rhetorical Closure, and Safe Spaces in Feminist Sexual Discourse Communities." *Rhetoric Society Quarterly*, vol. 51, no. 2, 2021, pp. 79–93.

Hsu, Hua. "The Year of the Imaginary College Student." *The New Yorker*, 31 December 2015.

Kissel, Adam. "New FIRE Video: How *Firefly* Fans Saved Free Speech on Campus." *FIRE.org*, 28 Dec. 2011.

Lange, Maggie. "Statue of Underdressed Man Terrorizes Wellesley College." *New York Magazine: The Cut*, 5 Feb. 2014.

Lukianoff, Greg. "Browncoats—1, Alliance—0: College Changes Tune on Censorship of *Firefly* Poster." *The Daily Caller*, 7 Oct. 2011.

Lukianoff, Greg. "Censoring Joss Whedon's *Firefly* and the Chancellor Who Cried Wolf." *The Huffington Post*, 29 Sept. 2011.

Lukianoff, Greg. "College Changes Course on Censorship of *Firefly* Poster." *The Huffington Post*, 7 Oct. 2011.

Lukianoff, Greg. "Don't Create New Avenues to Punish Provocative Professors." *U.S. News*, 30 May 2014.

Lukianoff, Greg. "*Firefly*, Free speech, and the Danger of Questioning Authority on Campus." *Ricochet*, 19 Dec. 2012.

Lukianoff, Greg. "Neil Gaiman and Fans of Sci-fi Classic *Firefly* Save Free Speech on Campus." *Fire*, 28 Dec. 2011.

Lukianoff, Greg. "Trigger Warnings: A Gun to the Head of Academia." *Unsafe Space: The Crisis of Free Speech on Campus*, edited by Tom Slater, Palgrave Macmillan, 2016, pp. 58–67.

Lukianoff, Greg, and Jonathan Haidt. "The Coddling of the American Mind." *The Atlantic*, Sept. 2015.

Malik, Nesrine. "The Myth of the Free Speech Crisis." *The Guardian*, 3 Sept. 2019.

"Move the 'Sleepwalker' Inside the David Museum," *Change.org*, 5 Feb. 2014.

O'Neal, Sean. "College Campus Police Save Students from Threat of *Firefly* Poster." *The A.V. Club*, 27 Sept. 2011.

Orem, Sarah, and Neil Simpkins. "Weepy Rhetoric, Trigger Warnings, and the Work of Making Mental Illness Visible in the Writing Classroom." *Enculturation: A Journal of Rhetoric, Writing, and Culture*, vol. 20, 16 Dec. 2015.

Poirot, Kristan. "Domesticating the Liberated Woman: Containment Rhetorics of Second Wave Radical/Lesbian Feminism." *Women's Studies in Communication*, vol. 32, no. 3, 2009, pp. 263–92.

"Put Some Pants On! Incredibly Realistic Statue of Man Sleepwalking in His Underwear Causes a Stir at All-Female Wellesley College." *Daily Mail*, 5 Feb. 2014.

Robillard, Amy. "Confronting the Real: The Trigger Warning Debate and the Rhetorical Space of the Classroom." *Pedagogy: Critical Approaches to Teaching Literature, Language, Composition, and Culture*, vol. 20, no. 2, 2020, pp. 327–47.

Rose, Steve. "How the Word 'Woke' Was Weaponised by the Right." *The Guardian*, 21 Jan. 2020.

Sloan, Sam. "P.C. Run-a-muck: *Firefly* and Anti-Fascism Posters Get Professor Threatened with Criminal Charges on University of Wisconsin Campus." *Slice of SciFi*, 27 Sept. 2011.

Smith, Michelle. "Containment Rhetoric and the Public Sphere: Imagining Amana, Inscribing America." *Rhetoric Society Quarterly*, vol. 40, no. 2, 2010, pp. 128–45.

Thrasher, Steven W. "Yes, There is a Free Speech Crisis. But Its Victims are not White Men." *The Guardian*, 5 June 2017.

Weldon, Laura Grace. "First They Came For the *Firefly* Poster." *Wired*, 27 Sept. 2011.

CHAPTER SEVEN

THE CASE AGAINST TRIGGER WARNINGS

David J. Morris

In June 2008, less than a year after I'd survived an improvised explosive device (IED) attack in Baghdad, I was so triggered by a scene in *Ironman*, starring Robert Downey Jr. that I leaped out of my seat and ran out of the theater. Looking back, what was so shocking was that it seemed to come out of nowhere. I'd sworn off war movies years before when, after my first trip to Iraq in 2004, I'd discovered that Hollywood didn't know the first thing about actual war—spoiler alert: there is little about war that is actually cinematic or entertaining. Not knowing anything about the *Ironman* comic books, the last thing I expected to see in a movie about a man with a magic red exoskeleton was a highly realistic IED attack scene.

It all happened so fast that it didn't fully register in my brain—I just bolted from the theater and, before I knew what was happening, I was pacing in the hallway outside the theater wondering how I'd gotten there.

Soon after watching *Ironman*, explosions became the leitmotif of my dreams. In time it became a sort of nightly museum exhibit in my head. A dialogue between my past and my amygdala. Later, I would come to see this period of my life as a war between different parts of my brain, one scared, the other addicted to a sort of perverse nostalgia.

Sometimes inoffensive items exploded at random in my head—garbage cans, an apple, a box of Chinese takeout. Then it was airplanes and helicopters exploding and crashing into the canyons behind my San Diego apartment, reminders of a close call in a Marine helicopter over Fallujah in 2006. My nightmares metastasized and, after several more months of this, I decided to check-in at my local Veterans Administration hospital where I was eventually diagnosed with post-traumatic stress disorder (PTSD).

Given my personal history, you might be forgiven for thinking that I support the current campaign to issue trigger warnings in the classroom and online, but I do not. In fact, I find trigger warnings, well, *triggering* and part of a larger trend that threatens the vitality of our culture by obscuring certain central truths about human existence—life (to paraphrase Conrad) is like the sea, cold and relentless, and trying to disguise these basic facts strikes me as deeply unethical, the moral equivalent of telling a child that everyone in the cemetery is merely taking a nap. One of our jobs as educators is to try to explain life and its myriad consequences to people who have seen less of life than we have. I've been blown up, mortared, shot at, been tortured, seen people waterboarded, and fallen off mountains. The idea that books like *The Great Gatsby* need to be preceded by a trigger warning, wrapped in gauze, and handled like atomic waste because it accurately depicts the misogyny in American society strikes me as ridiculous.

Still, up until very recently my opinions on trigger warnings were pretty much just a loosely held notion. Students have gotten along pretty well without them for centuries, so why the big hullaballoo over them now? While I'd found *Ironman* upsetting, I've never been triggered by a book or a song or a photograph or a comment in class. This sudden shift toward the use of trigger warnings that began in the 2010s seemed to me to be yet another example of Ben Shephard's "culture of trauma," which has metastasized into a broader, even more problematic movement that critics like Greg Lukianoff and Jonathan Haidt refer to as "safetyism" in their 2018 book *The Coddling of the American Mind*.

One of the most recent and misguided expressions of the culture of trauma is the widespread use of "trigger warnings" in the college classroom (over half of professors use them according to a 2016 NPR poll).

That there is no scientific evidence to support trigger warnings and, more to the point, that they inadvertently serve as a kind of white privilege status marker, doesn't seem to occur to the professors who use them. Furthermore, their broad, un-interrogated adoption speaks to how deeply ingrained and sacrosanct the "culture of trauma" has become in America today—especially in certain very expensive private East Coast schools, where an obsession with absolute student safety has come to dominate campus discourse.

Human beings are inherently fragile, like store-bought eggs, and it is the job—job? No, it is the *life mission, the raison d'être*—of parents and teachers everywhere to serve as a kind of 24/7/365 all-inclusive life egg carton, ensuring that young people today are insulated from all the various bumps and bruises of life and are delivered to adulthood complete and pristine, without any damage.

Or so the thinking goes.

In 2021, a group of Harvard researchers released two major studies that examine the role of trigger warnings among college students and trauma survivors, respectively. What they discovered sheds new light on what the actual lived experience of trigger warnings is in the classroom and beyond. For the study on college students, published in the *Journal of Experimental Psychology: Applied*, the researchers took 462 college students and gave some of them trigger warnings before asking them to read potentially distressing passages from world literature. A control group received no trigger warnings. The Harvard team found that trigger warnings were not helpful for the college students, and actually caused small increases in anxiety in response to potentially distressing passages.

The study on trauma survivors included 451 participants, and was published in *Clinical Psychological Science* in September 2020, in the midst of the ongoing pandemic. The research report article, co-authored by Benjamin Bellet, an army Afghanistan veteran, concludes, "We found no evidence that trigger warnings were helpful for trauma survivors, for those who self-reported a PTSD diagnosis, or for those who qualified for probable PTSD... We found substantial evidence that trigger warnings countertherapeutically reinforce survivors' view of their trauma as central to their identity."

In 2019, a group of Australian psychologists reported in the *Journal of Experimental Psychology: Applied* that they had conducted an experiment similar to the Harvard study in which they issued trigger warnings before showing some subjects a slide show involving "emotionally ambiguous" photographs. The researchers found that "warned participants experienced a negative anticipatory period prior to photo viewing that did little to mitigate subsequent negative reactions."

Not sure what to make of all this, I decided to informally replicate a portion of the Australian study on the literature class that I teach at the University of Nevada, Las Vegas (UNLV) in February 2021. I chose six stock images drawn from the internet that showed ambiguous situations such as a child waving at an airplane at a major airport and a patriotic halftime show at a college football game. Another showed flight 175 crashing into the World Trade Center south tower. My admittedly unscientific study had very similar findings as the Australian study—in nearly all cases, the students who received a trigger warning rated their emotional distress as being higher than those who did not receive a trigger warning.

A week before, I'd described my experience bailing out of the theater during *Ironman* to my students and so I posed the following question to my class: given what you know about me, am I being a hypocrite for not issuing trigger warnings to you? A few students raised their hands and said, yes, that they thought I was being hypocritical.

The day after my experiment, I reached out to a local friend beginning her Master's in Social Work, having last attended college in the nineties, well before trigger warnings arrived on the scene. She said: "I once received a trigger warning at the beginning of a presentation and had to wait ten minutes before viewing the 'concerning material.' Your anxiety builds as you wait and it distracts you from the lecture as you're wondering what they're going to show you that could possibly be so 'upsetting.'"

Discussing her experience reminded me of James McGaugh, a pioneering neuroscientist at University of California, Irvine who I'd interviewed a few years before. In his 2006 book *Memory and Emotion: The Making of Lasting Memories*, McGaugh describes how physiological activation relates to the strength of memories in mammals. (While most of his experiments were conducted on rats, his work is widely understood to relate to humans.) McGaugh writes, "Research from many laboratories has revealed that there are different forms of memory [and that] emotional arousal activates stress hormones that, in turn, stimulate a specific brain system that regulates the consolidation of recently acquired information in other brain regions. A little stress is good for making lasting memories."

The question to me seemed to be: what if by warning students of an impending disturbing event ahead of time, teachers were inadvertently re-enacting McGaugh's research—what if they are actually causing harm by helping to induce a state of heightened stress in their students? Is it possible that trigger warnings could actually be paradoxically harmful—causing the very damage that they are intended to prevent?[1]

Not sure what to make of all this, I decided to email Benjamin Bellet, the author of the most recent Harvard study and asked him about my *Ironman* experience. He replied:

> While that sort of experience would doubtlessly be distressing for many with trauma histories, they can also be an impetus for seeking treatment for PTSD symptoms. However, if trigger warnings become a widespread phenomenon, people who have experiences such as you had may be incentivized toward a far less desirable alternative: using trigger warnings and other blanket protective measures to structure their world in a way in which they will never have to confront their anxiety, and never seek treatment.

To Bellet's comments, I would add that there is something qualitatively different from my experience watching an action film in a movie theater from a student being assigned to read *Lolita* for a literature survey. At the risk of being obvious, films move at the speed of the projector and moviegoers have no choice but to exit the theater if they are triggered by something on-screen. A student reading *Lolita*, by contrast, can set the book down, or flip forward a few pages to avoid the upsetting content. Books, powerful as they can be, simply aren't immersive in the same way as modern films and the idea of requiring trigger warnings (as many universities do) for written material strikes me as conspicuously misguided.

But beyond the evidence suggesting that trigger warnings are specifically harmful, their usage contributes to a larger messaging trend on campuses today that encourages students to avoid any material that they find upsetting. More than a few critics have pointed to this sort of campus culture, in some cases claiming that colleges are being turned into "emotional daycare centers" and "snowflake factories." Indeed, Donald Trump Jr.'s bestselling 2019 book *Triggered*, essentially built an entire political theory using trigger warnings as an example of everything that is wrong with modern liberalism. The book opens with a satirical trigger warning: "Do not continue reading this book if you don't like conservative ideas or if the thought of reading bad words scares you. Do not continue reading if you don't have a sense of humor."

Far more disturbing for the campus community that I belong to was an event in 2019 when Tomi Lahren, a right-wing media personality, gave a lecture on campus titled "Stay Triggered, Snowflake." After the event, a written threat was discovered scribbled in a nearby bathroom, threatening to lynch all the Black people on campus on a given date. This hate-speech incident—which the UNLV police department dubbed "serious and credible"—upset and frightened many on campus, and most of my colleagues canceled at least one of their classes in response.

While professors who issue trigger warnings are hardly to blame for these sorts of hate crimes, the incident does serve to illustrate how trigger warnings have become weaponized in our current political climate. Further, the broader cultural response to academia's use of trigger warnings and its larger engagement with trauma culture has, in certain cases, served to diminish the perceived value of a college education and its applicability to the real world. Comedians like Bill Maher have even gone so far as openly advising against going to college because of trigger warnings and the academic culture that created them.

While it would be a mistake to take Don Jr.'s fatuous book or the UNLV incident too seriously, I think it is worth questioning whether trigger warnings aren't abusing the language of trauma and the diagnostic concept of PTSD, asking us to approach college curricula in a way that is contrary to its central purpose—to expose students to new and possibly disruptive ideas, to show us how the adult world really works, warts and all.

Finally, in the wake of the COVID crisis, it's unclear what role trigger warnings will play in our educational environment. It's worth noting that, while there may be mental health fallout from the pandemic, it's unclear if the pandemic led to a nationwide outbreak of PTSD. To be sure, there will be nurses, physicians, EMTs and other frontline workers who will suffer from trauma as a result of the ongoing pandemic, but the idea that the average American will develop PTSD as a result of having to stay home for a few months or wear a face mask to the grocery store is an insult to trauma survivors everywhere. Whatever else the pandemic has taught us, it has given many Americans an education in pain, loss, and trauma, and I hope that this education will help professors think more clearly about trauma and death and see trigger warnings for what they truly are: an empty form of virtue signaling that achieve nothing.

NOTE

1 Later, I emailed McGaugh and he replied, "Yes, I think you are correct in seeing the implication of my findings. And such trigger warnings could result in a sort of 'stage fright' as well."

WORKS CITED

Bellet, Benjamin W., and Payton J. Jones. "Helping or Harming? The Effect of Trigger Warnings on Individuals With Trauma Histories." *Clinical Psychological Science*, vol. 8, no. 5, 2020, pp. 905–17.

Lukianoff, Greg, and Jonathan Haidt. *The Coddling of the American Mind: How Good Intentions and Bad Ideas Are Setting Up a Generation for Failure*. Penguin, 2018.

McGaugh, James. *Memory and Emotion: The Making of Lasting Memories.* Columbia UP, 2003.

CHAPTER EIGHT

NOW WHAT? WHEN AN ENTIRE COURSE NEEDS A CONTENT WARNING[1]

Michele Parker Randall

As a Pixar fan, when the film *Up* came out, I packed up my kids, and we went to the movies. How cute will this be—an old man and a floating house? Very early on, there is a montage that portrays the life of the old man and his wife, their wedding, purchase of a fixer-upper home, and painting a nursery. The next scene is a shadowy meeting with a doctor and the wife weeping. And I was weeping and ugly crying into my popcorn, remembering the moment a doctor told me I could get pregnant, but I couldn't stay pregnant. I wasn't ready for that scene; I didn't expect that content in a children's film. For sure, I was affected by the material. Would a content warning have made a difference in my choices that day? I honestly don't know.

I understand why we use content warnings, but I question their effectiveness. Semester after semester, I observe my students and wonder if content warnings accomplish what they are supposed to. For whom?

The courses I teach that need content warnings are *Intro to Writing Poetry, Personal Essay, Fairy Tales*, and *The Literature of Mental Health (Neurodivergent Literature)*. As you would guess, each class has vastly different content, and not just the texts I've chosen for the syllabus. Students in Poetry or Personal Essay workshop share their lives—some students are fine with sharing about a personal trauma, but other students in the workshop may not be okay reading those works. In The Literature of Mental Health, we read many first-person narratives by neurodivergent writers. Those narratives help us better understand what another's life is like. The issue arises in the variety of topics, types of media, videos, articles, and the student contributions, and including content warnings for every potentially difficult situation becomes far more complicated than a blurb on a syllabus.

Content warnings on course materials are not comparable to movie or music content warnings. They come with too many variables. First, which students need the warning? Second, is one blanket warning in the syllabus enough for all the material? All classes? Are content warnings given just before a presentation problematic? Should instructors monitor or pre-approve class discussions when students are offering their opinions, observations, or experiences? When does that become censuring or limiting? All valid questions.

There is no one-warning-fits-all solution, but I have experienced and observed successes and failures where uncomfortable topics frequently came up in conversation or literature—different catalysts and different solutions; same university, same instructor.

FAIRY TALES AND "ME TOO"

I did not have a content warning attached to my Fairy Tales class until 2017, after the Harvey Weinstein stories became daily news. The #MeToo movement took off, and I was surprised at how quickly the classroom conversations changed. Previous semesters focused on character actions, potential allegorical theories, and whether the story met the moral given at the end. Suddenly, I was fielding questions such as:

> *So they thought she was dead and they sold her to the Prince—because he wanted to look at her some more?*[2] (Um, yes.)
>
> *Wait, her father chopped down a tree with an axe because he thought his daughter was hiding in it?*[3] (Also, yes.)

The author's moral was that women should not be curious, but blindly obey their husband instead of confronting him about the bodies of his former wives in the basement?[4] (That's what the author wrote.)

You get the point.

On one hand, students came ready to apply a current-event mindset to the stories we read, which was great. They wanted to talk about ideas like how far can we push our current norms onto works that are hundreds of years old? What about art? Laws? This was exciting—contemporary relevance alongside age-old texts. However, after the first few semesters, the classes began to suffer from a reluctance to move beyond the #MeToo lens to see anything else in the tales. For example, in Cinderella-type stories, discussion prompts of what those stories say about how horribly women treat each other were flat out ignored. Maybe the content warning ended up leading us toward #MeToo discussions instead of a type of promised protection.

Needing a workaround, I leaned heavily on teaching students to contextualize stories. For example, in Paul Delarue's version of *Little Red Riding Hood*,[5] a cat calls Red a "slut"[6] and the wolf is a *bzou*,[7] and female. That last detail pushed back on the scholarship about *Little Red Riding Hood* being about maturity through puberty or losing her virginity and leads to one of my favorite discussions every semester: *In so many stories, why do we assume the wolf is male?* For many semesters, this worked and we had lively conversations about how the gender of the villain changes what we think about stalking, grooming, enchanted animals, name calling, murder, cannibalism, and being held hostage while tied to a werewolf (all in that one version of *Little Red Riding Hood*).

Post-COVID, with Fairy Tales, it didn't seem to matter what warnings were given. The last time I taught it, when I offered content warnings about *Bluebeard*[8] and *Snow, Glass, Apples*,[9] some students turned right to them. As I was talking. A few students were offended by the content—a few days later, one of them told me they tore one story out of the textbook they were so disgusted. Their book; their choice.

I now discuss the content during the first day of class, out loud, and invite students to write down any questions they have, anonymously.

I begin the next class with the answers to those questions. Interestingly, since I've started that practice, not once has any student asked about what to do if the content sparks discomfort. Although that is working for my Fairy Tales class, I am not sure it would work for Literature of Mental Health.

LITERATURE OF MENTAL HEALTH (NEURODIVERGENT LITERATURE) AND COLLEGE STUDENTS

The Literature of Mental Health (Neurodivergent Lit) course starts out with discussions of language, how language in and about mental illness is fraught with misunderstandings and wrong information passed on through media. We agree to assume good intent by everyone in the class. We all have the potential to say something harmful unintentionally, and we will trip over our words—what we can't be is afraid to speak and learn. We agree to co-create a safe space.

The first day of class we spend much time discussing that the content of most mental health narratives contain circumstances that are traumatic. Everything you'd expect is mentioned in the non-fiction narratives, poems, novels, and films: suicide ideation, suicide attempts and completions, sexual assault, assault, abuse, homelessness, prison, school located traumas including school shootings, bullying, gender dysphoria, stigma, social shunning, becoming illegal depending on laws created to target or strip rights from large groups of people, lack of access to mental health care,[10] insufficient care or malpractice from healthcare providers, loss of jobs, loss of families and friends, and more.

Before the end of the first day, I ask students to seriously consider if they are in the best place to take the course *that semester*.[11] We speak bluntly and compassionately about how taking all of the uncomfortable parts out of the narratives would be a disservice not only to the authors but to our own desire to understand another's life. If students choose to stay in the course, they choose to read and discuss the authors' whole lives, everything they were brave enough to share. I do say if something becomes too difficult to skip ahead ten pages and pick it back up.[12] I remind them to use context clues—you can usually tell what's coming up in a story. Not all stories.

As college students are the age at which lifetime mental illnesses present,[13] this course fills with students desperate to understand or to be understood. Some students want to help their family member(s), and others plan to get a job in the mental health industry. Everything we read and discuss has the potential to spark an emotional or anxious reaction, from narratives to news, to the personal stories students offer during discussion. None of these fit into a blanket warning, but at least can be given before that day's class. Sometimes.

Student presentations, though, are an example of in-the-moment content warnings which may create more problems than they solve. Imagine that midterm presentations are on the schedule, and each presenter has their own content warning offered right before they start speaking. If the warning is about sexual assault,[14] a student who might genuinely be dealing with that trauma is now offered a chance to stand up and leave, but that choice also publicly outs them as a victim of sexual trauma. Even if a student took the opportunity to step out for a phone call in that moment, every other student is watching that student leave. From my vantage point, students whisper to each other, shake their heads. When that student comes back, they walk in to every student staring at them. (They also get a friendly check in email from me later that day—just in case they need it.) Whether or not they are a victim of assault, assumptions are made. The other option to stay put and stiff upper lip until that presentation is over doesn't seem pleasant either. In-the-moment warnings have this effect, regardless of the age of the audience or the topic at hand.

If the goal of content warnings is to protect or assist, it fails in these circumstances. The class is also discussion heavy, and there is no way to know what will come up. Some students[15] are very open with their own family or personal experiences with mental health. Imagine that class involved "pre-approving" comments during class. We cannot know everything that may happen during class. I experienced this personally, while attending an active shooter presentation at my university: the speaker showed a slide with a photograph of a couple I knew, from my town, who had been kidnapped and held for ransom in Papua New Guinea—only one of them survived their rescue. My lungs burned. My jaw ached, clenched. I could not leave. I remember nothing else from that presentation. I was expecting school shooting imagery, I'd readied myself to see photos of

Virginia Tech where my father-in-law stayed locked in his office that day getting updates from us in Florida watching the news, but I did not expect to see the kidnappers' smiling faces in the background. At the same time, no one else in that room had the same memories or experiences I carry. How can we ever craft a content warning to cover every possibility?

Part of the issue may be that traumatic events are still pretty fresh. Statistically, college students are of an age where sexual assault more frequently occurs[16] and mental illnesses[17] present,[18] and the recentness of those events makes the mention of them hard to process. Films would be harder to watch—to see it, or eyes closed to hear a similar event. And, then, can the student trust what that film presented as true? Research done by USC Annenberg Inclusion Initiative studied the portrayal of mental illness in 300 popular films. Their results found that "when characters with mental health conditions did appear, they were often stereotyped and stigmatized" (Pieper). This can cause a young student with a new diagnosis to make devastatingly wrong conclusions about their own lives, especially true of someone in the middle of the process. Way too many variables to craft effective content warnings.

As the Neurodivergent Literature course progresses through the different texts, we keep returning to language—where words can illuminate or obfuscate meaning or truth. One of the first semesters I taught this class, one student asked if we could please change the language from "trigger" to "content" warning. There followed an animated discussion, but mostly in affirmation. Stetson University is three hours from Marjory Stoneman Douglas High School, site of the February 14 massacre. My students had family attending high school that day, and one student lost a close family friend. I wish I could remember the name of the student who asked the original question, but she sat in the second row, third column from the left, and was quick to smile and enter discussions. Her reasoning that day: "For our generation,[19] the word *trigger* has one connotation." Hard to argue with that.

POETRY, PERSONAL ESSAY, AND OTHER COURSES

My goal for this chapter was not to argue for or against content warnings, but to discuss experiences in the classroom and consider potential paths to a safe(r) space for our students. Every college class has the potential to include "uncomfortable" or catalytic language or information, and that depends entirely on the student's personal history, the student's family history, current societal trends, current political leanings, religion, race, gender...each student unique. There is no perfect warning. So, now what? Where do we go from here?

- Warnings inform that the content may cause discomfort. Should we also include steps to take if that happens? What should students do?
- What are instructors told to do? What is the science behind it?
- When is the best *time* to use a content warning?
    - Just the syllabus?
    - First day of class and syllabus?
    - End of prior class for next meeting?
    - Beginning of that class meeting?
    - Beginning of relevant discussion?
    - Top of relevant assignment?
    - How often should we repeat content warnings? Should we repeat?
- What feels ineffective? Is there a better way? Are we involving the students? What else is affecting this outcome?
- What feels effective? Why is it working: in that class/with that topic/in that major/with that age group? What else is affecting this outcome?
- Other potential language: content advisory, c notes, c review, c check, c concerns, c care, c factors, c issues, c elements, c survey, c study, etc.

College classes should be a time for students to ask questions, and maybe content warnings squelch that to some extent or encourage instructors to not teach particular works because of the traumatic elements found within the text: works about assault, war, the holocaust, psychosis, and recovery. You know, life. Not talking about difficult things doesn't make it easier for anyone, it just makes it harder for students to get their questions answered or even speak their questions out loud. If we never read or discuss the uncomfortable—in a safe space[20]—as a class, students may not be able to write the uncomfortable, write through the discomfort, or assist others by teaching them how to do so.

NOTES

1 For this chapter, I chose to use the phrase "content warning" as the word "trigger" brings up images and memories (for many of my students) of gun violence in their schools and communities.
2 Snow White
3 Ashputtel, the Brothers Grimm
4 Bluebeard
5 *The Story of Grandmother*
6 Original definition of "street-kid."
7 Werewolf
8 Charles Perrault (rumor has it, the story was based on an actual person).
9 Neil Gaiman (modern twist on Snow White)
10 Florida ranks 49th in access to mental health care. Florida ranks "30th for youth mental health" (Evans).
11 I hope not to connote any semblance of "you can't handle this" and instead allow a student to say, "not this term."
12 Our semester also starts with a visit from the counseling center on campus—the counselor knows this course well and speaks to action steps.
13 50% of all lifetime mental illness begins by age 14, and 75% by age 24 (NAMI).
14 81% of female victims and 71% of male victims report the sexual violence occurred prior to age 25 (Smith et al.).
15 Never a requirement to share personal stories in my classes.
16 "One-third of US adults (32.7%) reported sexual harassment and one-quarter (24.6%) reported sexual assault during early adulthood. Reported sexual harassment rates [and sexual assault rates] were similar for respondents who enrolled in college...and respondents who did not enroll in college" (Mumford et al.).
17 "Median age at onset for specific mental disorders mapped on a time continuum, from phobias/separation anxiety/autism spectrum disorder/attention deficit hyperactivity disorder/social anxiety (8–13 years) to anorexia nervosa/bulimia nervosa/obsessive-compulsive/binge eating/cannabis use disorders (17–22 years), followed by schizophrenia, personality, panic and alcohol use disorders (25–27 years), and finally post-traumatic/depressive/generalized

anxiety/bipolar/acute and transient psychotic disorders (30–35 years), with overlap among groups and no significant clustering" (Solmi et al).

18 National Institute of Mental Health reports "young adults 18–25 years had the highest prevalence of [any mental illness] AMI (33.7%) compared to adults… . AMI is defined as a mental, behavioral, or emotional disorder" (NIMH).

19 June 12, 2016, 49 dead–58 injured, Orlando Pulse Shooting; June 5, 2017, 6 dead, Orlando factory; February 14, 2018, 17 dead–17 injured, Parkland shooting; August 26, 2018, 3 dead–11 injured, Jacksonville Landing; November 2, 2018, 3 dead–5 injured, Tallahassee shooting…

20 This author is aware that not every classroom is a safe space for every opinion. It is my hope that it becomes so.

WORKS CITED

Evans, Arthur C. "APA Letter Addresses State of Florida's Request to Review Cambridge/AICE Psychology Course." American Psychological Association, 2 August 2023, https://www.apa.org/news/apa/2023/cambridge-aice-psychology-letter.

Mumford E. A., et al. "Sexual Harassment and Sexual Assault in Early Adulthood: National Estimates for College and Non-College Students." *Public Health Reports*, vol. 135, no. 5, 2020, pp. 555–59.

NAMI (National Alliance on Mental Illness). "Mental Health by the Numbers," https://www.nami.org/about-mental-illness/mental-health-by-the-numbers/.

NIMH (National Institute of Mental Health). "Mental Illness," https://www.nimh.nih.gov/health/statistics/mental-illness.

Pieper, K., et al. *Mental Health Conditions Across 300 Popular Films: A Research Update from 2016 to 2022.* USC Annenberg Inclusion Initiative, June 2023, https://assets.uscannenberg.org/docs/aii-mental-health-2023-06-28.pdf.

Smith, S., et al. *The National Intimate Partner and Sexual Violence Survey: 2015 Data Brief—Updated Release*. 2015, https://www.nsvrc.org/resource/2500/national-intimate-partner-and-sexual-violence-survey-2015-data-brief-updated-release.

Solmi, M., et al. "Age at Onset of Mental Disorders Worldwide: Large-Scale Meta-Analysis of 192 Epidemiological Studies." *Molecular Psychiatry*, vol. 27, no. 1, 2022, pp. 281–95.

CHAPTER NINE

TRIGGER WARNINGS AND A PEDAGOGY OF TRUST

Morgan Read-Davidson

As the director of two writing programs, it has now become a common and expected occurrence to have both students and contingent faculty come to my office expressing anxiety over course content. In my roles as the Writing Program Administrator of our rhetoric and composition program (GE courses, a minor, and courses in the broader BA in English studies) and the Director of the Creative Writing major, I supervise approximately thirty part-time faculty and graduate instructors, and provide programmatic advice to ten full-time faculty, advise one hundred fifty plus majors, and any general education undergraduates taking our GE writing courses. While the concerns range across a wide spectrum, from faculty fears of censorship or being "canceled" for assigning materials with discomforting content, to student complaints of offensive or triggering material (both in the assigned class material and in student writing), one thing remains consistent: they look to me to confirm their perspective.

While the larger conversation about difficult content and trigger warnings is not new, the sudden need for urgently scheduled meetings with me did not begin until the COVID-19 pandemic crisis and our move to remote instruction, and the subsequent adjustment back to the classroom. This seems to coincide with the increase of online and social media interaction during the pandemic, where the use of trigger warnings and content warnings on social media, particularly on Twitter, Instagram, and TikTok, have made the conversation far more visible. For students, this seems to have given them validation and confidence, as well as a discursive language, to express their concerns about content. While prior to the year of remote instruction (2020) I had heard from faculty now and again about tensions with students over discomforting content, it was after the return to in-person instruction (2021) that students seemed to feel confident to come to me for advice or just venting about what they felt was problematic or triggering course content. I appreciated the benefit such conversations have in helping us continually develop pedagogy and student support, but I also couldn't help but notice that often the conversation was first preceded by a grading conflict between student and instructor. Only when I pushed back did the student, as a secondary tactic, turn to a complaint about course content using the discourse of trauma. For example, after complaining about grading conflict in a class, an advisee student pivoted their complaint to the assignment of the novel *Kindred* by Octavia Butler and its use of the term "relationship" to describe the complex interaction between the protagonist and her abuser ancestor. The resulting conversation about discomfort, representation, language, and the rhetoric of fiction was very fruitful, but I also was secretly disturbed by what appeared to be a weaponization of trauma discourse in a conflict between student and instructor.

In creative writing courses, there has also been a post-remote-learning increase in complaints about the content of student writing in workshops. While the creative writing workshop in general still carries lingering fumes of the old Iowa Workshop model of a "safe place" for all content (typically misogynistic, homophobic/transphobic, and racist), it has certainly progressed in most classrooms to at the very least ask writers to provide content and trigger warnings. When this courtesy has not been followed or enforced, students have come to me to voice their concerns. Like in rhetoric and literature classes, students are bringing that discourse of trauma into the creative writing classroom, mostly with an awareness of mental and emotional health...but sometimes as a weapon against students with whom they have a conflict.

On the one hand, I understand faculty fears of censorship, the slippery slope of attempting to "shield students from words, ideas, and people that might cause them emotional discomfort," rather than confronting those factors to understand why they cause discomfort, as well as developing solutions to the larger societal problems they represent (Lukianoff and Haidt). Certainly there are plenty of anecdotes like those above of students who don't want to read or watch material that challenges, subverts, or offends their current world view and values, or weaponize trigger warnings against instructors with whom they have a disagreement—ideological, but even personal. Book banning events, happening not only in conservative states but even in my home state of California (prior to a state law banning the banning of books) are striking examples of content-based censorship, but so is left-leaning censorship of racial and patriarchal texts, even when taught in critical contexts. On the other hand, it is important to acknowledge the real effect of content commonly associated with triggers of psychological trauma—sexual assault, homophobia, transphobia, war, bullying, suicide, and self-harm—where reading, viewing and even discussing representations of such events can trigger memories, emotions, or flashbacks that result in panic attacks or other forms of post-traumatic stress disorder (PTSD) (Klieber 3).

For many faculty, student requests for trigger or content warnings appear as an imposition on academic and creative freedom. Rather than establish a context for *why* certain discomforting content is necessary to study, or in the case of student writing, allow in the workshop setting, they dig in their heels and repeat the "coddling" argument of Lukianoff and Haidt; that is, that this generation of students has been shielded from tough subjects, leading to a hyperfragility inhibiting the pursuit of knowledge (Klieber 4). Reading about the history of sundown towns and white supremacy *should* make white students uncomfortable, and most reasonable people would agree that protecting them from that discomfort undermines efforts of cultural progress. But BIPOC students may also feel distress as memories of their own repression surface through the representation of racist acts. Rather than trying to parse the differences between feeling discomfort and being psychologically triggered, we should focus on creating the most effective learning environment for *all* students.

The use of trigger and content warnings preceding potentially sensitive content should not be seen as a censoring imposition, but part of a student-centered pedagogy of active learning. As the University of Michigan guide effectively puts it, these notices provide individuals with PTSD and other anxiety disorders "the forewarning necessary for them to make use of [coping] strategies that will decrease the harmfulness of encountering triggering material." That's not censorship; that's empathy. When I first started as a Writing Program Administrator in 2014, the topic of trigger warnings came up in a pre-semester program meeting, and I distributed this guide for its helpful definitions and suggestions. Recently, however, I've focused on a particularly important section:

> While it is impossible to account for all potential triggers, which could include smells or sounds that recall a past trauma, some of the most common triggers include representations of sexual violence, oppressive language, gunshots, and representations of self-harm. *If you establish sufficient trust with your students* and make clear to them that you will do your best to supply any requested trigger warnings, you can provide personalized notices about any material that may be triggering for them. However, trust can be challenging to build and takes time, so the inclusion of warnings for common triggers can be helpful to students who may not feel comfortable telling an instructor they barely know very personal information about their mental health and past trauma. (UM Guide; my italics for emphasis)

The key portion I emphasized, and what has changed my approach as a teacher and a program administrator, is the phrase "establish sufficient trust with your students." The UM guide doesn't describe how we might do this, other than making the effort to provide warnings. But with the increase in discourse about trauma, trigger warnings, and content warnings in social media, our disciplinary communities, and in my own programs, I wanted to ensure that I was not only giving the right advice to my own community of faculty and students, but making the right pedagogical choices in my classroom. Though I certainly cite best practices, like the UM guide, I found more success in responding to faculty and student anxieties by discussing my own teaching practices as I also navigate these issues.

While I've been fairly consistent in providing basic content warnings for films and texts assigned in my courses, I'd not given much more thought to *why* those were so important, or how I might better prepare my students to be able to engage with that material in healthy, productive ways. My pedagogy has always had an "empathy-first" goal, but the disruption of spring 2020 and the subsequent foregrounding of a variety of student and faculty needs as a result of the abrupt move to remote instruction made me realize how woefully inadequate my approach actually was. The first thing I did was send out a confidential survey to assess each individual student's needs, and it was so successful in understanding where I needed to change policies, instructional strategies, and make accommodations, that I have used this survey, or variations, at the beginning of every one of my classes since.[1]

One of the most important results of using these surveys is an establishment of trust, a simple means of showing that I care, and that I am trying to the best of my ability to create an environment for successful learning. I ask questions about name pronunciation, preferred pronouns, learning styles, accommodations, and possible triggers. Rather than being forced to take that difficult step of reaching out to an instructor, not knowing how they view learning accommodations or trigger warnings, students are invited to tell me about themselves in an accessible form. In turn, I can get a feel for the personality and needs of my class, and design trigger and content warnings, as well as pre- and after-care activities that will help create the best learning environment for them.

For example, in one of my classes we play an interactive text-adventure that explores the author's grieving process after his brother was killed in the 2017 terrorist bombing in Manchester, UK. Prior to using my survey, I had provided a trigger warning and never had anyone approach me with concerns or questions, though I did have one instance where a student left the class abruptly during the discussion, telling me later that it triggered feelings about the recent passing of a family member. However, in the first in-class semester where I implemented the survey, I discovered that several students had experienced recent deaths of family members.

I didn't remove the text-adventure from my curriculum, but I did reach out confidentially to the specific students to discuss the upcoming content, and I also decided to incorporate pre- and after-care activities derived from trauma therapy, not only to help those students in question (all of whom decided to engage with the content and subsequent discussion), but any others who may not have reported a trigger, been aware of a trigger, or simply felt uncomfortable with the content.

My inspiration for turning to trauma therapy came from a former rhetoric and composition student, Cade Galal, who had entered a masters in therapy program. Galal pointed me to readings and resources that included pre-care and after-care activities like journaling, reflection, small and large group discussion, and mindfulness. I decided to have my students do a bit of in-class journaling about their anticipated response to a grief-process text-adventure prior to playing it, with starter questions like:

- Do you tend to internalize emotional material and get flooded with emotions?
- Are you more likely to get numb and dissociate?
- Do you need to take breaks while engaging with the text-adventure?
- Will you find discussion about this content difficult?
- During discussion, do you need to prepare to leave the classroom for a moment?

After journaling, I offered the opportunity for anyone to share, and many did, including one of the students I'd previously reached out to. This led to an intimate and collaborative discussion that seemed to not only normalize the idea of course content being distressing and containing possible triggers, but also the act of talking *about* how and why this happens, how we deal with it, and why such content is still important for learning.

Typically after playing the text-adventure, I ask students to post a response in our online discussion forum discussing it in the context of the theoretical reading it was paired with. This time, however, I encouraged students to also talk about their emotional experience playing the game, following up on the pre-care activity of journaling and discussion.

At least half the class chose to do so, and the reflection on emotional responses, rather than sidetracking critical analysis, actually deepened it by making connections between the rhetorical meaning behind the procedural narrative choices and the emotional responses students experienced. Students were able to articulate the necessity for representing trauma in this content in order to make a larger point about the social process of grief.

In *The Body Keeps Score: Brain, Mind, and Body in the Healing of Trauma*, Bessel van der Kolk calls these pre- and after-care activities "emotional-regulation techniques" (244). Rather than suppressing or avoiding emotions, emotional regulation attunes us to our mental and physical responses to disturbing and discomforting material and situations (Klynn). Journaling and discussion activities promote active reflection and articulation of what makes us uncomfortable, what we anticipate we might feel, what we feel in the moment, and how we feel after the experience. We can also use mindfulness techniques of centered breathing and sensory observation to help students take a moment to calm their mind and emotions (Hanh). I've recently begun to implement centered breathing before difficult subject-matter discussions in my class, and anecdotally it seems to have actually increased participation in the discussion among the quieter students.

More importantly, it communicates to my students that I take both their well-being and the learning situation (including the distressing content) seriously. Van der Kolk tells us that triggered responses "are irrational and largely outside people's control," making them "feel crazy... As a result, shame becomes the dominant emotion" (74). By sharing coping mechanisms and articulating possible intense feelings, we can validate our students' experiences with the material and hopefully create a community of support in the classroom. This in turn enables us to discuss triggering material in productive ways that meet our expectations of academic rigor and discourse.

So now when faculty come to my office with anxieties about content, about trigger warnings, and about fears of censorship or student pushback, I ask them how their pedagogy is preparing students for difficult or distressing content. What tools, like journaling, small group and full class discussion, and online discussion forums, are they already using?

How might they build trust with students by communicating that they take student concerns and needs seriously? How can they incorporate concepts of emotional regulation into the activities they already implement in class? While composition instructors are not trained therapists, nor should we be taking on those roles, we certainly deal with course material and student writing that accesses potentially traumatic memories and experiences, or at the very least can cause distressing emotions. It cannot hurt us to learn more about the way the body responds to triggering and discomforting material.

By preparing our students ahead of time for difficult material, we treat "them as adults who can and should attend to their own wellbeing with all available information" (UM guide). We're not labeling anything as off-limits to teaching, nor are we "coddling" or "infantilizing" students by shielding them "from words, ideas, and people that might cause them emotional discomfort" (Lukianoff and Haidt). In fact, by employing a pre- and after-care pedagogy, including active discussions of trigger and content warnings, we are directly communicating with our students that we are not fortune-tellers, that we cannot anticipate how every student will respond to every possible distressing text, video, or discussion—but that we *do* care for their learning and their well-being. Both students with psychological triggers and students who are uncomfortable with distressing content can be helped by these strategies, which means both are less likely to become resistant or defensive, shutting down their desire and ability to learn. In the end, shouldn't that be our goal?

* An earlier version of this chapter was published in *FEN Blog*, an online imprint of *Composition Studies,* March 27, 2023.

NOTE

1 Access my survey at https://tinyurl.com/y7jzszzp

WORKS CITED

Hanh, Thich Nhat. "Five Steps to Mindfulness." *Mindful,* 23 Aug. 2010, https://www.mindful.org/five-steps-to-mindfulness/.

Klieber, Anna. "On the Epistemology of Trigger Warnings, or Why The Coddling Argument Against Trigger Warnings is Misguided." *Feminist Philosophy Quarterly*, vol. 7, no. 4, 2021.

Klynn, Bethany. "Emotional Regulation: Skills, Exercises, and Strategies." *Betterup*, 22 June 2021, https://www.betterup.com/blog/emotional-regulation-skills.

Lukianoff, Greg, and Jonathan Haidt. "The Coddling of the American Mind." *The Atlantic*, September 2015.

UM Guide. "An Introduction to Content Warnings and Trigger Warnings." *University of Michigan*, https://sites.lsa.umich.edu/equitable-teaching/an-introduction-to-content-warnings-and-trigger-warnings/.

Van der Kolk, Bessel. *The Body Keeps Score: Brain, Mind, and Body in the Healing of Trauma*. Penguin, 2015.

PART THREE

QUEER/FEMINIST/ANTI-RACIST INTERVENTIONS

CHAPTER TEN

TRIGGER WARNINGS, OR AN AUTOETHNOGRAPHY OF TRAUMA AND MARKED SPACES

Ryan Ashley Caldwell

INTRODUCTION

I present three vignettes within this autoethnography that use trauma as a lens for understanding the classroom and its many triggers. These vignettes are intended to deepen the discussion about trigger warnings and associated anxieties within the classroom, those associated with teaching and learning, and to ultimately highlight that educational spaces are not *unmarked spaces*. Educational spaces require negotiation, as agents are diverse and have various lived experiences such that we all do not enter these spaces equally or similarly. In fact, a deeper understanding of trigger warnings and their use could teach us all more about those who experience trauma, how trauma shapes classroom and learning experiences, how systems of triggers exist from above and within institutions, and how to be more effective and empathetic as educators given the realities of navigating "marked" institutional spaces. Trigger warnings remind us that how we show up to such learning spaces matters. Within this chapter, I make a plea for the use of trigger warnings from my own lived experiences and provide hopeful teaching pedagogies and strategies associated with a trauma-informed approach to teaching.

Trigger warnings: institutional violence, police violence, heteronormativity, sexism, transphobia, queerphobia, domestic violence, suicide, neglect

VIGNETTE NUMBER ONE: THE TRIGGER OF SAFETY: WHEN INSTITUTIONS FAIL

I was born into multiple tragedies. As a young person I was faced with the trauma of navigating a toxic home environment, full of emotional and physical damages, of which I was one of the consequences. For forever, I was mostly my own adult. Our parents had a dance with each other that included acting out our ancestors' trauma with very little chance of escaping its grasp. We were the prints of the prints of those who previously did the printing. My home was unsafe—it was unpredictable. I routinely did not invite friends over because I was embarrassed and knew I had no way to control the levels of fighting that took place within.

Neglect looks different across families, and I assure you that my neglect probably seemed *unfathomable* given the outside performances of middle-class success and whiteness. As a child I thought we were really experienced in hiding family troubles from the outside world. My superhero power was living several separate lives and never confusing them. This allowed me to have control over knowing how or when anxiety might arise and defined spaces as "not home" as "mostly safe" (although this was not a foolproof practice). My neglect was of love, safety, and belonging, and so I grew up trying to manage as a young person who attempted to live within the walls of a flaming, toxic, burning house.

By the age of six I knew how to go inside myself for reprieve. When my auntie visited that year and saw the levels of despair and tried to leave, my dad ripped the phone off the wall so she couldn't adjust her flight. I showed her my closet and the back room where my brother and I went to feel safe and magical. I tried explaining to her in my head as we drove to the airport that evening that I wanted to go with her. I wanted somewhere else.

As a third grader, I found so much excitement in the part of the year where the book fair would come to school for a visit. I was transported through stories to new places that had so much possibility. I sought these spaces and saw myself embedded within them. I made myself within these spaces.

That same year, I remember meeting the school's counselor puppet named Duso. He was a shy dolphin and so we as a class would sing for him to come out and visit with us. "*Hey Duso, come on out. I like to listen and talk to you. I like your songs and your stories too!*" I remember he sang and asked us questions about happiness and safety and strangers. I think there was also a frog—Clyde maybe? Apparently, the collective of animal puppets were easier to speak to at this age than adults. As a young person of eight, and supported by Duso and Clyde, I asked to see the counselor in her office. I cannot remember to this day what was said or even what happened, but I know for sure I told her about the violence in my home, about the terror and the eggshells that were scattered on the floor in every room, and the abuse and how it had always been, and that I was scared. I was scared for my mom. I was scared for my brother. I left and had the feeling that things would be taken care of now and that I would be okay.

Although I don't have many clear memories of my early years, I remember going to family therapy in the late 1970s and early 1980s (the entirety of elementary school) and how it involved an hour of yelling. Sometimes my younger brother and I were asked to sit outside of the door, only to hear the yelling at a lower decibel. This was always followed by a formal fancy dinner. This awful family ritual took place every week until, at age 13, I fortunately began going to my very own private therapy session, likely to recover from family therapy itself.

Over the next few years, I realized that despite asking for help from everyone I knew, nobody was coming. The violence had scared away those that "should have," and any who "would have" also. Many pretended not to know. I learned that the police would not really do much, despite calling them to our home every time there was violence. Perpetrators would leave, those violated would lie, and during those times even if there was clear destruction and devastation, adults with state and local authority and power walked away. I had already experienced dissociation by now and learned the self-soothing ritual of counting shadows and collecting rocks.

My anger as a result of all of this would come out as I became a young adult, first by allowing additional abuse, and then causing it to others and ultimately to myself, and I maintain that there aren't enough apologies when you pass on violence from within.

VIGNETTE NUMBER TWO: THE TRIGGER OF SCHOOL: "THE TIME BEFORE THE METAL DETECTORS"

Tuesday, January 8th, 1991

...Try to forget this (try to forget this)
Try to erase this (try to erase this)
From the blackboard
...Jeremy spoke in class today

(Pearl Jam, "Jeremy," 1991)

As always, when I drive up to Richardson High School, I pass the campus and come around the far side to park on the street near the cafeteria. I like this side because I can easily leave when I want. It's the side of ultimate freedom. I don't have to deal with the security guard, whose job is impossible given the amount of parking areas he must oversee simultaneously.

At school, the teachers, counselors, and administrators are very kind to me: my mother works for the school district as the Director of Counseling and Student Services and I have the cultural capital to exist behind the scenes and in between; I am known as her child and so existing on campus as a ghost—sometimes there and sometimes not—is easy for me.

I might have been identified in the early 1990s as sort of a weirdo, but if anything, I had several parts to myself already and these seemed distinct to me. I existed at home as a captive, but at school I felt more confident in my abilities. I am an honors student making straight A+s and am already accepted into a handful of colleges by this point in the academic year. I am white and able bodied, and my mental health issues are largely not visible but have consequences, nonetheless. Many think I am a straight female, including myself, which changes in the future to non-binary and queer. I wear black and have pink hair or maybe sometimes blue or red. (I still do.) I consider myself fashionable and sell high-end clothes to the alienated (including myself) at the Dallas Galleria on weekends. Ru Paul and MAC makeup have released Viva Glam lipstick and Macy's is a center of rainbow capitalism and LGBTQ+ culture. I am not particularly aware at this age of much about queer culture other than that Viva Glam is being used to fund research for AIDS and that there are glorious nights of drag that we sneak into at the gay bars with our fake IDs. There are no LGBTQ+ courses or even sections in classes about LGBTQ+ anything, despite being almost two decades past when homosexuality was removed from the DSM as a psychological disorder. In the news, there are stories of gay men being targeted and beaten in Dallas's Oak Lawn and this is what I know of such local history. Even in school at Richardson High School, there are no LGBTQ+ groups on campus (although it is true that these sorts of student groups didn't exist yet on many campuses and wouldn't for at least a decade more). In fact, even trying to think of a gay-identified student in any of the three levels of students at school proves impossible. School is lonely but I am good at it. I am one of the leaders of a group called "Peer Helpers" at the High School. Despite doing "well" in school in terms of grades and testing, I am mostly bored there. I have a handful of friends, many a grade or two ahead, but school is the place where I can go that is away from home—*a safer space in fact.*

Today is a Tuesday and it is the beginning of January just after winter break. My second period is computer class, and this was considered revolutionary because we finally had Word documents and files we could save instantly instead of using a typewriter. From beyond our classroom there was the loudest of claps that I describe sounding like a huge pile of books being dropped to the floor—a slam! None of us knew what it was and only later realized it came from one hall over, from within an English teacher's classroom. We hear quiet chaos, crying, and hurried movement. A short while later an announcement comes on over the speaker system that asks us all to stay in our classrooms and "shelter in place" until another announcement is made. Ten minutes pass and an office assistant walks into the classroom with a pass for someone and I am called out of class and asked to bring my things to the front main office. I pack up my stuff and head immediately toward the front of the school. I use the stairwell that I didn't know held such a dark secret that day and downstairs I see students crying and sitting in the front few rows of the fancy auditorium among the red velvet curtains and gold piping. It had just happened.

My mother calls my name from down the hall in front of me and I walk toward her. Why is my mom at my high school? Am I in trouble again? She tells me, "*Ryan, listen to me, there has been a shooting. A suicide. The police have just arrived. I am here to oversee the student care and school response, so I signed you out of classes for the rest of the day while the school is on lockdown. Go home and I will call you in a little bit.*" I remember not being scared or really having any feelings at all and responding immediately to my mother's command. My mom and I knew how to behave in the face of violence and harm and so I felt confident as we exchanged glances that we each knew our roles. My mom went into the auditorium and shut the door behind her. About an hour prior, a 15-year-old student, Jeremy Delle, left class to go to his locker to retrieve a gun, held Mrs. Barnett's English class at gunpoint, and then shot himself in front of everyone.

It would not be until decades later that I would even know what a trigger warning was, but I believe my mother was using our shared history of family abuse to signal her understanding of terror and its effects for my body within the walls of RHS that day. Within our shared look I knew everything. Even before the school shooting, I had experiences that taught me what the anxiety part and protocol would be like around an emergency. My mom was the trigger warning embodied, but ironically the place I was going home to was more toxic than a space where a suicide had just happened. I became hypervigilant in leaving the school, walking unseen even between the police and ambulance services as I went back upstairs to my locker to get my keys and books, past the nurse in the hallway who was all bloody from giving impossible CPR to the shooter, and then finally out the front doors of the school. I remember the feeling of being above and watching myself move and moving within simultaneously—a split between the body and mind, both an object and subject and also neither. I wondered how anyone could possibly learn that day and thought everyone should be given the chance to escape from what they would soon understand happened.

Distinct parts develop around trauma, and so it won't be surprising to know that with each and every new classroom on the variety of campuses where I have taught, I imagine scenarios to exit if there is school violence, and worse, how exactly a confrontation in this sort of emergency situation might look. I imagine and plan every escape including how I might pile up furniture in front of the classroom door. It is an automatic thing that happens where my brain begins sorting and filing risk. It isn't surprising to me how personal experiences of violence and experiences associated with weapons in the classroom (and the increased levels of school violence scenarios in the United States) can infuse the mind with long-term anxieties associated with teaching and learning spaces that might function as a...trigger. For those with trauma brains, memories are encoded differently during traumatic events. Memories can be like flashes without context or representations of photos I had seen with stories I created for them. For example, even though the classroom where the shooting took place was locked and unused until every student in the school had graduated, there was not a single time that I passed the room and didn't feel an overwhelming fear and hypervigilant terror crawling over my body given everything I had witnessed. For me, it was as if it was still a dangerous room. In fact, it was my practice to avoid the hallway where it happened if at all possible, so as to avoid the trigger of previous trauma.

There are consequences to trauma for the body and brain. For example, it is difficult to manage teaching or learning spaces when there is a split-shift experience happening for the individual given the trauma of the mind and classroom—one-half of the self manages teaching or learning and the other half manages anxiety. Only half of the mind shows up to teach/learn as it were, and this makes a lot of sense to me now that I understand more about the neurobiology of trauma. When someone experiences a traumatic event or situations of extreme fear, one's brain chemistry changes and the brain begins to function differently. Usually this is described as a fight/flight response, but there is also a freeze response and experiences of dissociation. Dissociation is a survival reflex where a person relies on their socialization to habits (or "habitual modes of being"), and thus goes into autopilot as a way to avoid trauma (perceived or real). It is this safe space of the mind where when dissociating I see myself. I know what it means to freeze, not respond, and disappear within. Understanding this fear circuitry is important as it functions as a normal protective mechanism. Understanding the trauma brain and its effects are extremely important for creating and maintaining learning and teaching spaces that are ADA (Americans with Disabilities Act) compliant and provide for a diverse classroom experience associated with equity for both students and educators.

It wouldn't be until 1997 that I was diagnosed as having Complex Post-Traumatic Stress Disorder (C-PTSD), meaning there isn't one trigger that offsets my anxiety and that in fact it could be many, some even unknown. My personal regulation takes a lot of work because I have to think about how I can be *the least* triggered rather than *not triggered at all*. As it turns out, for me it is all about having a few seconds between the trigger and one's response to it. There will always be a trigger for someone with disordered anxiety like myself, and this likely won't change. The trigger will lead to a response—if given enough time (meaning a few seconds or a minute) it can be possible to calm and ground myself if I act with intention. The sooner I know to do this (regulate) the more likely my anxiety can be alleviated from the trigger, and I am able to be more in charge of my responses. This took me about five years of doing specific trauma-informed therapies called eye movement desensitization and reprocessing (EMDR) to fully realize in teaching practice, but I hope that my experiences can translate into trigger warning support for students and teachers in the classroom and associated pedagogy for learning and teaching.

VIGNETTE NUMBER THREE: THE TRIGGER OF PARTIAL FRAMES AND SYSTEMS IN JEDI TRAINING:THE REVERSE TRIGGER WARNINGS THAT SHOULD HAVE BEEN, OR ALTERNATIVELY, WE ARE MOST DEFINITELY NOT "BASIC QUEERS"

In response to a problematic healthcare journey spanning several countries and decades around gender for my spouse— and of course widely experienced by other queers and non-normative minority bodies, too—I was inclined to organize a series of Justice, Equity, Diversity, and Inequality (JEDI) trainings that would expand upon ways medical professionals "know" bodies. I sought to make interventions into the training medical students and healthcare practitioners receive so that future doctors, chiropractors, clinicians, nurses, and other medical professionals consider how their frames for knowing, learning, and engaging with patients are based on partial perspectives that should be expanded upon for holistic intersectional patient-centered care. Changing the approach could create trust, empathy, and more complete ways of knowing one's client-patient.

Ultimately, the triggers in this vignette are those of systems: racism, sexism, classism, ableism, heteronormativity, colonialism—**trigger system warnings**. In these systems, the trigger does not begin with individual anxieties but is reflexive to the ways that power systems themselves cause these individual anxieties. The result of such systems for medical knowledge and patient care are partial perspectives for knowledge claims. Within a justice-centered intersectional approach, the trigger of partial perspectives is elaborated upon as the consequence of the above systems, *where the "trigger warning" of incomplete ways of knowing affects healthcare outcomes as detriments to public health.* This conceptualization for trigger warnings made sense to me as it shows how power systems can harm the individual and I immediately recalled how "gender identity disorder" was reclassified to "gender dysphoria" in the DSM-5. Within this reclassification, the experience of gender dysphoria specifies that this diagnosis focuses on the gender identity-related distress that some transgender, non-binary, and gender non-conforming people experience, rather than on transgender individuals being transgender or transgender identities themselves as the essence of anxiety. Hence, the presence of gender variance is not the pathology; the "disorder" is from the distress caused by societal marginalization of gender variant individuals and is thus a reflexive understanding of normative power associated with cultural systems from top down.

It was exciting discussing covert forms of discrimination such as microaggressions, as these were the perfect examples of how bias and stigma are enacted in daily life, where when someone is stigmatized, they are labeled, stereotyped, devalued or othered.[1] These sorts of stigma frameworks have been used in public health when researching specific illnesses (e.g., HIV/AIDS, mental illness), whereas prejudice and discrimination are highlighted in studies of racism and health (Phelan et al. 358). "Within public health, researchers have tended to define and measure discrimination as the behavioral manifestations of prejudice, stigma, and bias, thus considering discrimination a real-world manifestation of oppression *with potential adverse health consequences*" (Paradies 559, my emphasis).[2] What is more, those with multiple intersectional identities likely experience similar oppression and in multiple complex ways (Link and Phalen).[3] The implicit biases of healthcare workers can unintentionally lead to providing lower quality care for patients, affecting providers' "quality of clinical encounters, diagnostic decision making, symptom management, treatment recommendations, referrals to specialty care, [and] interpersonal behaviors, such as communication, empathy and trust" (Rose and Flores).

Partial perspectives for "knowing" create impenetrable frames, which is one reason that disability, feminist, queer, indigenous, Black, and fat study scholars *argue for decentering the gaze to include cultural knowledge and lived experience.* We don't always recognize the gaps in our knowledge and we wanted the participants to be better equipped and prepared as practitioners, and to further create trust by valuing their patients *as people* and on their own terms connected to their personal histories.[4]

The second set of summer training took place the summer after the overturning of Roe vs. Wade, and so, using contextual legal frames, we argued that we become socialized to normative frames for making sense of the world regarding gender and sexuality. We asked participants to try and imagine how clinical education about reproductive healthcare might look different from when they were trained as providers. Additionally, we made the vital connection that transgender bodies were also vulnerable to the overturning of Roe vs. Wade, and to similar legal decisions that affect healthcare and its categorizing of appropriate medical responses vis-à-vis the legal system and specifically given current states that were banning or limiting both adult and youth transgender care. How might clinicians in these states, and their associated patients, all operating under current medical-legal structures, give meaning to bodies with or in opposition to new "allowable" frames? How are bodies shaped by their political context and location? A specific relevant example was teaching students about laws for consent within California around kink and BDSM, not to mention the vast state protections regarding gender they will encounter as providers, and suggesting they remain updated to such legal contextual protections and committed to updating themselves regarding changing state laws and contextual practices.

It was a joy to think we were challenging and hopefully thus changing how students made sense of bodies that would in turn benefit LGBTQIA2-S+ and queer bodies...well, *until it wasn't a joy anymore.*

During this second summer of training, our training group had just finished the section about socialization, and we were beginning to present information about the process of normalizing. We wanted students to understand that norms were themselves *culturally normalized*, and thus *they come to function* as the social set of standards, rules, or expectations that exist as forms of social control within modern societies.

Participants were asked to consider how sex as a category described bodies, and we pointed out that one's forcible assigned sex at birth is in terms of cognitive opposites used to delineate the sex binary (and that this binary functions as an implicit bias)—especially given intersex bodies which destabilize the myth of opposite sex categories. We discussed gender identity and gender expression and pointed out these were different from "sex," but that both concepts were associated with systems of opposites called the gender binary—the most common classification used to categorize both sex and gender. We encouraged participants to consider how heteronormativity constructs both sex and gender relationally, as the definition of cisgender stems from the culture of heteronormativity at its basis, a main and basic tenet of queer theory. At this point we further deconstructed limiting body myths for participants and pointed out that what these letters "LGBTQIA2-S+" have in common was their relationality to heteronormativity for conceptualization. In addition to our use of a kaleidoscope and the vast universe of stars as metaphors for gender itself (with all its constructions), we relied upon queer theory to show that assumptions of heteronormativity and gender binaries are reductive and are ultimately an example of colonial knowledge. *This was one of the main trigger system warnings of our trainings.*

However, during the training, we experienced pushback for describing such systems as based in racism, white supremacy, heteronormativity, and ultimately colonialism and empire. We heard students respond verbally with terms like "woke" and "this is soooo LA" in reference to our presentation materials.

To navigate this discussion, we decided to present additional global gender identities to engage the idea of cross-cultural gender differences and ways of knowing as globally contextual. With jest, we reminded students "We ALL have a little colonizer inside of us and we need to deal with these handed down ideas about bodies that come from how we have all been socialized by colonial systems. Ryan and I are also socialized to colonial ideas and while it's sometimes difficult, it's important to continually examine these ideas so that expanded ways of knowing exist for you and your patients—especially given you all have careers in healthcare. We do this together as colleagues all of the time!" This comment about cultural socialization and narrowed ways to "know bodies" was later deemed "aggressive" in feedback.

Within a day, we received an email from an interim Dean sharing some feedback from the class. It began by stating that the university itself is dedicated to creating a welcoming and all-inclusive environment for students, especially since they were going to be future healthcare providers. The university claimed a concern that students should develop a diverse and broad perspective with respect to their future patient populations. However, there were certain things that some students had deemed objectionable. These are but a few of those things:

1. Some students felt that while discussing the content last week it was implied or mentioned directly that all white people are either racist, bigots or white supremist.
2. Some felt that if they conformed to heteronormativity/ own personal beliefs they were being labeled as being white supremacist.
3. Some thought that the content should be presented in an unbiased manner with factual scientific studies to corroborate with the information being presented.
4. ...They thought it was not creating a safe space for discussion.

Our interim Dean liaison explained to students that being white is not equivalent to being racist, bigoted, white supremacists, and that we were not targeting anyone based upon their race, beliefs, and orientation. Additionally, they explained we were presenting about how these terms had originated and evolved and that we were not denigrating anyone's belief system. *However, they did not mention that the implicit bias to which we are socialized is in fact racist, bigoted, and white supremacist.*

As queer and gender variant academics we were disappointed at the student comments since we thought that these trainings presented a hopeful pedagogy and deconstructed the systems that had trapped us within our own lifetimes.[5] Some students seemed either unable (or simply refused) to receive our lessons, despite our extensive evidence and training. Even mentioning the shorthand account of colonialism and gender alongside partial perspectives seemed to unsettle students who have been for decades trained to a colonialized medical model of binaries, whiteness, and beyond—or the very trigger systems of partial cultural perspective and meaning that they were so used to relying upon for diagnostics, medicine, social reproduction, and for a sense of security (and community perhaps?) for doing medicine "correctly."

Despite handling the feedback professionally and with empathy for students, we were not asked back for the summer of 2023 (or beyond) to provide trainings, which was a misfortune as these events allowed us all to both educate and simultaneously heal ourselves. We felt transformative, honest, and vulnerable sharing our lived experience, but were not interested in providing a non-critical approach or easily digestible symbolic attempt at diversity (what I have seen called DEI-lite microbites and virtue signaling) in our education pedagogy. This was our educational teaching and learning autoethnographic method and praxis for the very real pedagogical application of materials associated with the intersections of queer theory, transformative justice, and intersectional interventions within collaborative social justice-informed community learning spaces.[6]

What I learned in these trainings is that trigger warnings at the systemic level are complex and that I will identify such trigger system warnings to students in the future regarding power, systems, and institutions and their culpable participation in white supremacist, capitalist hetero-patriarchy—where the trigger system warning is an alert and red flag regarding the well-documented history of the migration of colonial partial perspectives and assumptions to which many of us are socialized, and in favor of more complete ways of knowing (re-indigenized and cultural expansions of knowledge) that benefit how individuals make sense of their own bodies in relation to and apart from the medical gaze.

Ultimately our call was for students and medical practitioners to constantly seek, develop, and insert equity-based practices and frames for "knowing" within medicine in sustainable ways associated with decolonizing knowledge.[7] Additionally, we insisted on the continued use of educational resources that use an intersectional health equity lens for their healthcare practice, given "the potential and promise that intersectionality holds as a lens for studying the social determinants of health, reducing health disparities, and promoting health equity and social justice" (Lopez and Gadsen).[8]

MOVING FORWARD, ADVOCATING FOR MYSELF

> This presentation has themes and experiences which could trigger some of you. Please feel free to walk out of this presentation at any point if you need to take care of yourself. Maybe you need to chat with a friend? You don't have to come back either. What I am presenting here today is not as important as your mental health.
>
> (Trigger warning for Mauro Sifuentes and Sè Sullivan's film *We Just Want to Be*, March 2024)

I exist as an individual with multiple identities and lived experiences. I am a professor and someone who studies and serves communities they are part of. I am a queer activist and public sociologist. I exist as "trauma-survived for now," but still anxiously process trauma with an invisible disability over my entire lifetime.

I seek to make education spaces as accessible and equitable as possible and so considerations about trauma in conjunction with learning and teaching spaces is very important to me. Educational spaces become marked with experiences, memories, anxieties—in fact, they are not neutral unmarked spaces for many reasons. I can't always know someone else's trauma, but I must imagine its possibility there with mine, all of us together navigating this room and beyond. This is the primary reason I thus advocate for managing triggers within the classroom with trigger warnings, and view trigger warnings as part of an intersectional critical disability consciousness that allows me to situate teaching and learning materials. To be more effective and empathetic as an educator, have a deeper understanding of our students—their experiences and anxieties—and how their existing trauma shapes classrooms and learning experiences, it is necessary to engage both the micro-contextual goal of better supporting our students within classroom contexts, and to highlight trigger systems with the associated macro goal of decolonizing educational perspectives.

Imagine the effects and possibility of creating more trust in previously untrusting spaces.

NOTES

1 See Harvard Implicit Bias Test or the IAT (implicit association test): https://implicit.harvard.edu/implicit/takeatest.html.

2 See also Truong et al.; Shavers et al.; Van Ryn et al.

3 One of the studies we presented claimed, "Weight stigma is so prevalent and detrimental to a person's self-worth that people who internalized fat-shaming and weight stigma, or those who blamed themselves for their weight, were more likely to avoid healthcare altogether. ...Stigma is an enemy to health" (Puhl 6). Hoffman et al. highlight a continued "well documented problem of racial disparities within pain management," and provide evidence that "false beliefs about biological differences between blacks and whites continue to shape the way we perceive and treat black people—*they are associated with racial disparities in pain assessment and treatment recommendations*" (4296, my emphasis). Clinical assumptions in dermatology have also centered whiteness (Narla et al.), where a partial perspective uses white skin as normative within medical trainings (https://www.blackandbrownskin.co.uk/mindthegap).

4 See Gopal et al. Our training team made the case again and again that implicit bias is a contributing factor to health disparities and has deleterious effects on patient health. This difference in treatment and clinical decision-making could lead to failures in patient-centered care, resulting in impersonal treatment, poor communication, lack of trust, and lack of necessary contextual knowledge for best engaging patients' bodies, which include knowing how patients give meanings in a variety of cultural and sacred ways to their bodies. (See Commission on Justice and Equity Recommendations.)

5 It was validating to educate that beliefs and biases about sexual desire and gender relations assume heterosexuality as the primary model from which to understand individual experiences, practices, and identities. Moreover, given that our approach to education pedagogy was mostly normative for queer studies and intersectional issues associated with public health, I was puzzled how to respond. I personally had been seeking a space for open medical discussions in public health, as had all the consultants who were part of these presentations, and we were excited that this professional opportunity existed.

6 See Patricia Hill Collins Keynote at 2015 Social Theory Forum @ UMass Boston: https://www.youtube.com/watch?v=pqToqQCZtvg.

7 See Stanford Medicine 25: https://stanfordmedicine25.stanford.edu/blog/archive/2020/five-practices-to-strengthen.html.

8 We also suggested having continued conversations about social justice and public health with their peers and colleagues, being mindful about their care,

and working in groups to minimize bias. Importantly, we suggested all participants consider how modern medical knowledge currently emanates from larger trigger systems themselves and what this means for previous ways of knowing bodies (and more).

WORKS CITED

Commission on Justice and Equity Recommendations. 2021, https://med.stanford.edu/content/dam/sm/diversity/documents/Commission/Stanford_Medicine_Commission_Report_Final.pdf.

Gopal, Dipesh et al. "Implicit Bias in Healthcare: Clinical Practice, Research and Decision Making." *Future Healthcare Journal*, vol. 8, no. 1, 1 Mar. 2021, pp. 40–48.

Hoffman, Kelly M. et al. "Racial Bias in Pain Assessment and Treatment Recommendations, and False Beliefs about Biological Differences between Blacks and Whites." *PNAS*, vol. 113, no. 16, 4 Apr. 2016.

Link, Bruce G., and Jo Phelan. "Social Conditions As Fundamental Causes of Disease." *Journal of Health and Social Behavior*, 1995, pp. 80–94.

Lopez, Nancy, and Vivian L. Gadsden. "Health Inequities, Social Determinants, and Intersectionality." *NAM Perspectives*, vol. 6, no. 12, 5 Dec. 2016.

Narla, Shanthi et al. Racial Disparities in Dermatology. *PubMed Central*. 12 Dec. 2022.

Paradies, Yin et al. "Prejudice, Stigma, Bias, Discrimination, and Health." *The Cambridge Handbook of the Psychology of Prejudice*, edited by Chris G. Sibley and Fiona Kate Barlow, Cambridge University Press, 2016, pp. 559–81.

"Patricia Hill Collins Keynote at 2015 Social Theory Forum @ UMass Boston." *YouTube*, 18 June 2015.

Pearl Jam. "Jeremy." *YouTube*, 11 Aug. 2015.

Phelan, Jo C. et al. "Stigma and Prejudice: One Animal or Two?" *Social Science & Medicine*, vol. 67, no. 3, August 2008, pp. 358–67.

Puhl, Rebecca M. et al. "The Roles of Experienced and Internalized Weight Stigma in Healthcare Experiences: Perspectives of Adults Engaged in Weight Management across Six Countries." *PLOS One*, 1 June 2021.

Rose, Jillian A., and Melissa Flores. "Heightening Awareness of Implicit Bias and Its Impact on Patient Care During COVID-19." Hospital for Special Surgery, 8 May 2020.

Shavers, Vickie L. et al. "The State of Research on Racial/Ethnic Discrimination in the Receipt of Health Care." *American Journal of Public Health*, vol. 102, no. 5, May 2012, pp. 953–66.

Truong, Mandy et al. "Interventions to Improve Cultural Competency in Healthcare: A Systematic Review of Reviews." *BMC Health Services Research* vol. 14, article no. 99, 3 Mar. 2014.

van Ryn, Michelle et al. "The Impact of Racism on Clinician Cognition, Behavior, and Clinical Decision Making." *Du Bois Review: Social Science Research on Race* vol. 8, no. 1, Spring 2011, pp. 199–218.

We Just Want to Be. Directed by Mauro Sifuentes and Sé Sullivan. 2014, https://www.wejustwanttobe.org/about-our-film.

CHAPTER ELEVEN

HOW TO GIVE TRIGGER WARNINGS THAT DON'T SUSTAIN GLOBAL CAPITALIST WHITE SUPREMACIST HETERONORMATIVE PATRIARCHY AND ITS YEARNINGS?

Aneil Rallin

The story of how I came to embrace trigger warnings in the classroom may not be atypical for a queer educator of my generation. I was once very resistant to the idea of trigger warnings not only because I thought everything I teach is triggering (in more ways than one), but also because of the long enduring history of censorship around queer and/or sexual representations in the United States.

I lived through the 1980s and 1990s during what seemed then to be the heyday of queerphobic hysterias (reignited at this present moment, along with transphobic hysterias) that resulted famously in the cancellation of the Robert Mapplethorpe exhibition at the Cincinnati Contemporary Arts Center in 1989 as the American Family Association took offense at the show's photographs of naked gay men and the "NEA Four" fiasco in 1990 that saw funding from the National Endowment for the Arts for the four performance artists Karen Finley, Tim Miller, John Fleck, and Holly Hughes withdrawn on the grounds that the subject matter of their feminist and/or queer and/or sex-positive work contravened general standards of decency. In 1990, after publicly owned television stations in Los Angeles, San Francisco, and New York broadcast Marlon Riggs's documentary film *Tongues Untied*, an honest depiction of the lives, loves, and struggles of Black gay men in the US, PBS programmed the film to air nationally the following year as part of its *POV* series, showcase for independent nonfiction cinema. Opposition to the screening erupted even before the film was broadcast on PBS. It was denounced in powerful circles and by powerful brokers, such as US presidential candidate Pat Buchanan, as pornographic and offensive to (mainstream white straight) American moral sensibilities. A number of PBS stations, as a result, refused to broadcast the film or programmed it near midnight to minimize visibility. Infamously, the film was targeted by that most deadly US senator, Jesse Helms, single-mindedly going after queer work and queer creators and HIV/AIDS education efforts—work I was teaching and determined to teach—to make a case against government funding for the arts in the US. Jesse Helms's lethal proclivities spawned the Helms AIDS Amendments of 1987 that prohibited the use of US federal funding for any HIV/AIDS educational materials that would "promote or encourage, directly or indirectly, homosexual activities," passed overwhelmingly by a repugnant US House of Representatives and repulsive US Senate and signed into law by an admiring US president, the vile homophobe Ronald Reagan.

I was thus, hardly surprisingly and certainly not uniquely, concerned about how the use of trigger warnings may reinforce and sustain heteronormativity, and could lead to pathologizing and stigmatizing queer work and queer creators/teachers/students. But my students, mostly young, mostly self-identified BIPOC, many queer, increasingly wanted trigger warnings and my colleagues most hostile to trigger warnings were mostly older cishet men, mostly white, all full of themselves. This reality made it easy for me: I wanted to align myself with the students, not the portentous colleagues invested in and dedicated to upholding heteropatriarchy.

But giving trigger warnings has turned out to be challenging.

One challenge is logistic: I often assign work I haven't read or viewed myself, sometimes as I come across work that seems particularly pertinent and/or timely as a class is underway, frequently as a pedagogical practice. I find studying work for the first time along with students and making this clear to students disrupts the conventional student/teacher hierarchy and troubles fruitfully that tiresome notion of the expertise of the teacher. It can have the effect of making class discussions feel immediate, as well as underscoring knowledge production as joint and collaborative. But even when I assign work I have read/viewed before, I don't always remember the work well and I don't always have time to look at it again until the day before class.

The other challenge is more philosophical: how to give trigger warnings that don't reinforce/sustain global capitalist, white supremacist, heteronormative patriarchy and its yearnings?

I don't want to discount the PTSD and/or the traumas my students struggle with. I want to try to ensure I give trigger warnings for the content many students find triggering and would like trigger warnings for. These include but are not limited to racist, sexist, misogynist, heterosexist, queerphobic, transphobic discourses/depictions, and sexual/gender violence—especially sexual/gender violence, not surprisingly, given how endemic sexual/gender violence still is. At the same time, I also want to attempt to give trigger warnings for the horrors of colonialism, ongoing US imperialisms, the British monarchy, American exceptionalism, US-centrism, Christian fundamentalisms, Zionism, Hindu fanaticisms, capitalism, neoliberalism, and globalism that continue to cause so much misery, so much trauma in the world.

I've come to think of trigger warnings as inquiry, as learning, as teaching tool in service of creating inclusive classroom communities, but in the spirit of queer propensities for unsettling, for play/playfulness, without undermining the seriousness of the traumas trigger warnings aim to address and the care that students are rightly seeking and deserve.

For instance,

- TW: presents only white cishet middle-class perspectives
- TW: reinforces white language supremacy
- TW: standard white English

- TW: zero BIPOC
- TW: understands poverty as inevitable
- TW: gender constancy
- TW: assumes there are only two genders
- TW: celebrates the monarchy
- TW: Israel
- TW: Judeo-Christian-centric
- TW: Hindu-centric
- TW: Islamophobic
- TW: Orientalist
- TW: weaponizes women's rights to justify western imperialism
- TW: represents the US as free and just
- TW: assumes the US is a democracy
- TW: epitomizes the US as peace-loving
- TW: normalizes Israeli apartheid
- TW: Zionist
- TW: normalizes US/Israeli genocide of Palestinians
- TW: sexist double standards
- TW: shows only bodies considered "beautiful" by hegemonic standards
- TW: assumes women should be judged primarily by their looks
- TW: no sexual diversity represented
- TW: no gender diversity represented
- TW: glorifies white, middle-class, able-bodied, cis gay men
- TW: glorifies labor/productivity
- TW: derides laziness
- TW: exalts veterans
- TW: vilifies Asians
- TW: vilifies immigrants of color
- TW: reproduces colonialist ideologies
- TW: nationalistic
- TW: human-centric
- TW: assumes readers/viewers are from the US
- TW: doesn't consider non-US perspectives

- TW: demonizes polyamory
- TW: demonizes China
- TW: Russophobic
- TW: homogenizes all of Africa
- TW: US-centric

CHAPTER TWELVE

TRIGGERS IN TEACHING AFRICAN AMERICAN LITERATURE

Gregory Shafer

Perhaps the first lesson professors learn in teaching African American literature is the long and ignominious legacy of ensconced racism that exists in both our society and inside the minds of our African American students. It is an insidious seed that was planted with the first shipment of slaves in 1619 and is evinced repeatedly in the voices of African American writers as well as the comments of their students. In teaching this class at my community college in the winter 2023 semester, I was both happy and intrigued by the triggers that came to the fore during our reading of various short stories, poems, and novels—much of it written by and about women of color. As we read about Phillis Wheatley and the slave narrative of Harriet Jacobs—as we explored the "passing" that has existed since those first ships landed in Virginia—a bubbling anger came to the fore, one that reveals the legacy of structural racism in our culture and the many ways our pedagogy can be used to address and mollify the triggers that accompany discussions of intelligence, equality, and the ubiquitous issue of trauma and healing.

The first step, as I quickly found, was to create a safe place for students to both acknowledge and confront the words and people that trigger them and evoke specific responses. As many of us know who have taught for more than a few years, triggers are ubiquitous, incendiary, and must become part of every language arts instructor's playbook. A psychological trigger is any language or depiction that reminds students of trauma, forcing them to face the trauma again—often in a place of vulnerability. And while some research (Jones et al.) has questioned the use of trigger warnings as a way to mitigate the pain of traumatized students, I found that my literature class on African American literature and language actually empowered students to confront the abject racism in their lives while establishing themselves as active agents—as liberated readers and writers—in working to become part of the solution. The key is perhaps best articulated in the words of Toni Morrison at her Nobel Prize address: "Language alone protects us from the scariness of things with no names."

TRIGGERS AND AFRICAN AMERICAN LITERATURE/LANGUAGE

Let me begin by suggesting that African American students—at least in my classes—are triggered by the constant presence of linguistic racism that places them at a structural disadvantage on a daily basis. For those who think this is not an issue, I suggest a simple discussion of how African American English works as a systematic language and how often students of color are slighted and marked down—and even killed—because they fail to speak for their white audience. How many jobs are lost because one cannot speak "good English"? How many implicit decisions are made about the character of a person because they speak the language of their grandparents—a language that has clear rules of grammar and syntax and that has been appropriated constantly by American media while being maligned in the classroom? How many men and women of color have been killed because their language does not comport with the vision of a police officer? Early in my class, Eugene,[1] an African American student, commented that "language is the most modern way, most acceptable way to keep Black people down in 2025, because the oppressor can say that they are simply correcting 'incorrect' English. But what makes my language incorrect? Is it because white people say it is?"

When Andrew Hacker asked his students about being Black in America and posed the question of how much they would demand before assuming the life of an African American, the students asked for 32 million dollars. The assumption was calculated with an eye to the many ways Black people must confront racism on a daily basis. While many white students think that racism is waning and our society is becoming color blind, most implicitly acknowledge the daunting life of people of color. According to Hacker:

> And this calculation conveys, as well as anything, the value that white people place on their own skins. Indeed, to be white is to possess a gift whose value can be appreciated only after it has been taken away. And why ask so large a sum? ...The money would be used, as best it could, to buy protection from the discriminations and dangers white people know they would face once they were perceived to be black. (32)

Before I ever began our first book on Phillis Wheatley, I asked students to read an essay on African American English and the prejudice experienced by the author. The essay begins with a former student from my community college class proclaiming that he is an African American man, someone who speaks African American English and who has loved it since he first recognized its beauty and connection to his grandparents and nuclear family. For the author, speaking White Mainstream English is itself a trigger, since its presence reestablishes the implicit inferiority of his language and the people who use it and love it. Going to school removes him from a language that is exulted by cousins, singers, and provides linguistic passageways to humor and subtle sarcasm. Further, the author laments the legacy of being denied the right to learn in school or thrive economically in society without having to adopt the language of another group of people. According to Jamal, my student:

> The fact is, Standard English is not any better than African American English. What separates the two is not a gulf of quality or clarity but POWER. My language reflects my color, so it must be considered unacceptable. It's the only way I can be kept down. (Student essay)

Jamal's response is one of many examples of how language has become a special place for contesting linguistic racism, which invariably lead to triggers. In discussing the dilemma of confronting linguistic racism, Wiley reminds us that it often leads to "hegemony," a situation in which the African American victim comes to accept their language as inferior, and their inability to master the White English of the classroom and greater society is their fault—further evidence of their inferiority. According to Wiley:

> Linguistic hegemony is achieved when the dominant group creates a consensus by convincing others to accept their language norms and usage as standard or paradigmatic. Hegemony is ensured when they can convince those who fail to meet those standards to view their failure as being the result of the inadequacy of their own language. (11)

In introducing students to this essay, which goes on to discuss the rule-governed way African American English works, I am providing students with an opportunity to discuss triggers and to probe the many ways academic life is a constant, ongoing quagmire of micro-aggressions and subtle insults. Indeed, this is a real issue. John Baugh argues that "many students who lack fluency in dominant discourse norms may suffer alternative forms of linguistic stereotype threats, and this might easily compound their educational risk" (280). When students of color enter our community colleges, they are subject to a series of insults simply because of the way they speak. In fact, many in my class supported the idea that they are "profiled" as a result of their dialect or language. In essence, they were judged and later demeaned because they spoke African American English. This supports Nicholas Henriksen and Matthew Nuebacher who write, "In a period of widening social inequality, the existence of and potential increase in linguistic profiling can be especially harmful" (347).

At the same time, I am acknowledging that such triggers have the potential to be both constructive and transformative. By broaching these topics and feeling license in effecting change, students stop being victims and assume an active role in combating the racism that this involves. Indeed, in language in the context of how it can exclude—and how African American English is rule-governed and eloquent—my students transcend the role of victim and become practitioners in both healing and solving long-standing racist practices.

In her book *Linguistic Racism,* April Baker-Bell discusses her own class and the need to broach the subject of racial bigotry with her Black students, helping them to see that "their voices matter" (40). In doing this, Baker-Bell is able to see

> how their experiences with language counter the dominant story about Black Language and what Black students need in a language education. Their counter stories confirm that eradicationist and respectability approaches to Black Language education do not account for the emotional trauma, internalized Anti-Black Linguistic Racism, or consequences these approaches have on Black students' sense of self and identity. (39–40)

This, of course, is the best approach to what Freire would call "liberation" education, a pedagogy in which students are active creators of truth and refuse to accept what he called the "banking system"—one that is employed when teaching students of color about the need to fix their language (66). Freire long advocated for an approach to education that is predicated on "praxis" or the notion that students become empowered when they engage in "action and reflection" (66). For students in my class, trigger points came often and with a sense of torrential anger, but being able to confront these triggers and the racism that accompanied them, made them conscious players in a classroom that was dialogic—that listened to their perspective and that gave license to their positions.

bell hooks has addressed this often in her scholarship. Central to her argument is the idea that students of color must refuse to be "the other" (29), the entity that is defined by white people, and seen as an inferior outsider seeking to gain acceptance to their world. hooks talks about classrooms where white people are shocked that Black people "think critically about whiteness because racist thinking perpetuates the fantasy that the other who is subjugated, who is subhuman, lacks the ability to comprehend, to understand, to see the working of the powerful" (29). She argues that the key to transcendence and change is to recognize and contest the ubiquity of whiteness in our classrooms—to demand a voice, a place in the making of literacy and language that is diverse. This, of course, begins when students contest the language and literature that triggers whiteness.

RESPONSES TO AFRICAN AMERICAN ENGLISH

The student essay I read and discuss with students is ten pages and introduces participants to a perspective on the legitimacy of African American English they have never considered. In that way, the essay is a trigger for white students as well, as it forces them to confront the racism they have long considered solved or improved to the point where they see education as fair, equal, and beyond racial consideration. Many become animated when discussing the following lines from the essay:

> People don't realize the dilemma. They are white so they don't know that this double consciousness lurks around every corner, making life a constant decision—a dilemma of allegiance to America or to family. (Student essay)

Such arguments trigger responses from both white and Black students, leading to a dialogue on the injustices of elevating one language above another while questioning the superiority of White Mainstream English. "I never thought of Standard English as being part of the white world. I just always thought it was proper and correct," proclaimed Stanley, a white student. Added Latrice, a Black student, "This is the dilemma that people of color must face in America. We are always judged by white standards but if we question them, we are told the standards are equal for everyone—that it is simply the 'correct' way to speak and write."

Such animated discussions help my students of color—and many white students—to grapple with injustice in a way that is constructive, that provides self-actualization and growth. "This is the first time I have recognized why I resisted learning English or doing my best when writing papers," argued another Black student. "I was always a little resentful that I had to put on this mask when doing school English." Added a white woman, "I think it is time we become bilingual, since white people have been given a huge advantage for centuries. It's something that has made me feel ashamed and more aware of my own place in the world."

Another part of the student essay that evokes a lot of passion is the following quotation:

> If I want to be respected, I have to turn my back on who I am, and speak like people who often don't like me that much anyway. The same was told to Native Americans or indigenous people. They were indoctrinated with the idea that their language was inferior. And, you guessed it, if their language was dirty, so too were they. So they eviscerated their language. And when they did, they took away a part of what made them a culture. (Student Essay)

Much like the other parts of the paper, the above quotation yields a variety of comments. White students are initially defensive but must finally come to terms with the trauma that linguistic racism has created for the "others" they have seen as equal. "I knew that we took away the indigenous languages of the Native Americans," said Bill, but I never considered this racism to be so close to home—so close to my own experiences and privilege." All of this discussion reminds us that linguistic racism has always haunted students. To return to bell hooks, she writes that "many of us pretend to be comfortable in the face of whiteness only to turn our backs and give expression to intense levels of discomfort" (31). I would argue that facing these linguistic triggers and contesting them in a classroom is the first step in engendering solutions and places for equal empowerment.

LITERATURE IN THE CLASSROOM

And so, as we worked our way from language to literature, the triggers that Black students have faced throughout their lives became moments for legitimacy and empowerment. Instead of being compelled to write like someone else or read from a perspective that was decidedly not their own, they used the language that triggered them to educate the other students in class. Our first piece of literature was Henry Louis Gates' book *The Trials of Phillis Wheatley*. In this wonderful work of scholarship, Gates chronicles the life of Phillis Wheatley, an enslaved person who was brought to America, emancipated by her master Susanna Wheatley, and who then proceeded to write some of the most eloquent poetry of the eighteenth century. Central to her story is, of course, the journey of proving her legitimacy by showing her ability to write like the white men around her. Such circumstances, unfortunately, are not foreign to my African American students and quickly generate a series of comments.

"I'm not sure how many of you know this, but Black students have been performing for white teachers for centuries," declared Derek. "We need to write in White Standard English or it's wrong. This blows my mind that this happened back before we were even a country."

Added Clara, a diminutive African American student in the same class, "We can learn from Phillis. We can learn that language is power and we need to fight for some."

As we continued our reading and discussion of Wheatley, more triggers were exposed. And despite the obvious anger that these triggers caused, there was also a sense of empowerment and healing as well. Many students saw Wheatley's circumstances—which included a series of questions to prove her poetry as original—as ironic. "How can a Black woman, a slave, write white poetry to prove she is legitimate? She is writing like white men and asking others to accept her into this group of writers who never will accept her as one of them," said Jerome.

Throughout the many days of reading and discussions, students grappled with the contradictions that are implicit in the life and work of Wheatley. Here, a recently emancipated slave was proving her "whiteness" to white men, while also asking them to see her as an individual—as something more than an imitator.

Argued yet another African American student, "I think this is still relevant. We are like Wheatley in wearing a mask, in doing something that is basically a performance. It has to stop. We want to keep it real in class."

The phrase "keeping it real," is, of course, an expression that derives from African American culture. And yet, the entire class both understood and admired it. "See we appropriate African American language every day," added Tamika, "but we don't want it as part of a regular English class. How isn't that messed up?"

A second piece of literature that cultivates a positive approach to triggers is Nella Larsen's *Passing*. It is a classic twentieth century novel about two African American women who are navigating the racial politics of passing as white. While one dabbles in it, the other, Clare Kindry, lives her life as white—even marrying a white man who is openly racist. As students in my class read about the lives of Clare and her friend Irene Redfield, they again feel a sense of consonance in their daily conundrums. The Black students begin to openly respond to the many times in their lives that they feel obligated to be "white" at jobs and even while in academic settings. White students see the issue of race from a perspective that triggers their own sense of guilt as well as times where they chose to try to be someone they are not. While Clare lives wanting to be part of the Black community she has walked away from, many of the other characters wonder about their lives in a white world—in a world in which race is never an issue.

Again, as with the Wheatley work, *Passing* evokes a torrent of reactions. Students of color are triggered by the examples of Black people—especially women—confronting a white world that compels them to negate their culture, world, and heritage. "I think we all pass," argued Marcus, "but the reality of having to pass on a daily basis, to turn your back on who you are, is incredible." Interestingly, this triggers other students who are immediately galvanized by this piece of literature and Marcus's response. "This brings back memories for me, and I'm glad I am facing them," said DeAutra. "My mother married a white man and spent much of my childhood trying to please him—to be white and to immerse me in a world of white kids and influences." Central to what many of my students argued related back to the quandary all of the African American students face in terms of loyalty to who they are and what compromises they are forced to make to succeed in a racist society. At the same time, facing these triggers, confronting these series of racial aggressions makes the African American students empowered and conscious of their place in society and the need to create change. This, I would contend, is the essence of using triggers as catalysts for change and growth. Once they feel liberated to challenge entrenched racial issues, students begin to deconstruct the reasons for them and possible ways to contest them. According to April Baker-Bell:

> While developing linguistic consciousness is crucial to their sense of self and identity, awareness is not enough to bring about social change. An Antiracist Black Language Pedagogy is designed to provide Black students with critical literacies and competencies to name, investigate, and dismantle white linguistic hegemony and Anti-Black Linguistic Racism. (86)

CREATING SOLUTIONS FROM TRIGGERS

After completing our reading of *Passing*, I asked students to create an assignment that would reflect a more inclusive, more just assignment. Many wanted to write simple responses to racism in and out of the college but many others wanted to create a literature of their own—one that featured a world of languages that were often subordinated in academic contexts and that exulted the culture they lived on a daily basis. After more discussion, we settled on stories and reflections that were ethnographies, focusing on the language and cultures of the writer. If a student lived in the city of Flint, that writer would construct a story that featured the values, customs, and language that were part of that world. In the same way, if students were from one of the many suburban towns that surrounded the city of Flint, they would craft papers that revolved around their world. In short, students would challenge the triggers that too often undermined their performance and become writers "dismantling the hegemony" Baker-Bell discussed earlier. Of course, the key to such an assignment is to find agency in the many ways students are triggered. Instead of avoiding or tolerating, they create spheres of empowerment, ways to respond in their own way. So often, students are told what to do and what is right. In this paper, they would provide a portrait of what they live and treasure.

Not surprisingly, the papers were imbued with investment and voice. The papers emanated from a place of warmth, of family and heritage. Instead of being triggered by yet another caveat in what they must do to earn a passing grade, they told the academic world what their discourse looked like and why it is precious. Tania wrote a paper about her family of Central Americans and African Americans. At home, she explained, "our voices ring with words of humor and linguistic variation that is filled with family knowledge." Tania discussed the use of double negatives—something they would never use in an academic setting—and the ways it was used to emphatically expose the absurdity and humor of a family member's remark.

"If we are loca/loco, if you are crazy, you get more negatives. It's just a comical way of exposing the person to your feelings and doing it without hurting anyone," she explained. Added a second paper, "my family is divided between older and younger generations and we learn so much from the polite and solemn words of our grandparents. We respect their words because they come from wisdom and often pain." In writing about this, the author elaborated on the use of African American English, especially the use of words from the 1960s (Boy, you on thin ice) (Girl you fixin' to head off a cliff) as ways to warn them of terrible decisions they were contemplating. "There is something profound about hearing it in those words," said the author. "It's authentic and pulsating with passion."

TRIGGERS, RESPONSES, AND THE COMMUNITY COLLEGE

Those of us who teach at community colleges know that it is the chosen place for many African American students in our communities. Research shows that "over 50 percent of African Americans in postsecondary education are enrolled in community colleges, while only 40 percent of their white peers select this institutional type as their point of entry" (Morrice). With this in mind, our jobs as community college instructors become more aligned with the notion that racial triggers must be addressed. Especially in a class that features African American writing, the goal of addressing and responding to triggers—and the trauma that accompanies these experiences—must be something we see as integral to our classes. Because, in the end, every image of a slave, every racial term that might seem innocuous to a white teacher, might have a devastating effect on a student of color, even resulting in feelings of alienation. In this class, I worked with students to create a safe place for students to confront and challenge those common triggers and traumas that often are debilitating. In doing this, students found they could transcend the subjugation often felt and engage in discussion, turning trauma into transcendent learning. As we consider our role as community college teachers, and our growing responsibility to writers on the margins, such assignments become invaluable.

NOTE

1 All student names are pseudonyms.

WORKS CITED

Baker-Bell, April. *Linguistic Justice.* Routledge, 2020.

Baugh, John. "Linguistic Diversity, Access, and Risk." *Review of Research in Education*, vol. 33, no. 1, 2009, pp. 272–82.

Freire, Paulo. *Pedagogy of the Oppressed.* Continuum, 1988.

Gates, Henry Louis. *The Trials of Phillis Wheatley*. Basic Books, 2003.

Hacker, Andrew. *Two Nations: Black and White, Separate, Hostile, Unequal.* Scribner, 2003.

Henriksen, Nicholas and Matthew Nuebacher. "Unmuting Voices in a Pandemic: Linguistic Profiling in a Moment of Crisis." *Being Human during COVID*, edited by Kristin Ann Hass, U of Michigan P, 2021, pp. 344–56.

hooks, bell. "Representing Whiteness in the Black Imagination." *White Privilege*, edited by Paula Rothenberg, Worth, 2016, pp. 29–33.

Jones, Payton, B. W. Bellet, and R. J. McNally. "Helping or Harming? The Effect of Trigger Warnings on Individuals with Trauma Histories." *Clinical Psychological Science*, vol. 8, no. 5, 2020, pp. 905–17.

Larsen, Nella. *Quicksand and Passing*. Rutgers UP, 1988.

Morrice, Pelema Imhotep. *It's the Perfect Baby Step: African American Students' Community College Choice and Transfer to Four-Year Colleges and Universities*. Dissertation. University of Michigan, Ann Arbor, 2011.

Morrison, Toni. Nobel Prize Speech for Literature, 1993.

Wiley, Terrence G. "Language Planning and Policy." *Sociolinguistics and Language Teaching*, edited by S. L. McKay and N. H. Hornberger, Cambridge UP, 2000, pp. 103–47.

CHAPTER THIRTEEN

AT THE GATES

The Strange Career of the Trigger Warning

Walter Lucken IV

In February 2023, writing on the Heritage Foundation's official website, conservative education researcher Jonathan Butcher applauded recent efforts by state legislators to "combat racism the right way," noting that state lawmakers were increasingly considering "proposals that defend teachers and students from being forced to believe ideas that clash with their personal values and America's founding ideals, including ideas that violate the Civil Rights Act of 1964." Butcher was referring to a wide range of state laws across the United States which seek to limit the discussion of controversial political issues in high school and college classrooms, in addition to required training programs in state agencies. These laws often focus on concepts like white privilege, the role of slavery in the founding of the United States, and gender identity.

The "personal values" Butcher spoke of could be anything within the standard range of conservative positions, from the notion that gender is immutable to the view that same sex marriages are illegitimate. Butcher makes a point to note that Florida's HB (House Bill) 7 states that a public employee cannot force a teacher or student "to believe" that they should "feel discomfort, guilt, anguish" because of their race. In context, Butcher strongly implies that the primary victims of critical race theory (CRT) are white students and teachers, analogous to how heterosexual (and indeed anti-LGBT) students and teachers would be the primary victims of pro-LGBT content. Critics of laws like HB 7 argue in turn that the effect of this legislation is to shut down critical discussions of race in classrooms and other public contexts, for the simple fact that a white teacher or student who claimed that they had been forced to feel discomfort, guilt, or anguish because of their whiteness would as a result have a credible claim to have been discriminated against. Thus, in practice, any discussion or exercise which might cause any white person to feel shame would be de facto banned. In a way, laws banning "gender ideology" content in schools and state agencies go a step further by officially creating legal safeguards to defend opponents of LGBT rights from being forced to participate in lessons or programming which cause them to feel discomfort because of that opposition. Thus, the laws in question essentially codify a right to homophobia, transphobia, and so on.

Students of United States public discourse will observe that these laws, on their face, serve a similar purpose to trigger warnings, ironically so because conservatives claim that trigger warnings shield students unduly from material they might find upsetting or offensive. For many, the right wing has again demonstrated its hypocrisy and made another characteristically bad faith intervention, mocking liberal students as "triggered snowflakes" while authoring laws to protect conservative students from being made to feel anguish. This riposte is often accompanied by the observation that right-wing critics of "critical race theory" lack a basic understanding of the concept, which is primarily taught in law schools and not in kindergartens across the country, as right-wing activists have claimed. Thus, liberal critics of laws like Ron DeSantis's "Stop WOKE Act" and "Don't Say Gay" law critique these laws on two accounts: first, that the right are inconsistent and hypocritical, and second that they are uneducated and lack any understanding of the academic concepts they criticize.

In the public conversation about higher education in particular, battles over trigger warnings, critical race theory, academic freedom, and controversial campus speakers have been largely characterized as a two-sided culture war debate, with left-wing values of diversity and inclusion on one side and right-wing values of tradition and meritocracy on the other. Adding to this perception are the voices of a great many "centrist" moderate commentators who have in fact opposed these new state laws with the same vigor that they critiqued trigger warnings throughout the 2010s. A cursory glance beneath the surface, however, reveals that the various debates about trigger warnings and state regulation of course content are much more complex than the simple dichotomy that most commentators refer to. Indeed, an excavation of the rhetorics of trauma, harm, and repair demonstrates that these discourses can and have been applied in service of any ideological position, a hypothesis which I argue is self-evidently borne out by the choice of conservative activists to use the term "racialist abuse" in their critiques of "critical race theory," as part of a larger strategy of appropriating rights-based discourse, social justice terminology, and in some cases even charges of genocide and incitement to genocide. As Jack Halberstam and others have argued, the recent "re-emergence" in public discourse of a "rhetoric of harm and trauma" which had dominated earlier feminist movements serves to "cast all social difference in terms of hurt feelings," dividing up "politically allied subjects" into "hierarchies of woundedness." In what follows, I push this reading a step further, arguing that rhetorics of harmful and traumatic speech, in the absence of any discussion of material dimensions of political and social power, in fact serve to foreclose on and frustrate any counter-hegemonic or anti-systemic argument.

In the context of 2014, Halberstam was writing about the pernicious impacts of the rhetoric of harm and trauma both on social movements and the academic post-disciplines they inspired, naturally so given Halberstam's position at the intersection of the two. Almost a decade later we see the implications of their argument borne out in terms of how the rhetoric of harm and trauma simultaneously withstands any counterargument (other than a posture of open callousness or ironic detachment at the very least) and finds itself open to manipulation by powerful forces in contemporary United States politics, particularly in their efforts to influence higher education. Taking seriously Halberstam's suggestion that the rhetoric of harm and trauma can indeed be used to shut down important or challenging discussions by any speaker who claims to be harmed by another's speech or a piece of writing, we might observe varying cases or trends wherein individuals claim to have been harmed or traumatized by speech or writing to see which individuals, organizations, or groups have fared the best in their efforts to employ these rhetorics of harm and trauma. In what follows, I will examine a few cases which draw out the larger contours of how the rhetoric of harm and trauma take shape in contemporary public discourse, particularly in cases where speech itself is limited, prohibited, or even punished.

At first glance, it is self-evident that a flattening of all harms and traumas caused or reignited by speech is problematic in terms of how rhetors are real people situated within history and existing social and political conditions. For an easy example we can imagine a student who claims immense distress at finding anti-Black graffiti on campus counterposed with another student who claims the same distress seeing a "Pride" flag. The factor that makes one claim credible and the other specious, rather than some inherent characteristic of the speakers, in both cases is the social context in which clear power dynamics and disparities are visible in the present and generally understood to have occurred in the past. This raises the question of what would motivate groups and individuals to articulate claims about issues of sexual or racial politics in the register of harm and trauma, as opposed to arguing that a given speech was part and parcel of a larger social context of oppression. In response, I argue that students often make this choice not only because the use of that register is encouraged by their institutions, but also the fact that those institutions mark any discussion of social justice issues beyond the rhetoric of harm and repair as fundamentally illegitimate, and in some cases threatening. In my view, this strategy of flattening all student complaints about social justice issues on campus into the register of harm and trauma serves two purposes: First, it draws the attention of students and their audience away from the material conditions of oppression, which make claims of harm credible and thus normalizes those conditions. Second, it ultimately reinscribes the authority of university administrators to assess claims of harm and administer consequences, restorative processes and accountability, and so on. Thus, the larger impact of the shift to a rhetoric of harm and trauma is in fact the closure of social justice politics into strategies which ultimately reproduce the same conditions which make claims of harm and trauma credible to begin with.

Even more instructive, however, are instances in which speech is construed as harmful or traumatic by members of groups which historically and currently enjoy power, privilege, or other advantages over the speaker. A timely example is the controversy in summer 2023 over the singing of the song "Dubul' ibunhu" (translated literally as Shoot the Boer or Kill the Boer) by members of the South African political party Economic Freedom Fighters (EFF), especially its use by party leader Julius Malema. United States audiences were introduced to the controversy when Elon Musk, the owner of X (formerly Twitter) among other companies, posted that Malema was "openly pushing for the genocide of white people in South Africa" by singing it. Musk, who was himself born and raised in South Africa, tagged that nation's president in the post, demanding an explanation. Malema's post in reply read "O balela masepa," translated literally as "you are talking shit." Conservative commentator Benny Johnson added to the discussion by noting that "this is all downstream from the rotten secular religion of wokeness and CRT plaguing America today. You have been warned" (Nkanjeni). Thus, in the context of United States politics, conservatives claimed that "Kill the Boer" was a case of incitement to genocide against white South Africans, and a harbinger of what was to come in the future.

At first glance, the argument that the EFF's use of the song is downstream from contemporary United States politics is specious, but if we consider its rhetorical contours we can uncover an important truth in Johnson's equating the song with "wokeness." Earlier, we mused that United States conservatives had endeavored to protect children from being "abused" by critical race theory by using the power of the state. In this case, we can connect efforts to protect presumably white teachers and students from harmful or traumatic speech to Musk's horror at the use of "Kill the Boer" at EFF political rallies, an interesting turn of events given Musk's promises to protect "free speech" on his social media platform and allow a space for controversial positions and speech that others would label "hate speech," including but not limited to openly anti-Semitic arguments and insults to transgender persons. A further examination of recent controversies about the song reveals an even closer connection between the racial politics of the two nations, specifically how anxieties about "white genocide" and social collapse animate larger public discourses about harmful speech.

In response to Musk, EFF supporters noted that South Africa's Johannesburg High Court ruled that the song did not constitute hate speech and was most properly understood in the context of the struggle against apartheid. The word "Boer," which commonly refers to a subgroup of Afrikaner people in South Africa, literally translates to "farmer" and can be taken to refer to institutional forces like the National Party, members of the South African Police, and other armed forces who fought to preserve the apartheid system during Black Africans' struggles to overturn it. Thus, as Malema and his supporters maintain, the meaning of the song primarily hinges on the historical context of the struggle against apartheid and should not be understood literally as calling for indiscriminate violence against white South Africans. In effect, the EFF's riposte to Musk depends most strongly not on whether the song could be understood as harmful to white South Africans, but whether the larger political context of the struggle against apartheid and continuing racial inequality in post-apartheid South Africa should carry greater weight in the evaluation of speech than the feelings of individual white South Africans.

Musk's claim that the song incites genocide against whites in South Africa itself has a larger context of its own, namely the larger effort by activists in the Afrikaner advocacy group AfriForum to draw attention to their position that Afrikaners and other whites in South Africa are under an existential threat from groups like the EFF, farm attacks, and the policies of post-apartheid South Africa writ large. AfriForum campaign officer Ernst van Zyl, writing in Claremont Institute funded online magazine *IM-1776*, writes that "the time has come for Western communities to stop running and start digging trenches," arguing that "people of a Western heritage" like he and his fellow Afrikaners must defend "the ground of identity and the mountains of heritage." AfriForum as an organization has often been accused of fomenting the "white genocide conspiracy theory," the idea that various elites are conspiring to eradicate white people as a group, and has sued media outlets and other organizations which have made this accusation in its direction. Thus, the accusation that "Kill the Boer" calls for genocide is itself linked to a larger and more ambiguous rhetorical ecosystem in which various right-wing organizations and speakers either explicitly state or insinuate the existence of plots to exterminate whites. Leftists and antiracist commentators have also pointed out that more extreme manifestations of the "white genocide conspiracy theory" posit that the supposed ongoing genocide against whites is masterminded by Jews, and Musk himself has publicly agreed with posts on X alleging that Jews have intentionally fomented anti-white sentiment among racialized groups in the West. Thus, while Musk signals his agreement with the Nazi talking point that Jews manipulate the global majority to hate and attack whites, an accusation which, among others, incited a real genocide, he appropriates claims of incitement to genocide for his own purposes. If we flatten all claims of harmful or traumatic speech to an essentially liberal view in which all are entitled to equal claims of being harmed by another's speech, we find ourselves here: accepting that South African struggle songs are no better or worse than Nazi propaganda against Jews. This liberal impulse ultimately serves the right wing, not only by obscuring relations of power but also entitling them to protections against speech which would reveal or transform them.

Murkier, however, are the motivations for "centrist" or "moderate" commentators to oppose limitations on speech from both sides of the political spectrum. These perspectives generally hinge on the premise that the values of liberal democracy are best preserved by allowing a wide range of perspectives to be debated within the public sphere, because the strongest arguments will inevitably win in the end. From the perspective of writers like Andrew Sullivan (an outspoken critic of trigger warnings as well as state laws restricting critical race theory and LGBT topics), the public sphere must be preserved as an ideologically neutral space based on the values of free expression, tolerance, and reasoned debate. As an example of the potential consequences of failing to heed this warning, Sullivan has in recent years presented his own supposed persecution by his peers in the media, based most acutely on his choice to platform the view that intelligence is hereditable and that differences in average intelligence across racial groups can be empirically observed. Thus, Sullivan has found within his own experience a cautionary tale about what can happen when unpopular or out of vogue positions are policed or punished by academia and the mainstream media.

In one column from 2018 he claims that attacks on researchers who study the connection between race and intelligence in fact inflame and contribute to racism by polarizing a complex subject into two discrete sides. Sullivan summarizes the work of David Reich as exploring the notion that genetic differences between racial groups "will lead to subtle variations in human brains, and thereby intelligence tests, which will affect social and economic outcomes in the aggregate in a multiracial, capitalist, post-industrial city," which he takes to be a self-evident position. In the current context, we can assume that the social and economic outcomes he refers to would include the stark social inequalities between racial groups in the United States in every area of life from life expectancy itself to rates of incarceration and infant mortality. Sullivan performs here a similar move to Musk and AfriForum in that he flattens the social and historical context that might explain present inequality in twenty-first century Global North cities, reducing all speech to a fundamental ontological sameness regardless of its origins. Thus, attacks on David Reich and Sullivan's ostensibly harmful speech are definitionally illegitimate and actually cause greater harm than racist theories of intelligence because they seek to limit speech. In Sullivan's formulation, it is attempts to limit speech which somehow produces worse and more harmful speech, which run the risk of creating great social harm at some point in the future.

Thus, for Sullivan, a set of ideas about race, genetics, and intelligence which explain and naturalize racial inequality in multiracial societies comes in for attack by radical leftists and many liberals because it challenges the basis for their politics, which is the idea that inequality in human societies is in fact created by humans and thus can be unmade. Sullivan's logic is circular, but there is an important kernel of truth in his argument in the sense that it reveals to us the truth of his classical liberal worldview and that of his peers, which is that any utterance which defends and reifies the status quo of late capitalist modernity must not be censored or attacked, as to do so runs the risk of upsetting that same balance of power. He goes on to argue that while similar ideas to his views on genetics and intelligence have a "hideous history," this history should not foreclose on the important work of those "striving for truth." His reasoning here is striking as well, that liberalism must not base itself on something which can be empirically disproven (intellectual equality between racial groups, as he claims) because of an even worse right-wing backlash that would be sure to follow the continuously failing social reforms which would result from the assumption of intellectual equality between racial groups. That present inequalities will persist is not so much of concern for Sullivan as the idea that our society would be overturned by an even worse set of political conditions. Thus, any position which justifies the status quo can belong within "liberalism," and any position which questions the status quo is misguided at best or dangerous at worst.

Thus, for Sullivan, the correct position on race and intelligence is the one which most closely preserves current conditions, especially in the instance that those conditions are challenged by social movements and "wokeness." Right-wing positions follow a different logic, which is that present conditions are intolerable because they are unfair to whites and/or heterosexuals individually and as a group (either explicitly named as such or referred to in coded terms). Increased economic inequality and related social ills have indeed impacted whites across the United States, with most whites enjoying a declining quality of life relative to the small and increasingly diverse upper crust of United States society. The far right argues that "regular people" have been betrayed by "cosmopolitan elites," a category which generally either includes Ashkenazi Jews or casts them as the primary culprits of this situation, along with possible charges of their complicity in "white genocide." In their worldview, the present situation is intolerable not because of the existence of poverty, but because some whites are poor and white collectivity is internally divided and undermined by the persistence of economic and social inequality. Arguments which take this form can largely be grouped under the category of "white nationalism."

For an example of the kinds of slippage that can occur when different forms of argumentation are marshaled to question and transform current political conditions, we can in fact look to the same column in which Andrew Sullivan defended David Reich. After sharing his sentiments on Reich, Sullivan went on to comment on a recent controversy concerning an ostensibly anti-Semitic mural in East London, concluding that UK

Labor Party leader Jeremy Corbyn's response to the controversy about the mural was proof of Corbyn's latent anti-Semitism. The mural in question, before its removal, depicted six men seated around a table which represented the world and included a stylized rendering of the world's masses holding the table and men on their backs, symbolizing the mass of the global population being oppressed and controlled by a small ruling elite. Los Angeles street artist Mear One, who created the mural, stated that he intended to depict the small "banking cabal" which, in his view, controls the world and includes, in his words, both "Jews and Anglos" (Cohen). Thus, according to Mear One, his intention was to call attention to and critique the status quo wherein global financial institutions exert undue influence over global affairs and oppress the world's largely impoverished population. During Corbyn's 2018 campaign, his critics unearthed Facebook comments wherein he said that Mear One was "in good company" and compared the mural to one by Diego Rivera which had been removed elsewhere following the discovery that it included a portrait of Vladimir Lenin.

It would seem obvious that Sullivan is able to recognize anti-Semitism when it is packaged alongside an anti-systemic critique of inequality but the legacy of eugenics is excusable for him when it appears in a form which normalizes inequality and argues for its fundamental inevitability in human societies. Before we give ourselves too much credit for putting this together, however, we should note with interest that Sullivan makes this argument fairly explicitly. Observing that both reactionary and leftist lines of argumentation share a rejection of the status quo, he notes that "hostility to global capitalism is often imbued with conspiracy theories about the masters of capital," which can "veer into classic Jew hatred" (Sullivan). In this way, Sullivan argues that lines of reasoning which unduly critique the present political condition are fundamentally illegitimate, dangerous even because they run the risk of being operationalized and acted on if promoted or even allowed to persist in the public sphere.

Thus, for Sullivan, David Reich's theories of intelligence, which offer the promise of justifying and perhaps entrenching present inequalities, must be protected from censorship. Conversely, Sullivan holds that Mear One's mural was rightfully removed because of its anti-systemic content and critique of those same inequalities. Thus, Sullivan fully demonstrates an awareness that public speech can and does lead to changing political realities, implying that all counter-hegemonic political programs are equally destructive. He mirrors this argument in his thoughts on rhetorics of whiteness and white supremacy, noting that when whiteness is described as "an invisible force subjecting millions to profound oppression" it necessarily runs the risk of morphing into anti-Semitism. Building from this point, he states that Jews are (in Sullivan's words) among the most prosperous and successful whites, and thus white supremacy eventually can morph into "Jewish supremacy." This critique of anti-Semitism from Sullivan and his peers in the political center necessarily accepts as true the idea that Jews as a group are more prosperous and successful than their fellow whites (erroneously racializing all Jewish people worldwide as white and Western) and proceeds from this premise to the conclusion that this differential in success and prosperity is just and based on innate characteristics of Jewish culture or genetics ("Andrew Sullivan Hints").

I have spent time on Sullivan's thought in observation that he is a primary voice in the political center. On this basis, he has criticized both trigger warnings and the de-platforming of campus speakers by leftist activists on the one hand and right-wing laws banning restrictions on educational content on the other, on the grounds that both instances threaten civil society and the classical liberal order by placing undue limits on speech. Ostensibly, for Sullivan, threats to the public sphere from both the left and right are identical, especially so because they threaten what he imagines to be an existing natural hierarchy between different groups that manifests itself in contemporary political conditions. As I argued earlier, however, institutional efforts to control harmful speech place not only strict limitations on speech deemed to be harmful but also simultaneous limitations on how that speech can be interpreted and responded to, insisting on institutional mandates as the horizon of legitimacy or legibility of claims of harm. Indeed, social justice efforts within educational institutions are often predicated on the premise that social justice issues can be resolved within institutions and society writ large by adjusting institutional practices and not changing fundamental power relationships between groups.

Elon Musk, perhaps indirectly, makes a similar argument to Sullivan in identifying Julius Malema's recitation of "Kill the Boer" as a threat to the continued future of whites in South Africa. To reiterate an earlier point, both the Economic Freedom Fighters and academic commentators explain that the song is best understood as a rallying cry for Black South Africans to come together and transform the oppressive political conditions which "the Boer" is meant to stand in for. Malema's resurrection of a "struggle song" from the struggle against apartheid, then, serves a dual purpose insofar as it calls the audience's attention to the fact that the basic character of South African society has remained unchanged. Being unable to recognize a future for white South Africans outside of these political conditions, Musk concludes that "Kill the Boer" must be a call for genocide, imagining the continuance of racial inequality in South Africa as the condition of possibility for white existence. Sullivan's worldview is not so different, as he too imagines that any effort to transform present political conditions will not only fail but also be destructive in the end. This raises the question of whether, when debating institutional limits on speech, we truly explore which speech is harmful or rather whether we debate which speech is most conducive to fomenting the continuation of present social conditions. If the answer is yes, we must ask whether we find current conditions to be tolerable. If the answer there is no, then we must question which speech will best move others to transform intolerable conditions.

Ultimately, we can look back on Halberstam's warning of "hierarchies of woundedness" and how rhetorics of harmful and traumatic speech often foreclose upon or frustrate genuine counter-hegemonic or anti-systemic political speech by marking it as harmful to groups enjoying power or privileges over the speaker. In the case of post-apartheid South Africa, and the "post-racial" United States, empirical evidence and basic historical reasoning demonstrates that Black South Africans, Black and Indigenous Americans, and other oppressed groups need not resort to claims of being harmed by speech to justify continued counter-hegemonic politics. The persistence of inequality in itself is evidence for the necessity of continued action to transform material conditions. Similarly, an epidemic of violence and political warfare against queer and trans persons across the world, particularly those who are multiply marginalized, demonstrates the necessity for a radical LGBT political program without resort to claims of harmful speech. Indeed, the only parties which benefit from a flattening of all rhetors as equally vulnerable on the one hand or a hierarchy of woundedness on the other are, in both cases, those wielding the most power and the most leverage to socially operationalize their claims of being harmed by speech.

WORKS CITED

"Andrew Sullivan Hints he Thinks Jews are Genetically Smarter than Other Groups." *The Times of Israel*, 1 September 2020.

Butcher, Jonathan. "State Lawmakers are Combating Racism the Right Way: Here's What You Need to Know." *The Heritage Foundation*, 9 February 2022.

Cohen, Ben. "Freedom for Humanity: A Cautionary Tale of Antisemitism." *The Algemeiner*, 26 January 2021.

Halberstam, Jack. "You Are Triggering Me! The Neo-Liberal Rhetoric of Harm, Danger, and Trauma." *Beacon Broadside*, 4 July 2014.

Nkanjeni, Unathi. "Malema Slams Musk for Accusing EFF of Calling for Genocide of White People." *Sowetan Live*, 1 August 2023.

Sullivan, Andrew. "Denying Genetics Isn't Shutting Down Racism, It's Fueling It." *Intelligencer*, 30 March 2018.

Van Zyl, Ernst. "A Time to Dig Trenches." *IM-1776*, 2022.

PART FOUR

POLITICAL PREDICAMENTS

CHAPTER FOURTEEN

FROM SEA TO SHINING SEA

Trigger Warnings and Rhetorical Decay in California and South Carolina Classrooms

Paolena Comouche

INTRODUCTION

Discourse surrounding trigger warnings in academia has become increasingly political in the United States, following the same trend in public discourse. Things that have no business being considered "political" issues—take bodily autonomy and the rapid decline of the biosphere—have made their way into the two latest identifiers of the US political binary: "Woke" vs. "Anti-Woke." In "Defining Wokeness," J. Spencer Atkins shows how the term "woke"—stemming from African American Vernacular English—was initially defined by the Black community as being informed and conscious of social injustices pertaining to racial inequity, its use dating back "at least to William Melvin Kelley's *New York Times* article 'If You're Woke You Can Dig It' from 1962" (322). By 1963, the term was being used "to describe people who [were] socially conscious," particularly of institutional racism (Atkins 322). During this time, the Black community was being internally encouraged to "wake up"—or become aware of the institutional nature of the inequalities/oppression they faced as a method for inducing change. Wokeness has since evolved into a cultural slang term that has been adopted by leftist/liberal communities across the nation, expanded to include awareness of inequalities beyond just race. For instance, I've been called "woke" for supporting media representation of the LGBTQIA+ community and for using reusable bags at the grocery store. In these instances, my being called "mad woke" was intended as lighthearted praise.

But since being aware of social injustice is inevitably a politicized mindset, there must always be an opposition to said mindset: enter "anti-woke." On the opposite end of leftist/liberal communities are right-wing conservative communities, who have "taken *woke* as a derogatory term for progressive policy"—or for progressive people, or for anything that seems like it could be progressive in any way (Atkins 321). Take the clothing choices of fictional, animated chocolate candies, for example: conservative public figure and former *Fox News* host Tucker Carlson expressed outrage in a 2022 report when the M&Ms company changed the female green M&M's footwear from long-heeled boots to tennis shoes, subsequently becoming "woke" by apparently disrupting her previously established gender role in which she was the "sexy" M&M. Through instances such as this, right-wing media has declared itself "anti-woke," rallying conservative communities to contextualize wokeness as hyper-sensitivity, as the source of absurd, unnecessary changes in cultural norms, or, overall, as everything that's wrong with America. This anti-wokeness therefore stems from alt-right beliefs that "wokeness" perpetuates hyper-sensitivity that disallows people from reliving the good ol' days. You know, when female M&Ms were sexy. Or when hateful speech was normalized, when there were no gays in the movies, and when advertisements casually advocated for male superiority and white supremacy. Thus, depending on the context of the term's usage—as well as the user—wokeness can either reflect its original definition in support of progressive ideals, or it can reflect the criticism of these same ideals.

My latest action that resulted in being called woke—and *not* in the good way—was my delivery of a trigger warning in the Southern college classroom I teach in. The accusing student believed that the trigger warning was "woke" for being sensitive to the possibility that students may be triggered by the material. He also assumed that I would be perpetuating wokeness in this discussion—though it had not started yet—because the trigger warning indicated my "clear bias." This supposed "clear bias" clearly disgruntled him, as all of these assumptions had him immediately disinterested in being part of the discussion at all. This association between trigger warnings and wokeness thus sparked my consideration of the rhetorical relationship between trigger warnings and "wokeness" in a classroom setting.

After this experience, I began to think about anti-wokeness as rhetorical decay (RD). Holly Fulton-Babicke defines RD as "a state of discursive degeneracy that results from particular derailing and blocking rhetorical tactics...it impedes the production of new knowledge—consensus, well-defined dissensus, or simply new understandings of a problem" (278). In the context of anti-wokeness, RD takes place via the "generalization of [a] topic that creates an unactionable rhetorical situation," this "topic" being anything involving the oppression or maltreatment of marginalized groups (Fulton-Babicke 278). Put simply, anti-wokeness causes RD when one is unwilling to participate in the production of new knowledge, or to attempt developing new understandings of a concept, because they refuse to listen to—and instead immediately act against—ideas that may not align with their own.

I seek to understand how this all comes together in classrooms with different student demographics. I've taught college composition in my home state of California during my master's program at Chapman University, and now, during my PhD program, I'm teaching college composition in South Carolina at the University of South Carolina (UofSC). These experiences have been similar in some ways, but *very* different in others—some of this, I assume, due to the differing regions and student demographics. In both classrooms, I've delivered trigger warnings prior to any display or discussion of content involving racial injustice, gun violence, sexual violence, homophobia, slurs of any kind, etc. In this chapter, I will reflect on and analyze how students in each state responded to trigger warnings—specifically those about race—in an effort to better understand the relationship between trigger warnings, anti-wokeness, and RD.

BACKGROUND

Methods and Methodologies

It's relatively common knowledge that California is a politically liberal state, while South Carolina is most certainly conservative. However, while the voting demographics of each state are relevant to the scope of my reflective analysis, I'd like to specifically focus on race and gender, as my methods for this study are purely observational, and these particular demographics are what I was best able to observe without asking students about their political affiliations. While observational methods can be problematic in some ways, I do take precautions to avoid assumptions about racial and gender identities to the best of my ability. For instance, my observations regarding gender are not mere assumptions of students' gender identities but are instead based on self-declaration by students, as I have all of them share their preferred pronouns on the first day of classes. In terms of my observations regarding racial identities, many of my students also disclose this in assignments and discussions prompting them to think critically about race, although not all of them do. I realize that those who don't disclose their racial background may be white passing, though I make my assumptions based on what I know of the students and the institutional demographics. This is not a foolproof method, of course, but I can say with confidence that the few students mentioned in these analyses were among those who had—at some point or another during their time in my class—disclosed their racial identities. I'm sure factors like sexuality and socioeconomic background may also play a role in their responses to trigger warnings, but again, these sorts of demographics are more difficult to observe without explicitly asking students about their personal backgrounds.

Drawing upon the racial methodologies presented in Asao B. Inoue's "Racial Methodologies for Composition Studies: Reflecting on Theories of Race in Writing Assessment Research," my observational methods for this study specifically attend to race by "[accounting] for racial formations in collecting data, forming hypotheses, making observations, and drawing conclusions" (128). In his critique of "raceless" methodologies that do not acknowledge whiteness as a racial category, Inoue demonstrates how data pertaining to student research is only "racialized" when students of color are involved, leaving race among white students otherwise unimportant (131). These methodologies thus "do not assume a need to investigate whiteness," consequently failing to consider racial formations related to whiteness and how it functions in classroom spaces (Inoue 131). In response to this lack of attention to whiteness as a racial category, my observational methods are focused on analyzing responses to trigger warnings in relation to both race and gender—even among predominantly white students—specifically "[calling these samples] white and [drawing] conclusions that explicitly mark these student reactions as white student reactions" (Inoue 131). By racializing and gendering my data, hypotheses, and conclusions, it is my goal to contribute to scholarship that investigates whiteness, racism, and racial formations within and outside the composition classroom.

Student Demographics: California vs. South Carolina

In terms of race/ethnicity, Chapman University and the University of South Carolina differ considerably. According to each university's website, in 2022, Chapman's undergraduate student population was 48.1% white and 4.7% unknown, leaving the remaining 47.3% as students of color. While white students still make up the majority of the population, the rate of student diversity is significantly higher than that of the University of South Carolina, which reported in 2022 to have an undergraduate student population of 73.6% white students, 1% unknown, and 25.2% students of color. My classes certainly reflected these demographics, as those I taught in California were noticeably more racially/ethnically diverse than those I teach in South Carolina. And this difference in diversity seemed to—at least somewhat—contribute to how students responded to trigger warnings involving race in the classroom. Additionally, with Inoue's racial methodologies in mind, the limited diversity among students in South Carolina does not make the data collected in this region any less informative, as it provides insight into how whiteness functions in relation to trigger warnings, anti-wokeness, and RD, because "even when our universities serve mostly white, middle-class students, we have an obligation to understand these racial formations as such" (Inoue 135).

In terms of gender, Chapman and UofSC are a bit more similar. In 2022, Chapman reported its undergraduates to be 59.9% female, 40% male, and 0.1% nonbinary/unknown. In comparison, UofSC reported its undergraduates to be 56.1% female and 43.9% male—with, unsurprisingly, no category for nonbinary/unknown (but that, along with UofSC's current labeling of non-US students as "Non-Resident *Alien* students," are conversations for another time). Ultimately, both institutions have an undergraduate student body predominately made up of women. This was also reflected in both of my classrooms, as my female students most often outnumbered my male students while teaching in both states.

Course + Activity Overview

During each of my graduate programs, I've had the privilege of building my own themed syllabus to teach first-year composition as a graduate teaching associate. My chosen course theme was/is film, as I want to give students the opportunity to think critically about—and write about—their favorite films, as well as popular films that act as a segue to understanding the world around them. I also use this theme as an opportunity to integrate discussions about important social issues, as films are representative of culture and the issues that exist within any given culture at any given time.

The trigger warnings I delivered in each of these courses typically occurred before an activity I call "Scenes from a Hat" (a play on the segment from the popular TV show *Whose Line is it Anyway*). During this activity, I would prepare a collection of movie scenes relevant to each unit and write these scenes down on small pieces of paper to draw from a hat. We would then watch whichever scene I drew together, and students were instructed to write a response rhetorically analyzing the scene. Afterward, we would discuss their responses and the scene as a class.

I give trigger warnings before I play scenes from films like *Straight Outta Compton,* which showcases police violence against the Black community in 1990s Los Angeles. Of course, I select scenes that are appropriate for a university setting, but still ensure these scenes have some sort of weight to them, hence the need for trigger warnings. For instance, in the case of this specific film, I warn students of police violence and racial slurs that take place in the scene. My experiences with delivering such trigger warnings in California vs. South Carolina were distinct enough to notice a difference, though I do acknowledge that the amount of time I've had teaching in each state is not enough to collect sufficient comparative data. I also acknowledge that I cannot say with absolute certainty that it was only the race/ethnicity and gender of students that influenced their responses, as I am fully aware that there are multiple other factors that could contribute to these responses. Yet, my observations still broadened my understanding of the role student demographics can play in defining the relationships between trigger warnings, anti-wokeness, and RD.

SOUTH CAROLINA: ANTI-WOKENESS AND RHETORICAL DECAY

According to Holly Fulton-Babicke in "Impediments to Productive Argument: Rhetorical Decay," RD is particularly useful for disrupting or combating arguments for social change (cue angry rant about the green M&M's unfeminine, unsexy boots) (279). In order to be considered RD, two essential qualities must be present: a derailing affordance and a suppressive act. The prior "alters the 'trajectory' of a conversation" to derail said conversation, and—as a result— "the rhetorical outcomes striven for (establishment of understandings, solutions, altered social practices, etc.) become extremely difficult to achieve" (Fulton-Babicke 279). The latter quality—a suppressive act—is the deliberate action of silencing or suppressing dialog to "impede or even entirely dissolve discourse, undermining the construction of new conceptual scaffolds and/or action," most commonly in an effort to "block rhetorical interventions that disrupt existing social hierarchies and cultural norms (including norms of gender, race, etc.)" (Fulton-Babicke 280). Think the banning of books, the censorship of American history, and the deliberate fear mongering that takes place at the mere mention of critical race theory.

To best understand the connections between trigger warnings, anti-wokeness, and RD in relation to the student demographics in these opposing states, I am using a singular point of reference: how students reacted to racially based trigger warnings delivered during my "Scenes from a Hat" activity. While teaching these lessons at UofSC, anti-woke responses to trigger warnings usually consisted of both derailing affordances and suppressive acts. I'll start with the derailing affordances, which occurred via critical comments and questions from students upon hearing that the movie scene we were about to watch consisted of police violence against the Black community and/or racial slurs.

I've noticed a sort of defensiveness among the students who responded in this way. For instance, one question I received when giving a trigger warning before showing a scene from *Straight Outta Compton* was, "Why are we talking about this? Obviously not all cops are like that. Woke media just makes it seem like more of an issue than it really is." Whew, lots to unpack here. These comments are a direct implication of two things: the first being the student's reluctance to converse about this topic, and the second being that there is no need to discuss said topic because "not all cops are like that," and it's really not as big of an issue as the "woke media" makes it seem. This effectively derailed the conversation from the original topic, as it forced me—the rhetor in this situation—to first defend the need to have the discussion at all, putting me "at a discursive impasse (off the tracks, so to speak)" (Fulton-Babicke 279). More specifically, I had to explain that although "not all cops are like that," this doesn't dissolve systemic racism from being an issue, nor does it dissolve the need to talk about it. I also explained how the "not all cops," "not all white people," "not all men" types of argument are tactics of denial designed to ignore the issues at hand. Looking back, I now understand that those who make "not all" arguments are enacting derailing affordances in an effort to avoid or impede the development of new knowledge regarding these issues.

I also had to address the student's comment about "woke media," as I felt it would be irresponsible not to use this as a learning opportunity. The mentioning of "woke media" in and of itself suggests that the student assumed the film fell within the category of wokeness simply because my trigger warning involved police violence against the Black community. And it was this association and generalization that seemed to lead the student to react by blocking my rhetorical tactics with critical questions and comments on account of his disdain—and distrust—toward anything "woke." In the end, addressing all of this ultimately shifted the point of the conversation from discussing the issue with an open mind, to defending the fact that it's a real issue at all—and one that is important to talk about, nonetheless.

Other similar comments/questions that acted as derailing affordances were things like: "Why are we always so focused on the bad things that cops do? They do so much good and nobody ever talks about that in these woke movies. If we only focused on the bad things people do then we would always just be talking about bad things." Again, there was an immediate show of disdain toward "wokeness" in the mentioning of "these woke movies," indicating a connection between the student's perception of my trigger warning as being woke, and his objection to the discussion. In response, I had to once again defend the need for this sort of discourse, and even provide examples of the overwhelming number of movies and other pieces of media dedicated to celebrating all the good that police officers do. However, this did not satisfy the few bothered students in this class enough to finally allow the real discussion to begin, as I then received another condescendingly delivered question: "Doesn't this scene have a Black police officer in it? Doesn't seem like it's a racial issue to me then." As mentioned by Fulton-Babicke, this sort of response is a particularly common instance of RD:

> One recurring example in the current conversation of violence, race, and policing is a respondent redirecting the line of conversation to instead emphasize "black-on-black crime"—a troubling trope much discussed by cultural critics, activists, and scholars. Such blockages redistribute energy and focus (drawing attention and effort away from policing practices and racism) and impede efforts to solve the original issue (by insisting that the conversation instead discuss intra-racial violence, a fraught and often-weaponized idea). (281)

And around and around we go.

Even the first instance I mentioned in the introduction to this chapter acted as a derailing affordance. The student who commented that trigger warnings were "woke" derailed the discussion by prompting me to ask why he thought this, altering the trajectory of the conversation from one thing to something entirely different. Despite my many attempts to explain in these situations, I was at times met with resistance and more blocking of rhetorical tactics. This demonstrates the unwillingness of the few students making these derailing comments to actually listen and learn in the face of what they deemed "woke," this "woke" thing being my trigger warning. And so commences rhetorical decay.

This brings me to the second quality of RD: a suppressive act. In the contextual circumstances of my UofSC classroom(s), this quality was present twofold: first within the above derailing affordances. The critical comments and questions referred to above were not only intended to derail, but also to suppress dialog pertaining to the bigger picture issues I was attempting to focus on. The students posing these questions/comments were directly "undermining the construction of new conceptual scaffolds" by deciding the issues at hand were not real issues and therefore did not require contemplation (Fulton-Babicke 280). Through such assertions, these students were suppressing and impeding any dialog that suggested otherwise. And by suppressing such dialog, they were blocking rhetorical tactics intended to create space for the production of new knowledge. Thus "in short: such responses suppress the larger argument by derailing it" (Fulton-Babicke 281).

Second, suppressive acts almost always took place in the form of refusal to participate in or listen to discussions about race following my trigger warnings. As previously mentioned, students who associated these trigger warnings with wokeness typically responded with annoyance, often expressed via the above noted comments or implicative body language. This made the discussions that followed more difficult to have, as those students who were annoyed by what they considered "woke" topics would often scowl for the remainder of the class, quietly protesting by using their silence to disallow discussions from progressing or extending beyond those who were willing to participate. More specifically, their refusal to engage acted as a "silencing maneuver—efforts to suppress interventions against dominant social norms" (Fulton-Babicke 280). Overall, encouraging the anti-woke students to establish understanding and open their minds to the development of new knowledge regarding the racial issues that plague the United States was—at least at times—like pulling teeth. Through these experiences, I've learned that anti-woke perceptions of racially based trigger warnings have the potential to produce RD in college classrooms.

Yet, I only received these types of anti-woke responses to racially based trigger warnings while teaching in South Carolina. These reactions were by no means applicable to all my students in the South, but enough of them to notice at least a handful belonging to a specific demographic in each class I taught. Though my classes most often consisted of more female students than male, those who responded negatively to trigger warnings about race were almost always male, with the exception of only a single instance. This is not an attack on male students, but potentially reveals a pattern that may—upon further analysis—be related to gendered social conditioning. And in terms of the racial/ethnic demographics of the students who reacted in this way—yes, they were always white. My students of color—though they were few and far between, never more than three in a twenty-four-student class—were generally eager to discuss these topics, often demonstrating their passion and engagement through frequent participation and excited comments about how they had never been allowed to discuss such topics in an academic setting before.

However, I'd again like to clarify that this reflective analysis is by no means an attack on white students (as I am white myself), or an attack on South Carolina, as one or a small handful of students "representing the sentiments of a particular group is never adequate" (Inoue 131). This is merely an observation that reveals the tendencies of some white students in the Deep South—specifically *those who openly subscribe to anti-woke ideals*—to cause RD when discussing the topic of race. It is also important to note that the lack of representation of students of color within these classrooms makes it difficult to draw conclusions about any students who are *not* white. But this lack of data pertaining to students of color does not negate what these observations can tell us about how anti-woke whiteness functions in relation to trigger warnings and RD.

A Question of Performance

This experience is also not an indication that anti-wokeness and racism only exist in the South, as these issues are prevalent not only across the nation, but around the world. Claiming something as simple as South Carolina = racist and California = not, is of course, far too essentialist and reductive. However, it would be irresponsible not to recognize that regional differences—specifically when speaking of California versus the South—as well as differences in diversity rates may play at least *some* role in the willingness of students to vocalize their disagreement with certain issues, particularly within the context of this small classroom space. It is entirely possible that these students' willingness to respond to trigger warnings in this way could simply be an example of performances intended to reflect the commonly known ideals of the region. More specifically, perhaps the regional expectation for white men to be anti-woke in the South leads white male students to put on a performance that fulfills this expectation. And this might look differently in California, where it's more common for self-righteous, self-proclaimed liberals to engage in performative "activism" while denying their inherently racist behaviors and casually spewing microaggressions.

Another possibility is that these responses could represent a level of comfort with expressing these opinions when whiteness is the dominant race inhabiting the space. If all the other students in the room are seemingly white save for 1–3 students of color, white students may be less inclined to keep their anti-woke ideals to themselves. This possibility is supported by the difference between white male student responses to racially based trigger warnings versus gender-based trigger warnings, as again, female students almost always outnumbered the male students in these classrooms. Specifically, the same white male students who were turned off by trigger warnings about racial inequities/injustices, were always respectful and accepting of trigger warnings about gender inequities/injustices. This makes me consider whether the equal—if not majority—presence of female students in the room could inspire performances in support of women, or potentially incline male students to keep misogynistic opinions to themselves. And while I cannot jump to conclusions without further study and observation, this could also suggest that these self-identified anti-woke students have sensitivities of their own, as—based on my experiences alone—they seemed more open to "woke" trigger warnings when they pertained to gender yet were prone to causing RD when they pertained to race. Though student response to racial vs. gendered trigger warnings is not necessarily within the scope of this reflective analysis, it's definitely worth mentioning because it either demonstrates a prioritization of some social hierarchies over others, or supports the above considerations of performance in relation to regional expectations or the demographics of persons inhabiting the space (or maybe all of the above). Curious, is it not?

CALIFORNIA, ON THE OTHER HAND

While there is not currently a term that works as an antonym for rhetorical decay, I am going to make one up. I assume this is fine considering all terms are made up, and because the notable Stacey Waite once told me, "If there is not a word for what/who you are/mean/do, make one up. Words become words when we say, write, and circulate them. Invent more words; we need them" (37). This advice in mind, I'm inventing an antonym for rhetorical decay, and I'm calling it **rhetorical flourishment** (**RF**). Rhetorical flourishment can be defined as a state of openness and growth that results from thoughtful engagement and contemplation of rhetorical tactics; it creates space for the production of new knowledge and new understandings of a problem. RF can only be achieved through rhetorical listening, which is practiced through interventions such as good faith questioning, genuine consideration, and open receptivity. And this sort of engagement is mostly what I witnessed when delivering racially based trigger warnings at Chapman University in California. Whether or not this experience was a result of inauthentic performances remains to be seen, but my trigger warnings in this region at the very least *seemed* to prompt students to rhetorically listen, which in turn fostered an environment of rhetorical flourishment.

Contrary to my experiences at UofSC, I was always met with eagerness to discuss topics of race after giving trigger warnings at Chapman. Again, while this is not a declaration of California's superiority over South Carolina, it does bear implications for how regional norms and student demographics may influence displays of open-mindedness toward certain topics in academic spaces. It also provides further insight to how whiteness functions regionally in these spaces as well. While teaching in California, my racially based trigger warnings (and all trigger warnings, for that matter) were consistently accepted with respect and an absence of annoyance or irritation. I did not notice negative body language that was implicative of disdain, and I never received any objections to the pre-supposed presence of "wokeness." In place of derailing affordances and suppressive acts, I was often met with "legitimate (or 'on-task') topic clarification efforts," or what I understand to be good faith questioning that acted as a form of rhetorical listening and therefore allowed for rhetorical flourishment rather than decay (Fulton-Babicke 281).

These sorts of good faith questions are demonstrative of how trigger warnings open up space for rhetorical listening, which again, is essential to rhetorical flourishment. As defined by Krista Ratcliffe, rhetorical listening is "a stance of openness that a person may choose to assume in relation to any person, text, or culture" (xiii). More specifically, as an "active communicative act that highly emphasizes understanding others" (Zhu 3) while encouraging those involved to "develop a more nuanced understanding of the self" (Zhu 5), rhetorical listening promotes careful consideration of others in addition to self-reflection that can aid in pinpointing personal bias and encourage openness (Zhu). This sort of openness is foundational to rhetorical flourishment, as it creates space for the development of collective knowledge and understanding among humans. The clarifying questions described below are examples of students actively engaging in rhetorical listening, as their inquiries are reflective of seemingly open-minded approaches to the discussions, and careful consideration of the issues at hand. More specifically, rather than questioning the validity of the issues in response to my trigger warnings, the students took them as an opportunity to better understand said issues by rhetorically listening, or asking clarifying questions that gave root to productive discussion.

For example, upon giving trigger warnings prior to the same *Straight Outta Compton* scene I showed at UofSC, a student in my Chapman class said/asked the following: "I've seen this movie before, and I remember that the African American cop was the most antagonizing. Can you explain what that means? I never really understood it, but I know it was done on purpose." The student's non-aggressive, curious tone when asking this question was the first indicator of intentions to better understand the issue, therefore creating space for the development of new knowledge/understanding instead of stifling it with condescension and denial. Furthermore, his claim that he knew there was important meaning behind this specific detail and his admission that he could not understand this meaning, followed by his action of asking for help in doing so, shows that this question was not intended to invalidate the issue, but was "foundational, [helping to establish] better understandings of the argument's 'building blocks' (assumptions, intended outcomes, etc.)" (Fulton-Babicke 281). Because he asked the question in this specific way, I was not forced to defend the validity of the issue, but was instead given the opportunity to explain its depth and gravity—thus laying the foundation for more complex understanding. (Also, this student was white. But more to come on that later.)

Rhetorical listening in the form of good faith questioning was also present in responses like, "What year was this movie based in? This is clearly still happening all the time so I'm wondering how long it's been allowed to go on." Similar to the previous question, this sort of inquiry does not invalidate the issue of police violence against the Black community, but instead creates space to provide more foundational information regarding the issue. It also showcases a level of understanding of—and openness to—the issue's legitimacy, and even a sort of anger toward the fact that it has been "allowed" to prevail. Rather than attempting to defend social hierarchies of race, the student's irritation that this issue has been "allowed to go on" suggests a desire for social change, working directly in opposition to RD, which is a "useful tool for disrupting arguments for social change" (Fulton-Babicke 279). Therefore, contrary to the questions/comments I got at UofSC—which masqueraded as clarification questions while "moving progressively further away from the initial problem space…so far from the original issue that the issue is entirely neglected"—my students at Chapman responded to my trigger warnings by asking questions that helped them better understand the issue overall (Fulton-Babicke 281). And so commences rhetorical flourishment.

Additionally, in contrast to the silencing maneuvers/suppressive acts that some students enacted at UofSC, my students at Chapman were frequently outspoken about these issues and would engage in conversation each time they came up. Following my trigger warnings and the "Scenes from a Hat" activity, I was usually met with multiple hands in the air. Students asked questions, shared thoughts and experiences, provoked new questions, and willingly continued to do so even past the official end time of class. They also often expressed noticeable anger toward the racial injustices we spoke about, commenting about how these things would "make [them] so mad," and how they "don't understand how people can be like this," among other things. These interactions, as well as the number of willing discussion participants, imply a certain level of openness and thoughtful engagement with racial topics in my California classrooms. Not only were the students intellectually invested in these topics, but they consistently demonstrated their capacity to rhetorically listen when faced with such discussion: they actively tried to understand these topics—and to understand each other—more deeply. These more positive responses to trigger warnings occurred numerous times during my time at Chapman, while infrequently at UofSC, where I have now taught for much longer. In the few instances they have occurred at UofSC, it was students of color that enacted such positive responses, with the exception of one white female student.

It was a lot more difficult to discern patterns in the racial/ethnic demographics of the Chapman students who reacted in this way, however. I usually had a pretty good number of both students of color and white students in these classrooms. But my white students were equally as outspoken, engaged, and open to racial topics/trigger warnings as my students of color were, which was not the case in South Carolina. This leads me to again consider questions of performativity. As previously mentioned, the regional expectation for California is woke liberalism (this isn't to say there are not right-wing extremists in California, only that the common stereotype/perception of California is left-wing liberal), so it's possible that the students in my California classrooms enacted performances that are reflective of this expectation. It's also possible that the higher number of students of color present in these classrooms may have inspired white students to speak up in support of marginalized groups, or even caused potential anti-woke students to refrain from outing themselves as such. So many possibilities, all equally important to consider.

Other external factors that may contribute to this phenomenon could be the influence of student residency in relation to overall state diversity. For instance, most of my students at Chapman were originally from California (Chapman's website reports that anywhere between 60 and 63% of undergraduates over the last four years have been California residents, with anywhere between 31 and 36% being out of state residents).

And according to the 2020 Census, 64% of Californians are people of color, predominantly LatinX, and 35% are white. This could mean that the majority of Chapman's Californian student body—including those who are white—are likely to have been more exposed to more culturally diverse populations throughout their lives than the University of South Carolina's student body.

Most students at UofSC, similarly, are South Carolina residents (UofSC's website reports that about 60% of undergraduates over the last four years have been South Carolina residents, leaving the remaining to be out of state residents). And according to the 2020 Census, 68.9% of South Carolinians are white, leaving only the remaining 31% as people of color, predominantly Black. This could indicate that students who are South Carolina residents are more likely to have grown up in an environment with much less cultural diversity than that of California. This is partially backed by my observations, as I commonly asked students where they were from as a way to make conversation before class started, and the majority of my students at Chapman were Californian, and the majority of my South Carolina students were South Carolinian. I only consider this a potential factor because I myself have experienced a drastic decrease in exposure to cultural diversity since moving from California to South Carolina, both within academic spaces and within any general public spaces outside of Columbia—UofSC's home city—itself. I therefore believe this could contribute—at least somewhat—to why racially based trigger warnings were accepted with more ease in California versus South Carolina.

My observation of the gender demographics of students who contributed to rhetorical flourishment at Chapman also differed from South Carolina, but not in the way that's expected. While my female students outnumbered my male students in both states, the male students were always more likely to speak in class, regardless of state. Therefore, male students in South Carolina were most prone to causing RD, whereas male students in California were most prone to contributing to rhetorical flourishment. I do believe that male students being more likely to speak out—whether in negative or positive ways—in either state further suggests the role gendered social conditioning may play in student behavior in academic spaces.

Yet, I still noticed a discrepancy within this comparison that suggests deeper complexities beneath this behavior. While it was always male students who caused RD in South Carolina aside from a single instance, a large number of both male and female students caused RF in California (with only a few more male students speaking out than female). So why did almost no female students speak out to contribute to decay at UofSC, whereas multiple female students spoke out to contribute to flourishment at Chapman? Are female students just less likely to be anti-woke? Or are they just more likely to see the value of trigger warnings, since they are statistically more likely to be victims of the kinds of events such warnings precede? Or are they just less likely to challenge academic authority figures due to social conditioning? Or does this social conditioning differ by state—specifically for women—making them more likely to speak up in California than in South Carolina? Or is this all just coincidental, and nothing means anything? I don't know the answer to any of these questions. There's a good chance I never will, as there is no real way to find out without first developing clairvoyant superpowers. And I don't see this happening in the near future, so thinking about it will have to do (I mean, what is academia if not a career that encourages us to think about things?).

CONCLUSION

And so here we are. All in all, these experiences have helped me to understand the complex potentialities that exist between student racial and gender demographics, trigger warnings, anti-wokeness, and RD. Essentially, anti-woke, white male students in the Deep South often perceive racially based trigger warnings to be woke. This perception leads to the derailing and suppressing of conversations about racial oppression, thus causing RD. In California, the opposite seems to be the case, as racially based trigger warnings usually led students of all demographics to respond with openness, thus causing rhetorical flourishment. This could be due to a variety of things, including but not limited to pressures to conform to each state's majority political affiliations, awareness of the in-room demographics, or exposure/lack of exposure to diverse populations. Beneath the few demographics I considered in this reflective analysis are endless possibilities and questions that still need answering. And while these conclusions are only based on my own minimal experiences, they sure are interesting and important to contemplate.

So, what can we do to make our classrooms spaces of rhetorical flourishment rather than spaces of RD? How do we encourage the production of new knowledge when anti-wokeness is so dedicated to impeding it? That brings me to my pedagogical suggestion: the integration of rhetorical listening as a skill that is essential to doing rhetoric. More specifically, I believe that teaching rhetorical listening can provide us with a potential solution to the decay that takes root via anti-wokeness in the composition classroom. Although I didn't specifically *teach* my California students how to engage in rhetorical listening by adopting an open stance and seeking to better understand others, their doing so—whether authentic or not—is what led to productive discussions and therefore rhetorical flourishment in these classrooms. So, what if I purposefully taught these skills to my students in South Carolina? Or all my future students, wherever they may be? What if my introductory lessons on rhetoric were focused on developing skills for rhetorical listening? How would this hinder anti-woke responses to racial trigger warnings, or to anything at all, for that matter? So my proposition is simple: teach rhetorical listening in *all* classrooms, and teach it early. Before teaching students how to *compose* rhetorically, teach them how to *listen* rhetorically. Teach them how to be open, how to consider the experiences of others, and how to reflect on their own experiences. Teach them how to ask productive questions, and how to actively seek a more nuanced understanding of the world around them. This will lead to intellectual productivity born from mutual consideration, in addition to well-developed worldviews that are formed as a result of legitimate contemplation rather than assumptions of personal correctness. And with that, voilà: we will have rhetorical flourishment.

I also propose that while teaching students how to rhetorically listen, we frame trigger warnings as a form of rhetorical listening, thus communicating the value and importance of said trigger warnings. While the above experiences showed me how trigger warnings can create space for rhetorical listening and thus flourishment, they also showed me that trigger warnings are a form of rhetorical listening in and of themselves. Let me explain: being that rhetorical listening is itself a stance of openness that emphasizes the understanding and consideration of others, I now realize that my decision to deliver a trigger warning acts as a form of rhetorical listening, as I only deliver the warnings in direct consideration of the possibility that one of my students could be negatively affected by a course text. Delivering a trigger warning is thus an indication that one is *open* to—and considerate of—the experiences of others. More specifically, I consider the potential experiences of my students, and in my attempt to understand how this text could be painful or harmful to them, I provide a warning and the option not to participate. When providing trigger warnings, instructors are thus rhetorically listening to what students may leave unsaid. If we integrate trigger warnings as an example of rhetorical listening when teaching such skills to our students, we can likely reduce combative, anti-woke responses to such trigger warnings while helping students to better understand the value of rhetorical listening.

We often teach our students how to "do rhetoric" without considering the fact that rhetoric can only be "done" if the audience involved in any given rhetorical situation is willing to listen. So, when we teach our students how to compose, how to speak, how to negotiate and renegotiate their identities, we must be diligent in also teaching them how to *listen*. If we find ways to teach rhetorical listening as a skill that is essential to "doing" rhetoric, we can combat anti-wokeness and RD while creating space for open-mindedness, critical thought, and human connection in the composition classroom. Through this, we can elicit synergetic responses among previously unreceptive or disconnected audiences while inciting real change within a world riddled with social injustice. And while this suggestion is short and sweet, it's open to your interpretation and creativity, so I hope you will consider it.

WORKS CITED

Atkins, J. Spencer. "Defining Wokeness." *Social Epistemology*, vol. 37, no. 3, May 2023, pp. 321–38.

Fulton-Babicke, Holly. "Impediments to Productive Argument: Rhetorical Decay." *Rhetoric Society Quarterly*, vol. 51, no. 4, Aug. 2021, pp. 276–92.

Inoue, Asao B. "Racial Methodologies for Composition Studies: Reflecting on Theories of Race in Writing Assessment Research." *Writing Studies Research in Practice: Methods and Methodologies,* edited by Lee Nickoson and Mary P. Sheridan, Southern Illinois UP, 2012, pp. 125–39.

Ratcliffe, Krista. *Rhetorical Listening: Identification, Gender, Whiteness*. Southern Illinois UP, 2005.

Waite, Stacey. "How (and Why) to Write Queer: A Failing, Impossible, Contradictory Instruction Manual for Scholars of Writing Studies." *Re/Orienting Writing Studies: Queer Methods, Queer Projects*, edited by William P. Banks et al., Utah State UP, 2019, pp. 42–53.

Zhu, Hua. "Rhetorical Listening: Guiguzi and Feminists in Dialogue." *China Media Research*, vol. 15, no. 1, Jan. 2019, pp. 3–13.

CHAPTER FIFTEEN

(UN)COMFORTABLE SUBJECTS

How Trigger Warnings and the Experiences of Military-Affiliated Students Compel Us to Reflect on Agency, Engagement, and Belonging

Corrine E. Hinton

In a *Task & Purpose* article adapted from his *Carrying the Gun* blogpost, US Army veteran Don Gomez reflects on trigger warnings from his experience as a student veteran attending college classes at a time when "the Iraq War was at its height both in terms of unpopularity and casualties" (n.p.). During his classes, many of which focused on "the Middle East and international relations," Gomez describes how "professors spoke about the war as a self-evident failure. It was a joke and an embarrassment." He laments, "Not once did any of my professors ever ask, 'Are there any veterans in the class?'" (n.p.). Gomez's experience echoes a common critique of the practice: to identify a trigger, one must identify what could be triggering and for whom. To identify *what* and *for whom* requires the individual offering the warning to be well versed in a variety of lived experiences and pathways by which particular discussions, concepts, projects, environments, or pedagogies might generate feelings of harm, vulnerability, or a lack of personal or psychological safety. Students often perceive trigger warnings as an instructor's acknowledgment that the students' affective or corporeal experiences can impact their learning experiences. While they seem to promise students the opportunity to exercise agency in maintaining their psychological safety, trigger warnings also communicate to students the issuing faculty's perceptions of vulnerability: who the faculty believes might suffer psychological or emotional harm as well as what (and whose) experiences, identities, and traumas matter.

Despite calls in higher education for culturally responsive, trauma-informed, inclusive practices and policies to foster student engagement and belonging (both seminal to student retention and success), Gomez's experiences, and those of other student veterans and military-affiliated students, highlight a critical fracture between the *philosophies* of student belonging to which higher education institutions and their personnel ascribe and the *practices*, including trigger warnings, individuals employ to signal their alignment with those philosophies. Although historically excluded from perceptions of marginalized groups in academia, student veterans and military-affiliated learners often cite their experiences with stigmatization and microaggressions, exposing the inequity and subjectivity of practices like trigger warnings and validating cautions about the politicized nature of student belonging in higher education. Here, I will begin by reviewing key aspects of student belonging and highlight trigger warnings as a specific practice that attempts to foster belonging. Next, I will focus on the limitations of how trigger warnings are conceptualized and enacted, rendering them a problematic and politicized practice in the cultivation of student belonging. Finally, I will offer research with and firsthand accounts by student veterans and military-affiliated learners that further elucidate the limitations and complications of practices like trigger warnings and notions of student belonging. By featuring military-affiliated students[1] as a specific population whose experiences unveil gaps in institutional attempts to create and sustain environments that support belonging, I hope to demonstrate how postsecondary educators and administrators must confront implicit bias and subjectivity as well as expand current conceptions of belonging if we hope to generate learning environments where students feel safe to be (and share) themselves.

STUDENT BELONGING

Fostering a sense of belonging for students has become essential in the higher education landscape, but the more we learn, the more complex and seemingly impossible it becomes for institutions to achieve. Belonging is often defined as "an emotional attachment, feeling at 'home,' feeling safe and an act of self-identification *or the identification by others*" (Yuval-Davis 199, my emphasis). As part of the "new 'social contract'...that considers and recognises each learner's sense of identity whether that be 'cultural,' 'spiritual,' 'social,' or 'linguistic,'" belonging also attends meaningfully to student wellbeing (UNESCO as cited by Ajjawi et al. 2). More recently, conversations within postsecondary research, policy, and practice have progressed from how institutions can support or provide opportunities for fostering belonging to how they can identify and "remove 'barriers to belonging'" (Gravett and Ajjawi 1387). Additionally, research focused on the (un)expected spaces, places, and relationships that cultivate belonging for students as well as how students perceive their own identities and engage in their own unique ways of belonging continue to reveal how truly complex the idea of belonging is (Ajjawi et al.; Gravett and Ajjawi; Yuval-Davis). In their exploration of how students conceive of and cultivate belonging at their universities, Ajjawi et al. discovered students hold diverse and nuanced understandings of belonging (and the related concepts of *unbelonging*[2] and *not-belonging*[3]) as well as strategies by which they might test belonging across a variety of spaces and institutional contact points. Belonging, then, "does not just happen or not happen; belonging evolves along a spectrum, responsive to individual experiences and subject to changes in a student's dispositions and identities" (Hinton 84).

For postsecondary institutions, supporting student belonging is often multifaceted: organizationally (e.g., core values, strategic planning), structurally (policies and procedures), relationally (e.g., professional development for campus personnel, community partnerships), and curricularly (from program-level outcomes to what individual faculty do in individual courses). Gravett and Ajjawi speculate, "Many pedagogical models include belonging as essential to student success and retention," though in practice, such models are only as effective as the educator adopting them (1387). How faculty communicate and enact philosophies, practices, and pedagogies as well as instructional behaviors and dispositions attentive to notions of belonging are as diverse as the students they serve. And although students are essential to how an institution can assess its climate of belonging across all levels, and students experience their identities and aspects of belonging uniquely at various institutional connection points (including interactions with individual faculty), agents of the institution—rather than students—typically lead decision-making and organizational change efforts. Hence, belonging is politicized, "an ongoing process of negotiation" whereby those engaged in those negotiations do not operate from equal positions of power and privilege within the academy (Ajjawi et al. 4). I would argue that we can uncover similar inequities of power and privilege, particularly but not exclusively for military-affiliated students, when we interrogate the conceptualization and implementation of trigger warnings.

TRIGGER WARNINGS AS SUPPORTIVE PRACTICE FOR STUDENT BELONGING

Trigger warnings attempt to acknowledge the complex, integrated nature of students' experiences, the majority of which have occurred *outside* the institution, as a pathway toward cultivating belonging *within* the institution. Generally categorized within trauma-informed pedagogies as "protective measures," trigger warnings attend more holistically and compassionately to students by recognizing that we humans carry our emotions, lived experiences, and traumas with us as we engage in the world, including within a formalized learning environment like a college class (Bellet et al. 134). This nuanced understanding has catalyzed a shift in the roles and responsibilities of postsecondary institutions and faculty to their students. Josalin J. Hunter explains:

> Support for social and emotional learning, as well as mental and behavioral health, has now become a responsibility of educators and administrators in higher education. This responsibility is not only to provide resources, but also to attend to needs for effective teaching and learning. (27)

In some ways, then, trigger warnings have become a well-intentioned olive branch to students. Students can make their own choices about how and with what topics they engage within the instructional environment, challenging "dominant notions of instruction and education that perpetuate a false dichotomy between cognition and emotion and force students to adapt to the classroom rather than adapting the classroom to its students" (Grayson 414). Faculty who implement trigger warnings intend to provide students with agency over their trauma triggers by giving them options for avoiding or confronting potentially disruptive reminders of their trauma. Rhetorically, faculty also use trigger warnings as demonstrations of their compassion and concern for student wellbeing. While one could critique the offer as virtue signaling, most faculty who use trigger warnings genuinely want students to have (and maintain) feelings of psychological, social, and emotional safety (not *comfort* or *ease*, but *safety*). Thus, the very presence of a trigger warning statement could communicate something positive about the issuing faculty's dedication to providing a supportive learning environment. To that end, then, we can categorize trigger warnings as a deliberative practice to foster student belonging, not just for students who may need to avail themselves of the opportunities presented but also for any student who would feel comforted by a rhetorical demonstration of their faculty's concern for their wellbeing. However, a critical analysis of the limited, and limiting, conceptualizations and enactments of trigger warnings encourages us to reflect on their impact on student belonging, particularly for military-affiliated learners.

TRIGGER WARNINGS: LIMITATIONS AND COMPLICATIONS

Trigger warnings offer the rhetorical promise of empowering students to determine their own learning threshold when it comes to engaging with course content they deem as having a high potential for retraumatization or extreme emotional or psychological discomfort. However, conceptualizing a trigger warning relies on subjective perceptions of vulnerability and enacting them relies on a faculty's provisioning of student agency and coercive disclosure. I'd like to focus on these three limitations—*perceptions of vulnerability*, *provisioned agency*, and *coercive disclosure*—and then position these in context to the narratives and accounts of student veterans and military-affiliated students.

Perceptions of Vulnerability

Trigger warnings direct our attention toward certain kinds of trauma (or content/ experiences that might be retraumatizing) broadly based on the provider's perception of that trauma as well as the provider's perception of which individuals or groups might be vulnerable. Faculty create constructs of vulnerability based upon their knowledge, understanding, biases, and experiences. They then use these to shape how trigger warnings, designed to communicate concern and care as well as demonstrate support and belonging, function in their learning environments. Thus, trigger warnings generate from a faculty's (or institution's) assumptions about the "emotional incapacita[tion]" impact of trauma exposure and the identities and capacities of trauma survivors or trauma avoiders (Bellet et al. 135). While well intended, these assumptions and perceptions are subjective, limited, and have the potential to create harm. For example, in their study comparing participant responses to content with and without trigger warnings, Bellet and his colleagues found trigger warnings serve as "reminders" about trauma and trauma victims, reminders which "contribute to perceptions of heightened vulnerability," "of trauma survivors as dysregulated victims," and "to negative stigma concerning the very individuals trigger warnings are intended to protect" (135). Hence, drawing attention to (the potential for) trauma can intrinsically perpetuate trauma-related stigma.

In addition to potentially reiterating harmful assumptions and perpetuating negative stereotypes, trigger warnings also reflect limitations in our perceptions about what could harm and who could be harmed. In their critique, Khalid and Snyder call attention to the "arbitrary" nature by which trigger warnings are dispensed to confirm that faculty "don't... have the expertise or moral authority to make decisions about what kind of pain—not to mention whose pain—matters most" (n.p.). Since faculty cannot possibly account for all potential "pain" or how students' lived experiences shape how they might engage with course content, faculty have the potential to cause unintentional harm by leaving the unanticipated pain of others unprotected. In her work on the "politics of belonging," Nira Yuval-Davis explains:

> Belonging...is not just about social locations and constructions of individual and collective identities and attachments but also about the ways these are valued and judged. Closely related to this are specific attitudes and ideologies concerning where and how identity and categorical boundaries are being/should be drawn, in more or less exclusionary ways, in more or less permeable ways. (203–204)

When we consider the interrelationships of trauma, vulnerability, and identity at work, trigger warnings become rhetorical and linguistic outputs of the issuing faculty's perceptions and constructions (i.e., "values" and "judgments") of the "boundaries of the political community of belonging" (Yuval-Davis 204). By communicating divisions between those who could be harmed (and are worthy of a measure of protection and agency) and those who should not be harmed, trigger warnings draw boundaries of (un)belonging among students as well as between students and faculty.

Provisioned Agency

Whether as statements of official policy or of individual practice, trigger warnings generally outline a claim about the potential for harmful material and, often but not always, propose one or more actions by which students can protect themselves from harm. These warnings, however, do not provide an *assurance* of agency, merely an opportunity; they do not empower learners but provide an opportunity for empowerment. When warnings about potentially sensitive material lack an accompanying outline of actions the student might or could take in response, students are left to their own knowledge and decision-making about how they might protect themselves. However, not all students feel equally capable or safe to know or claim their agency. As Mara Lee Grayson, citing from scholars like Asao B. Inoue, reiterates:

> [Some students] may choose to tolerate their discomfort because they also don't feel comfortable approaching the teacher to request an alternative reading or assignment. [...] The students likeliest to feel agency in the classroom are those who already feel comfortable with self-expression in such spaces and are familiar with the discourse of the classroom, a discourse most readily available to White middle-class students. (429)

As the implied composers and enforcers of the policy/practice, faculty initiate the opportunity for agency to their students under the conditions the faculty dictate. Some students can access this agency, and this access is regulated by their ability to meet the conditions set forth. As such, faculty provision agency to their students, a step *toward* empowerment without the assurance of actual power.

Coercive Disclosure

For students to take advantage of the provisioned agency an instructor affords them via the trigger warning, they must explicitly or implicitly disclose their potential or actual discomfort or distress to their faculty. Explicit disclosure requires or encourages students to make direct contact with the faculty to reveal or explain their concern about content or topics as well as to request a responsive action (or request access to the alternatives provided in the warning). Implicit disclosure includes how a student might avoid the material by not engaging during class, not attending class/accessing content, or not completing an activity or assignment. Whether a student engages in explicit or implicit disclosure strategies, the faculty is presented the opportunity to identify affected students, and by virtue, access to their traumas, stressors, and other private experiences or information the student may not want to divulge. For composition scholars and pedagogues, this argument is comparable to what Lester Faigley, Sharon Crowley, Cathryn Molloy, and others have critiqued about the nature and consequences of some personal narrative assignments because they provide faculty (and sometimes other students) access to aspects of student's lives that could change the teacher-student dynamic without the student's awareness of or control over that change.

Grayson explains, "Instructors who include stipulations for how students should request alternative assignments or excused absences may inadvertently put the onus on students to out themselves as trauma survivors" (428). Hence, some trigger warnings, and the faculty who use them, rely on coercive disclosure as an accessibility pathway; subsequently, students may knowingly or unknowingly place themselves in more vulnerable positions through these disclosures.

While trigger warnings were initially conceived as a trauma-informed practice to help curtail retraumatization for individuals with formal diagnoses of post-traumatic stress disorder (PTSD)—including those who experienced, committed, or witnessed combat-related violence—they have evolved and now, more often, prioritize other forms or sites of trauma. Coalescing perceptions of vulnerability, provisioning (and regulation) of student agency, and coercive disclosure reveal limitations in how trigger warnings are conceptualized, communicated, and enacted. These limitations are especially relevant in light of trigger warnings that go beyond individual experiences of isolated (single event) trauma into systemic, institutionalized, collective, or long-term traumas like racism, sexism, homophobia, or xenophobia (Grayson). Faculty provide trigger warnings to help facilitate student learning, engagement, and belonging through an acknowledgment designed to communicate care and concern. However, faculty remain the primary authority and control agent as students attempt to engage in the course, and our perspectives are always limited and, potentially, limiting. Thus, even in our attempt to communicate an environment of care and foster a sense of belonging, we may end up creating more divisions in our learning spaces than we intend. Based on scholarly reporting and firsthand accounts of their experiences, student veterans and military-affiliated students may be an overlooked student population experiencing those divisions.

NARRATIVES FROM THE FRONT LINES: STUDENT VETERANS AND MILITARY-AFFILIATED LEARNERS

Student veterans and military-affiliated learners continue to have a notable presence within colleges and universities, but their feelings of belonging, like other student populations, can be influenced by the institutional culture. The Student Veterans of America's *2020 Annual Report* shares that more than one million student veterans currently access GI Bill education benefits, the majority of whom are enrolled full-time. The United States has periodically experienced surges in veterans seeking postsecondary education, often a combination of educational incentives (i.e., the GI Bill) and troop drawdowns following decreasing combat engagements (e.g., World War II, Vietnam, and the operations affiliated with the Global War on Terror after 9/11), as one pathway during the service-to-civilian transition. Many educational benefits for veterans can be transferred or expanded to include dependents, such as spouses, children, or caregivers, resulting in a more robust and diversified military-affiliated student population. Additionally, the presence of Reserve Officers' Training Corps (ROTC) detachments and military installations as well as Reserve Officer and National Guard units further expand the scope of military-connected learners.

Student veterans and military-affiliated learners bring a wealth of experience and skill to their college lives, but these are not always recognized or recognizable. Military-connected learners bring leadership and teamwork experience, a mission-first orientation toward accomplishing academic objectives, resilience, and a variety of specialized, transferable skills in the areas of their military occupational specialties (Institute for Veterans and Military Families and SVA). Additionally, scholars and educators have emphasized how student veterans bring writing, communication, and critical thinking skills along with global worldviews cultivated through professional experiences into classroom discussions (Conference on College Composition & Communication). Despite these strengths and contributions, some student veterans still routinely report difficulty during the transition to civilian life, generally, and to higher education specifically. Of relevance to this argument are individual identity negotiations (Bagby et al.; Blaauw-Hara; Hinton; Jones; Martin) and relationships with faculty and nonveteran peers (Alschuler and Yarab; Carter et al.; Elliott, Gonzalez, and Larsen). Student veterans and other military-affiliated learners are, like other student populations, susceptible to feeling a lack of belonging at their postsecondary institutions based on their interactions, some of which stem from a perceived misunderstanding about military culture and their identities (Bodrog, Gloria, and Brockberg; Eakman et al.).

A lack of awareness about the degree to which military culture can impact the identities of American military servicemembers is central to some student veterans' feelings of belonging on campus (DiRamio and Jarvis; Olsen et al.). Adjusting to civilian and campus life can, for some student veterans, generate a phenomenon scholars call "reverse culture shock" (Livingston et al.; Wade), "converse culture shock" (Carne), or "cultural incongruence" (McAndrew et al.). In one section of the Association for the Study of Higher Education's (ASHE) 2011 report, *Crisis of identity? Veteran, Civilian, Student*, David DiRamio and Kathryn Jarvis provide a comprehensive look into identity and cultural incongruity among student service members and student veterans. The report considers the varying degrees by which student veterans may be shaped by their military service and, as a result, the "additional layer of complexity of intersecting identities" that becoming a college student evokes (56). In the end, ASHE includes a framework of four typologies that students with military experience might inhabit, depending upon the veteran's commitment to their military identity and the student veteran's awareness of any identity tensions: "Ambivalent" student veterans (i.e., uncommitted to a military identity and unconcerned with developing a new one), "Skeptic" student veterans (i.e., strong military core with little desire to reconceptualize), "Emerging" student veterans (i.e., connected to their military identity but recognize it "may not serve effectively in other contexts"), and the "Fulfilled Civilian Self" (i.e., a balanced core identity) (60–63). As one might reasonably conclude, *Skeptic* and *Emerging* student veterans who inhabit greater degrees of attachment to their military selves may be more susceptible to feelings of nonbelonging than their *Ambivalent* or *Fulfilled Civilian Self* counterparts (DiRamio and Jarvis). Similarly, my own investigations of veteran identity, particularly as it relates to adopting a student (civilian) identity supports a nuanced understanding of veteran identity cultivation based upon several factors including veterans' self-described levels of attachment to their military identities while serving, length of military service, and combat experience (Hinton). Moreover, my interviews with several student veterans unveiled a range of qualities that shape how veterans perceive their own veteranness, illustrating a salient awareness of their various identities (including the identities they believe others craft for/onto them) that impacts how, when, and if they disclose their military affiliations to others on campus (Hinton). Yet, historically speaking, student veterans and military-affiliated learners are generally overlooked as specialized populations for whose feelings of belonging most institutions, save for those catering directly to veterans/active military learners, need to account (O'Connor).

Research with and firsthand accounts by student veterans and military-affiliated learners report microaggressions, stigmatization, and marginalization because of their service or service connections, exposing the impact that subjective perceptions of vulnerability, provisioned agency, and coercive disclosures can have. Existing literature continues to identify faculty/staff as one of the most critical contributing factors to student veteran and military-affiliated learner engagement and success (Alschuler and Yarab; Arminio et al.; Dean et al.). If trigger warnings rely, in part, on faculty perceptions of trauma, potential trauma triggers, and students vulnerable to such triggers, then faculty would need to conceive of student veterans and military-affiliated learners as a vulnerable or at-risk population in need of support (Carter et al.; Dean et al.; O'Connor). Research with both student veterans and faculty suggests such a perception is unlikely unless a faculty member has had some prior positive contact with the military "outside of academia" (Gonzalez and Elliott). This contact can also influence the faculty member's "willingness to help student veterans succeed in college" (39). Comparatively, Lucy Barnard-Brak and her colleagues found, "Faculty members who have negative feelings toward the Post-9/11 conflicts and the military service of student veterans have less self-efficacy around working with student veterans" (33). Carter and her colleagues expand upon these findings, contextualizing faculty perceptions and interactions within broader cultural conflicts and power dynamics between higher education culture and military culture. They propose, "Faculty/staff would benefit from reconsidering student veterans as a cultural minority on campus" (198). To further problematize faculty perceptions of the potential for veteran vulnerability, faculty and administrators must also recognize the intersectionality of veteran identities, identities that do not all present as physical signifiers and identities that challenge traditional notions of veterans and military-affiliated learners. Such difficulties often lead to faculty, staff, and civilian peer stereotyping.

Many nonveterans on campus tend to stereotype student veterans' experiences and make determinations about their values and beliefs based on how those student veterans present. In his book, *War & Homecoming: Veteran Identity and the Post-9/11 Generation*, Travis L. Martin powerfully articulates this nonverbal exchange:

> Somewhere today, a veteran walked into a college classroom. [...] Once a veteran signifies veteran status, the minds of others come alive with theories, expectations, notions of what, exactly, it means to be a veteran. In return, the veteran anticipates these unspoken beliefs. [...] From the time the student veteran walks from the doorway to their desk, an entire set of conscious and unconscious exchanges takes place. [...] [T]he veteran takes a seat, having played a localized yet pivotal role in maintaining a larger cultural narrative about their country, its beliefs, and fellow veterans. Not a word has been spoken. (38)

How might a veteran "signify"? Age, clothing, haircuts, tattoos, gear (like backpacks) reappropriated from service to campus might lead some faculty and students to (mis)label them as "combat vets," even without knowing the reality of their military experiences. Active duty, National Guard, ROTC, or other students actively serving are subject to mischaracterization by virtue of the uniform. Women student veterans and student veterans of color are often miscast as nonveterans, a carryover from the pervasive (misre)presentations of *veteran* as *white male* in American culture and media (Casavantes Bradford; Lau et al.). These stereotypes are misguided at least and catastrophic to students at worst. For example, two years ago, a colleague of mine recounted an odd experience he had during a class discussion very early into the fall semester. One of the class's core outcomes focused on students' ability to deliver arguments orally using evidence; to demonstrate an example of what *not* to do, the professor jokingly referred to President Joe Biden's speech wherein the President recounted the "extraordinary success" of the nation's disastrous and deadly withdrawal from Afghanistan. While my colleague's example was likely an attempt to connect to students using humor and by leveraging a story active in the news cycle, he failed to recognize the severity of the wider contexts at work for the student veteran, who had served in Afghanistan herself, in his room. She left class, without disruption, and *never went back*. Had this student not chosen to seek me out, as the department chair and a student veteran advocate, and share her story, my colleague would never have known how his insensitive misstep of trading in sarcasm created a learning environment she felt was unwelcome and unsustainable for her.

In addition to being at risk for misconceptions about how faculty perceive student veterans' potential need for support, some student veterans and military-affiliated students may have difficulty asserting their own agency or have been met with negative faculty interactions when attempting to assert their agency. Student veterans and military-affiliated students are imbued with a great deal of resilience as a mechanism for helping achieve their mission-first mindset within a collectivist culture. An admission of needing assistance could be, for some veterans, perceived as an admission of weakness or an attempt to take resources away from others who they believe may need them more. And because military learning systems place the instructor in the position of subject matter expert, student veterans and military-affiliated learners—especially those early into their civilian reintegration or college transitions—are likely to expect that their college faculty will share in the responsibility for facilitating student success and engage with them as equals (Blaauw-Hara). Consider, for example, the experience Travis L. Martin recounts as a graduate student with a faculty mentor:

> I walked into that professor's office feeling as though we were equals. And when I left feeling invalidated, the power differential didn't sit right. I respected the professor's research and expertise, but that respect didn't feel like a two-way street. My views had simply been shrugged off. (24)

The American postsecondary climate relies heavily on structures that expect students to recognize and assert their own agency despite being part of a system of which they may not have a comprehensive understanding. Trigger warnings are an example of how that system enacts itself in course policies and in faculty pedagogies. For student veterans and military-affiliated students, particularly for those attempting to navigate often hidden cultural norms and codes of higher education, asserting agency can be challenging for several reasons. Further still, if asserting that agency is met subsequently with unanticipated resistance or rejection by faculty who claim to hold values committed to mutual respect and student success, the consequences for student veterans and military-affiliated learners can be felt quite deeply.

As illustrated by some of the experiences and stories I've shared, for student veterans and military-affiliated learners actively readjusting to civilian and campus cultures, cultural incongruence and identity conflicts can be further exacerbated by negative interactions with and attitudes of faculty, campus personnel, and other students (Livingston et al.; Wade). These negative interactions can impact a veteran's willingness to disclose their military-affiliated identity to others on campus (Barry, Whiteman, and MacDermid Wadsworth; Herrmann et al.; Hinton; Lau et al.; McAndrew et al.). In their research, Herrmann et al.'s student veteran participants identified several challenges they faced in higher education, one area of which the authors categorized as difficulties with "campus culture." This list included several comments from student veterans that could certainly impact a veteran's willingness to disclose. For example, "a professor or some professors at my school openly make false negative statements in class about military service," "administrators at my school say anti-military or anti-veteran comments to students knowing they are veterans," and "non-veteran students at my school ask inappropriate questions about hazardous duty or combat experiences" (35–36). When confronted with class conversations about the conflict in Iraq, Don Gomez explains:

> Early in my college career, I'd challenge. I'd raise my hand offer my perspective. [...] I felt like as one of the few student veterans on campus, I had a duty and responsibility to say something. But it was exhausting. I learned quickly that once you "out" yourself as a student veteran, that's it. When people see you, you're now the "Army guy." It doesn't go away, and whenever a topic that has anything to do with "the war" or the military comes up in class, all eyes fall on you. (n.p.)

Here, Gomez is experiencing the tension that develops when others place his military-affiliated identity over that of his personal identity. They then leverage his veteran status to dictate his terms of engagement with the group (e.g., being expected to participate when "anything to do with 'the war' or the military comes up"). Gomez is, thus, depersonalized and *othered*, valued only for what his veteranness brings to his peers and the learning environment.

Because of actual or potential negative interactions that can ostracize, minimize, or stereotype student veterans from/by nonveterans, some student veterans choose to control how, when, and to whom they disclose their military-affiliated status. In his study with veterans, Mercurio concludes, "Participants generally preferred to control the time, place, and manner in which they divulged details of their service, espousing a preference for interactions with other ingroup members or when the directional orientation of the engagement was in their favor (e.g., they chose to disclose their military affiliation/experiences)," a phenomenon he refers to as *controlled disclosure* (9). His study reveals how some veterans occupy "a juxtaposition of enjoyment derived from countering stereotypes by disclosing military services...with the need to be guarded, worrying if the civilian is safe and can be trusted with the disclosure" (11). At the instance of disclosure, Mercurio explains, the veteran is "directing the course of the engagement and choosing to disclose their service. In doing so, they are also mediating whatever role or stereotype the other member(s) of the interaction had ascribed" (11). Through controlled disclosure, a veteran may also choose not to disclose at all. This silence, for some, may be a coping mechanism in anticipation of or in response to experiences with alienation or rejection by fellow students or faculty. In essence, some student veterans choose to hide in plain sight:

> This masking is usually not out of embarrassment or denial about their military service but rather an output of humility (not wanting to seek or receive preferential treatment), identity camouflage (to remove a potential obstacle from connecting with peers or faculty), or protection (to avoid self-disclosure and thwart uninvited interactions centering on their veteranness or military service experiences). (Hinton 96)

Silence may also be "an embodiment of power and agency in a classroom" rather than a defensive response, as Roger Thompson argues in

"Recognizing Silence: Composition, Writing, and the Ethical Space for War" (201). Contextualizing his arguments in consideration of whether or not faculty should engage in conversations about war, Thompson continues:

> The wartime experience is personal, that students' connections to war may be largely invisible to us as instructors, and that imagining our pedagogy as one that circumvents those invisible connections to war fails to create space for students to shape their own responses to the war experience, whether they be civilians, military family members, or veterans. Silence is one way they may do so, and as a legitimate, complex, and powerful response to war, silence is a particularly important rhetorical strategy that can embody the personal. (201)

I would argue a similar claim can be made about military-affiliated identity disclosure and concealment. The veteran identity is "personal," and a veteran's individual, unique connection to that identity "may be largely invisible to us as instructors" (201). As such, faculty must "create space for students to shape their own responses to" their military-affiliated identities, including the decision not to disclose that affiliation (201). Veterans and military-affiliated learners who choose not to disclose their military-affiliated identity to others are engaging, I purport, in a deliberative, rhetorical act of silence.

A NOTE ABOUT OTHER MILITARY-AFFILIATED STUDENTS

While the bulk of this chapter has focused on student veterans, faculty and other campus personnel should also consider the ways in which similar kinds of experiences can have comparable impacts on other military-affiliated students, such as military spouses, intimate partners, children, caregivers, and parents who might be enrolled in classes or engaging with the campus community. For example, caregivers who may never have experienced life in the military may still have been impacted by it, whether they knew their veteran during or after service. In their caregiving responsibilities, they have likely had to assist the veteran with navigating complex systems like the Department of Veterans Affairs, the Veterans Health Administration, Social Security Administration, or others and, as such, could be negatively impacted by campus experiences with others who may—knowingly or unknowingly—make unsolicited, offensive, or inappropriate remarks about the military, military personnel, or the families who support them. Children of service personnel and veterans also come onto campus with their own unique set of experiences, particularly if they lived abroad, endured parent or guardian deployments, or experienced frequent moves (Shafer et al.; Zurlinden et al.). Like their primary military family member, the identities of these military-affiliated family members may include aspects of their *selves* they may feel more or less comfortable sharing with others on campus based on perceived or actualized concerns with acceptance.

CONCLUDING REMARKS

Trigger warnings attempt to communicate to students that faculty are sensitive to their needs and that we trust them to navigate what is healthy for their learning *and* wellbeing. Yet, they often require a student's action in response to that notification (e.g., asking for an alternative reading or assignment, asking for latitude in not attending class). These warnings also imply our (namely, faculty's) willingness to accept those responses as students work to assert their agency through setting and maintaining the boundaries that they deem necessary. Such responses are rhetorical, and all responses—including *speaking out* and *staying silent*—are on the table. Otherwise, trigger warnings are simply performative, acts not actions, that claim to make space for students and to empower them to make choices for themselves while, instead, simply reasserting our (faculty's) subject position as controlling what we will and will not accept in exchange for providing the warning.

Here, I have advocated for greater understanding of the political complexities that trigger warnings have the potential to generate as well as for responsive practices and policies that recognize and attempt to grapple with those complexities. However, I would be remiss if I did not acknowledge the problems inherent to veteran advocacy work within higher education. The military, like higher education, is rooted in White epistemologies whose policies, structures, and systems historically, and contemporarily, perpetuate systematic injustices against those whose bodies, minds, or identities are coded outside of these dominant epistemologies. As such, my call for greater awareness and inclusion of student veterans and military-affiliated learners could be misinterpreted as support for this system, for the war machine, for the occupation of nations, and for state-sanctioned violence. In the same way I believe that every student veteran and military-affiliated learner is an individual with their own experiences, thoughts, values, strengths, identities, traumas, and stressors, I believe that *every person* brings the same multifaceted, unique personhood into our institutional spaces, and not all identities or experiences are visible or disclosed. This includes students (and faculty) whose lives have been transformed by the actions of military, paramilitary, or other occupying forces or regimes, generating associated traumas and stressors. Advocacy for one should not be interpreted as disregard for any other.

Truly inclusive pedagogy must begin with an explicit admission, to ourselves and our students, that we can never know, nor can we claim to know, what experiences have shaped them into the person they bring forward in the moments we have together. For Army veteran Don Gomez, providing classroom spaces that are "more considerate of people's past experiences" means including student veterans (n.p.). "Whether they are suffering from PTSD or not," he contends, "if they fought overseas—or even if they didn't, their minds and emotions are likely intertwined with that discussion. Veterans certainly don't need a trigger warning; the idea of being warned before they're offended is comical. But what they do deserve is a fair chance at being heard. And an understanding that they exist" (n.p.). Gomez's experiences, and those of other military-connected learners, reinforce concerns about how we reconcile higher education's cultural commitment to inclusion and belonging with practices that attempt to regulate or restrict, explicitly or implicitly, that inclusion and belonging. Ajjawi and her colleagues insist, "We need to handle belonging with criticality and care," and they propose:

> a need to avoid a singular "sense of belonging" becoming an expectation of university experiences, as well as inferring an onus on already pressured educators to provide something that is essentially unachievable. This is

not the same as the need for educators to work to support a diversity of students to engage and have an equitable learning experience, including foregrounding good curriculum design as a scaffold for belonging opportunities. (11)

Postsecondary educators and administrators must address implicit bias and broaden our limited notions of belonging to create and sustain spaces where students feel safe and empowered to be (and express) their authentic selves.

NOTES

1 To be clear, my focus here is not just about veterans with Post-Traumatic Stress (PTS) or related conditions whose traumatic histories may increase their chances of being triggered but on veterans and military-affiliated people who, by virtue of their connection to and relationship with military cultures, may feel excluded or experience exclusion at the hands of faculty, staff, or other students.

2 "Those who long to belong but are unable to achieve this state" (Ajjawi et al. 4).

3 "Those who choose not to belong" (Ajjawi et al. 4).

WORKS CITED

Ajjawi, Rola, Karen Gravett, and Sarah O'Shea. "The Politics of Student Belonging: Identity and Purpose." *Teaching in Higher Education*, 2023, pp. 1–14. https://doi.org/10.1080/13562517.2023.228061.

Alschuler, Mari, and Jessica Yarab. "Preventing Student Veteran Attrition: What More can we do?" *Journal of College Student Retention,* vol. 20, no. 1, 2018, pp. 47–66. https://doi.org/ 10.1177/1521025116646382.

Bagby, Janet H., Lucy Barnard-Brak, LaNette W. Thompson, and Tracey N. Sulak. "Is Anyone Listening? An Ecological Systems Perspective on Veterans Transitioning from the Military to Academia." *Military Behavioral Health*, vol. 3, no. 4, 2015, pp. 219–29. https://doi.org/10.1080/21635781.2015.1057306.

Barnard-Brak, Lucy, Janet Hall Bagby, Natalie Jones, and Tracey Sulak. "Teaching Post 9/11 Student Veterans with Symptoms of PTSD: The Influence of Faculty Perceptions and Self-Efficacy." *Journal of Vocational Rehabilitation*, vol. 35, no. 1, 2011, pp. 29–36.

Barry, Adam E., Shawn D. Whiteman, and Shelley MacDermid Wadsworth. "Student Service Members/Veterans in Higher Education: A Systematic Review. *Journal of Student Affairs Research and Practice*, vol. 51, 2014, pp. 30–42. https://doi.org/10.1515/jsarp-2014-0003.

Bellet, Benjamin W., Payton J. Jones, and Richard J. McNally. "Trigger Warning: Empirical Evidence Ahead." *Journal of Behavior Therapy and Experimental Psychiatry*, vol. 61, 2018, pp. 134–41. https://doi.org//10.1016/j.jbtep.2018.07.002.

Biden, Joseph. Remarks on U.S. Withdrawal from Afghanistan. 13 August 2021, https://www.c-span.org/program/white-house-event/president-biden-remarks-on-us-withdrawal-from-afghanistan/602343.

Blaauw-Hara, Mark. *From Military to Academy: The Writing and Learning Transitions of Student-Veterans*. UP of Colorado, 2021.

Bodrog, Bryan C., Albert M. Gloria, and Dustin Gregory Brockberg. "The Effects of Mattering and Combat Deployment on Student Service Members/Veterans' College Adjustment: A Psychosociocultural Approach." *Journal of Veterans Studies*, vol. 3, no. 2, 2018, pp. 109–25. https://doi.org/10.21061/jvs.v3i2.73.

Carne, Glenda Lynn. *Coming Back to College: Middle East Veteran Student Involvement and Culture Shock*. Dissertation, University of Colorado, Colorado Springs, 2011.

Carter, Carrie, Jae Hoon Lim, Claudia Interiano-Shiverdecker, and Jerry Dahlberg. "Unlearning As Learning? A Critical Analysis of Student Veteran Support at a Veteran-Friendly Campus." *Journal of Veterans Studies*, vol. 9, no. 1, 2023, pp. 190–202. https://doi.org/10.21061/jvs.v9i1.416.

Casavantes Bradford, Anita. "Latinx Veterans, Outsider Patriotism and the Motives Behind Minoritized Military Service. *Journal of Veterans Studies*, vol. 7, no. 3, 2021, pp. 4–22. https://doi.org/10.21061/jvs.v7i3.272.

Conference on College Composition & Communication. *Student Veterans in the College Composition Classroom: Realizing Their Strengths and Assessing Their Needs*, March 2015, https://cccc.ncte.org/cccc/resources/positions/student-veterans.

Crowley, Sharon. "The Invention of Freshman English." *Composition in the University: Historical and Polemic Essays*. U of Pittsburgh P, 1998, pp. 46–78.

Dean, Terezia, Carl H. Sorgen, and Cordelia D. Zinskie. "Social Integration of Student Veterans: The Influence of Interactions with Faculty on Peer-Group Interactions." *Journal of Veterans Studies*, vol. 6, no. 2, 2020, pp. 20–29. https://doi.org/10.21061/jvs.v6i2.188.

DiRamio, David, and Kathryn Jarvis. "Crisis of Identity? Veteran, Civilian, Student." Association for the Study of Higher Education (ASHE). *ASHE Higher Education Report*, vol. 37, no. 3, 2011, pp. 53–65.

Eakman, Aaron M., Adam R. Kinney, Michelle L. Schierl, and Kimberly L. Henry. "Academic Performance in Student Service Members/Veterans: Effects of Instructor Autonomy Support, Academic Self-Efficacy and Academic Problems." *Educational Psychology*, vol. 39, no. 8, 2019, pp. 1005–26. https://doi.org/10.1080/01443410.2019.1605048.

Elliott, Marta, Carlene Gonzalez, and Barbara Larsen. "U.S. Military Veterans Transition to College: Combat, PTSD, and Alienation on Campus." *Journal of Student Affairs Research and Practice*, vol. 48, no. 3, 2011, pp. 279–96. https://doi.org/10.2202/1949-6605.6293.

Faigley, Lester. *Fragments of Rationality: Postmodernity and the Subject of Composition*. U of Pittsburgh P, 1992.

Gomez, Don. "An Army Vet's Take on Trigger Warnings In The Classroom." *Task & Purpose*, Sep. 28, 2015.

Gonzalez, Carlene A., and Marta Elliott. "Faculty Attitudes and Behaviors Towards Student Veterans." *Journal of Postsecondary Education and Disability*, vol. 29, no. 1, 2016, pp. 35–46.

Gravett, Karen, and Rola Ajjawi. "Belonging as Situated Practice." *Studies in Higher Education*, vol. 47, no. 7, 2022, pp. 1386–96. https://doi.org/10.1080/03075079.2021.1894118.

Grayson, Mara Lee. "The Trigger Warning and the Pathologizing White Rhetoric of Trauma-Informed Pedagogy." *Rhetoric of Health & Medicine*, vol. 4, no. 4, 2022, pp. 413–45. https://doi.org/10.5744/rhm.4002.

Herrmann, Douglas, Charles Hopkins, Roland B. Wilson, and Bert Allen. *Educating Veterans in the 21st Century*. BookSurge, 2009.

Hinton, Corrine E. "'I Just Don't Like to have my Car Marked': Nuancing Identity Attachments and Belonging in Student Veterans." *Journal of Veterans Studies*, vol. 6, no. 3, 2020, pp. 84–100. https://doi.10.21061/jvs.v6i3.211.

Hunter, Josalin J. "Clinician's Voice: Trauma-Informed Practices in Higher Education." *New Directions in Student Services*, 2022, pp. 27–38. http://doi.org/10.1002/ss.20412.

Institute for Veterans and Military Families, and Student Veterans of America. *Student Veterans: A Valuable Asset to Higher Education*, Nov. 2019 https://ivmf.syracuse.edu/student-veterans-a-valuable-asset-to-higher-education/.

Jones, Kevin C. "Understanding Student Veterans in Transition." *The Qualitative Report,* vol. 18, no. 78, 2013, pp. 1–14, http://www.nova.edu/ssss/QR/QR18/jones74.pdf.

Khalid, Amna, and Jeffrey Aaron Snyder. "The Data Is In – Trigger Warnings Don't Work." *Chronicle of Higher Education*, 15 Sept. 2021.

Lau, Stephanie J., Susan McKelvey, Christine H. Groah, and Elizabeth E. Getzel. "Unique Needs and Challenges of Women Veteran Students with Disabilities: Conceptualizing Identity in Higher Education." *Journal of Veterans Studies*, vol. 6, no. 3, 2020, pp. 101–09. https://doi.org/10.21061/jvs.v6i3.212.

Livingston, Wade G., Pamela A. Havice, Tony W. Cawthon, and David S. Fleming. "Coming Home: Student Veterans' Articulation of College Re-Enrollment." *Journal of Student Affairs Research and Practice*, vol. 48, no. 3, 2011, pp. 315–31. https://doi.org/10.2202/1949-6605.6292.

Martin, Travis L. *War & Homecoming: Veteran Identity and the Post-9/11 Generation*. UP of Kentucky, 2022.

McAndrew, Lisa M., Sarah Slotkin, Justin Kimber, Kieran Maestro, L. Alison Phillips, Jessica L. Martin, Marcus Crede, and Austin Eklund. "Cultural Incongruity Predicts Adjustment to College for Student Veterans." *Journal of Counseling Psychology*, vol. 66, no. 6, 2019, pp. 678–89. https://doi.org/10.1037/cou0000363.

Mercurio, Nicholas J. "Beyond 'Thank you': Recommended Modalities for Meaningful Civilian-Military Discourse." *Journal of Veterans Studies*, vol. 4, no. 2, 2019, pp. 1–33. https://doi.org/10.21061/jvs.v4i2.103.

Molloy, Cathryn. "Multimodal Composing as Healing: Toward a New Model for Writing as Healing Courses." *Composition Studies*, vol. 44, no. 2, Fall 2016, pp. 134–52.

O'Connor, Ashley Ann. "Please Don't Assume: Development of the Student Veteran Stigmatization Scale." *Journal of Student Affairs Research and Practice*, vol. 59, no. 5, 2022, pp. 516–28. https://doi.org/10.1080/19496591.2021.1997754.

Olsen, Timothy, Karen Badger, and Michael D. McCuddy. "Understanding the Student Veterans' College Experience: An Exploratory Study." *US Army Medical Department Journal*, Oct.-Dec. 2014, 101–108.

Shafer, Leah, Bari Walsh, and Matt Weber. "For Military Kids, Resilience and Challenges." *Usable Knowledge*. Harvard Graduate School of Education. 9 Nov. 2016, https://www.gse.harvard.edu/ideas/usable-knowledge/16/11/military-kids-resilience-and-challenges.

Student Veterans of America (SVA). *2020 Annual Report*, https://studentveterans.org/research/sva-census/.

Thompson, Roger. "Recognizing Silence: Composition, Writing, and the Ethical Space for War," in *Generation Vet: Composition, Student-Veterans, and the Post-9/11 University*, edited by Sue Doe and Lisa Langstraat, Utah State UP, 2014, pp. 199–215. https://doi.10.7330/9780874219425.c009.

UNESCO. *Reimagining our Futures Together: A New Social Contract for Education*. Report from the International Commission on the Futures of Education, 2021.
Wade, Carmen M. *Perceptions of Military Veterans' Advisement and Mentoring Experiences during School Culture Reintegration* (Publication No. 10282204). Doctoral dissertation, Hampton University, 2017.
Yuval-Davis, Nira. "Belonging and the Politics of Belonging," *Patterns of Prejudice*, vol. 40, no. 3, 2006, pp. 197–214. https://doi.org/10.1080/00313220600769331.
Zurlinden, Taylor E., Michael W. Firmin, Aubrey L. Shell, and Hannah W. Grammer. "The Lasting Effects of Growing up in a Military-Connected Home: A Qualitative Study of College-Aged American Military Kids." *Journal of Family Studies*, vol. 27, no. 4, 2021, pp. 523–39. https://doi.org/10.1080/13229400.2019.1650800.

CHAPTER SIXTEEN

REHISTORICIZING TRIGGER WARNINGS AMID THE POST-9/11 US SECURITY STATE

Kevin C. Moore

The idea to reconsider trigger warnings against a broader post-9/11 media and security landscape first occurred to me in light of an unexpected request for a content warning from a group of my own students. This request took place in a required, sophomore-level writing and speaking seminar I teach regularly for the Program in Writing and Rhetoric at Stanford University, where my course theme is "Propaganda and Rhetoric." In this course, students not only investigate propaganda as mass persuasion, but also as an essential component of discourse in modern, democratic societies. Propaganda as I present it is not necessarily negative, and it can often be positive, for instance in the case of messaging promoting an anti-smoking or vaccination campaign.[1] Like rhetoric itself, it is pervasive, although researching the influence agendas of propaganda texts can be especially challenging, in part because those agendas often disguise themselves. For outside observers trying to analyze propaganda, it can be hard to recover the intentions, not to mention the intended audiences, of propaganda texts.

One of the texts I ask students to engage with as an instructive model for addressing the challenges of researching propaganda is Steven Soderbergh's 2011 pandemic thriller *Contagion.* This film was also the subject of an article I wrote a few years ago after that film saw a surge of renewed interest during the early days of the COVID-19 pandemic (for a few days in March 2020, it was a top-trending film on several major streaming platforms). In my course, I show students how the film was created in collaboration with organizations including the Centers for Disease Control and Prevention and the World Health Organization, as well as several prominent scientists (Douglas). We also explore how and why the film adopted a deliberate agenda to raise awareness about respiratory virus pandemics as a tangible threat and moreover as an urgent matter of national security (Moore 2). In fact the original release of *Contagion*, produced and distributed by Participant Media—the same production company that created the influential documentaries *An Inconvenient Truth* (2006) and *Food, Inc* (2008)—was timed to correspond with the weekend of the ten-year anniversary of the September 11, 2001 attacks. The film thus also marks a historical point of inflection midway between the crises and media shocks of 9/11 and the outbreak of the COVID-19 pandemic (Moore 3). For COVID-19-era audiences, many aspects of the film were not just realistic, but uncannily so, including both its depictions of the chaos wrought by an emergent virus as well as its portrayal of the government's response. This is no coincidence. As the film's screenwriter Scott Z. Burns explained in a 2011 interview, he and Soderbergh sought to create an instrument of education regarding what might happen should a real pandemic actually strike (Douglas). The film deploys familiar pandemic terminology, including the concept of "social distancing," and it is well versed in the Bush administration's push to securitize the handling of potential pandemics beginning in the mid-2000s after the SARS-CoV-1 crisis and amid fears of the spread of H1N1 avian influenza (a process continued by the Obama administration).[2]

Retrospectively, I suppose I should have foreseen that this content could be potentially upsetting for students who had all too recently experienced the COVID-19 pandemic themselves. Beyond its advocacy agenda, *Contagion* is a sensationalist thriller, and it contains harrowing scenes of pandemic fear, including panic buying and hoarding, closed businesses and schools, closed borders, botched government operations, as well as graphic renderings of suffering from severe respiratory disease. So perhaps it should have come as no surprise when I initially asked students what they thought of the film, which they had watched at home on their own, and several students commented that they wished there had been a warning issued about the film. Two or three other students nodded in emphatic agreement. It quickly became apparent that the film had been challenging for a number of students in this group.

This request stayed with me for a few reasons. On the one hand, I understood my students' response as the response of people who had all too recently experienced the collective as well as the personal trauma of living through a real pandemic, which in many ways might be considered the 9/11 event of their generation in terms of media shock and disruption. I offered a sincere apology for any distress it may have caused, and said I would consider prefacing *Contagion* with a specific warning about harrowing pandemic content in future quarters. Yet it felt significant that this film, in a class focusing thematically on propaganda, had prompted a request for a trigger warning, given that the film itself seeks to be a preemptive warning about lurking potential dangers. This sense was related to a lesson I present to students via the film: how research into the film's agenda reveals that *Contagion* and its renewed popularity in March 2020 was *not* evidence of it being "prophetic," as some commentators claimed at the time. Rather, the film was designed to shape our perception of pandemics, and indeed to mediate the nature of our response. It provides a kind of affective glossary, presenting feelings and experiences quite representative of what many people experienced during the response to the real COVID-19 pandemic on a spectrum running from the uncomfortable to the traumatic. Insofar as *Contagion* feels uncanny, insofar as it triggers us, that's at least in part because the film helped to construct the affective reality of the pandemic response we had all lived through, and to show us and perhaps even to influence how individuals as well as governments ought to respond to such a crisis.

This classroom experience also got me thinking about how a specific concept I present in the seminar when we discuss *Contagion* offers a lens for rehistoricizing trigger warnings (alongside other kinds of preemptive warning scenarios) as they emerged amid the twenty-first-century

US security state. In my earlier article on the film, I argue *Contagion* represents an especially compelling example of the post-9/11 phenomenon the media theorist Richard Grusin calls "premediation" (that's pre*mediation*, not premeditation). Unlike prediction, or for that matter even propaganda (although propaganda can premediate), premediation operates according to a more open cultural logic. It's about imagining possible futures in order to mitigate their potential trauma, whether in fictional genres, journalism, or other forms, including social media. This criterion becomes helpful for understanding narratives and framings from the years following the terror attacks, especially those that became a warrant for policy, such as the Patriot Act, or conflicts like the US-led Afghan and Iraq Wars. As Grusin explains it, "Premediation is not about getting the future right, but about proliferating multiple remediations of the future both to maintain a low level of fear in the present and to prevent a recurrence of the kind of tremendous media shock that the United States and much of the networked world experienced on 9/11" (4). Cultural productions like *Contagion*, which seek to warn about a possible future containing traumatic events or outcomes, may or may not offer a serious agenda or argument to make about the shape of the future. They may or may not be "right" about the future. That is because, according to Grusin, premediating texts have another, usually unstated function: imagining possible, traumatic versions of the future "to maintain a low level of fear in the present," which then becomes a new baseline or background state against which future deliberative action plays out. Premediation does not necessarily imply conspiracy, or even propaganda, although it can certainly be exploited by governments and politically motivated actors. Rather, premediation is a cultural logic, a distinct set of practices and conventions for rational, deliberative discourse that emerged in response to the historical pressures of 9/11 and its aftermath.

To what extent do trigger warnings participate in this logic, insofar as they echo and possibly emulate in their conventions other kinds of safety and security warnings? As I have already mentioned, premediating phenomena are not limited to narrative fictions like *Contagion*. They can include many other genres and forms of communication that transpire in the "networked world." For instance, Grusin explicitly cites the many different media predictions of how the Iraq War would play out between 9/11 and the invasion of Iraq. Countless statements by government officials and pundits forecasted detailed, wildly various scenarios for the possible conflict. In Grusin's view, these, as well as new formats for transmitting visual and narrative representations of those scenarios, "prepared the media public to accept [the war] as a *fait accompli* when it actually happened" (46–47). This need not be part of a concerted plan or propaganda agenda, although aspects of the coverage (in particular the discussion of weapons of mass destruction) were clearly designed to be deliberately deceptive. These practices have become part of the culture. In a line that may be Grusin's most portable definition of the concept, "it is precisely the proliferation of competing and often contradictory future scenarios that enables premediation to prevent the experience of a traumatic future by generating and maintaining a low level of anxiety as a kind of affective prophylactic" (46). Instances of premediation act as a kind of "affective" or emotional spoiler, which regardless of actual intentions create a "low level of anxiety" in order to prepare us for a "traumatic future," which, in Grusin's theory, may then become or at least feel inevitable. Especially as smartphones and the wireless internet became ubiquitous in the late-2000s and 2010s, efforts to preempt, warn against, and mitigate perceived threats—whether terrorism, mass shootings, natural disasters, or viral threats—have become pervasive features of our increasingly securitized daily life.

Can trigger warnings, as part of a broader ecology of security warnings and other gestures that seek to preempt future trauma, be explained as a species of premediation? Intuitively, the answer would seem to be yes, although there are some distinctions when it comes to thinking about how this phenomenon plays out in classroom spaces. Historically speaking, trigger warnings developed in tandem with the other forms of premediation described in Grusin's theory. They made their way to classroom applications after proliferating in networked, online spaces, originally mainly support groups for survivors of abuse in the 1990s and especially the 2000s (and their very tendency to proliferate perhaps bears a hallmark of premediation as well).[3] Yet trigger warnings—in online as well as postsecondary classrooms—differ from these other forms because they usually seek to address accidental encounters with reminders of potentially undisclosed personal trauma rather than by imagining potential, future-tense collective experiences. Instead of abstract, generalized threats, they usually warn about specific, potentially traumatizing aspects of course content, which of course may or may not be actually traumatizing for a specific student in a given classroom. Yet they still have the potential to create a "low level of anxiety" in classroom spaces, and they do seem to seek to serve as an "affective prophylactic." The irony that my students requested a trigger warning for *Contagion* thus directs us to several provocative questions: How might thinking about trigger warnings as an example of premediation, and thus as a feature of the post-9/11 US security state, teach us about the actual cultural work that they perform? What other features of the US security state might impact and shape the cultural work and meaning of trigger warnings? And although trigger warnings originally and organically evolved to promote safe forums to discuss challenging material, to what extent has the discourse been shaped or even captured by devious political actors?

I realize this line of questioning might sound precarious to some. Let me be clear: I make these observations not as a critic of trigger warnings per se. On the contrary, I am of the opinion that content warnings *do* have a role to play in some classroom settings when approached rhetorically rather than as settled institutional procedure. I deploy them in my own pedagogy, especially in the context of representations and discussions addressing sexual violence and self-harm. One might even wager that classroom trigger warnings are always primarily rhetorical, and determined by factors such as exigence and audience, and when treated rhetorically they can become the tools of community building they ostensibly are meant to be. As a teacher who nevertheless worries, and for that matter frankly assumes that our pedagogical practices and conventions are not always under our control, I believe it is important to think about the possible ways trigger warnings may inadvertently intersect with or even serve the structures of the broader security regime alongside which they emerged.

A further exigence for rethinking trigger warnings amid the security state comes from the shifting political valence of skepticism regarding the practice. During the first decade of mainstream and academic discourse about trigger warnings, ever since Amanda Marcotte called 2013 "The Year of the Trigger Warning" (*Slate*), criticism about trigger warnings most often came from conservative, libertarian, or classic liberal political orientations. Perhaps most notorious among these is Greg Lukianoff and Jonathan Haidt's essay in *The Atlantic* "The Coddling of the American Mind" (2015), which dismissed trigger warnings as elements of a broader, liberal culture of campus "safetyism." Yet today, criticism increasingly seems to emanate from the progressive left, which is significant to the present discussion not least because progressives have generally been among the fiercest critics of the post-9/11 security state. Recent work by rhetoric and composition scholar Mara Lee Grayson, for instance, offers a fairly scathing indictment of the deceptive effectiveness of trigger warnings in the context of class discussions of racial trauma. In a June 2022 *CCC* article titled "Who Is It Really For? Trigger Warnings and the Maintenance of the Racial Status Quo," Grayson asks postsecondary teachers to reconsider which students and groups trigger warnings actually serve, as well as what structural and systemic baggage they may propagate.[4] Citing a dearth of empirical primary evidence on the effectiveness of trigger warnings in rhetoric and composition research, as well as the difficulty of trigger warnings—even focused, specific warnings—to be "responsive" to the actual causes of racial trauma for marginalized communities, Grayson worries they "operate within a frame of abstract liberalism that advantages white students" (708–09). At best, trigger warnings might accidentally acknowledge a specific content trigger for a student in a given class. Far more often, they probably serve to paper over actual sources of potential discomfort or harm on campuses, as a form of distraction or even denial. On this point, Grayson cites sociologist Tressie McMillan Cottom, who in 2014 observed the uneven distribution of trigger warnings in campus spaces as a problem: "No one is arguing for trigger warnings in the routine spaces where symbolic and structural violence are acted on students at the margins...Instead, trigger warnings are being encouraged for sites of resistance, not mechanisms of oppression" (Cottom). Or they could even cause damage. Near the end of the essay, Grayson offers this fairly damning analogy to describe the practice: "Like a Band-Aid available in one beige flesh tone and placed over a festering laceration, the trigger warning does little to address the depth of racial wounding or the cultural hegemony responsible for the cuts, and it may cause additional harm in the process" (714). For Grayson, trigger warnings are not just an evasion when it comes to addressing racial trauma. They can become complicit in exacerbating harm: a participant in historical and ongoing cultural hegemony, or even an instrument for whitewashing racial trauma. Reiterating the provocation she offers in her title, she asks, "If the trigger warning is not for those who are both traumatized and marginalized, who is it really for?" (711).

Who for indeed. To ask this question is not to suggest that many of those who deploy trigger warnings in the classroom or on syllabi are not earnest in their intentions to empathize with students' experience and mitigate harm. Nor is it necessarily to claim that all trigger warning practices are inherently harmful, although if harm or benefit from trigger warnings could be reliably quantified one suspects those metrics would fall along a nuanced spectrum, and would vary depending upon different kinds of warnings and contexts as well as who was offering them. Rather, Grayson's warranted skepticism raises the important question of how structural and systemic racism may contaminate trigger warnings despite ostensibly good intentions, which classifies them among other "seemingly just social practices" that "in fact uphold white cultural hegemony and perpetuate educational inequity" (Grayson 694). Like corporate statements of solidarity with protest movements or marginalized groups, trigger warnings may in some cases ring hollow and evade rather than confront responsibility for injustice, as well as draw attention away from (or take the place of) more meaningful practices of classroom community care. They can become but a box to check off rather than a practice that actually does productive social justice work, which in the case of Grayson's study means the work of antiracism.

Grayson's skepticism raises the question of what embedded structures and stakeholders the discourse of trigger warnings actually serves, and who it may harm as collateral in the process. A further dilemma emerges from the possibility that some of these stakeholders may be quite devious, in particular those operating in the shadowy background of contentious debates over campus free speech. According to Ralph Wilson and Isaac Kamola, campus free speech discourse has been so disrupted by an ultrawealthy "radical plutocratic libertarian movement" seeking to dominate the conversation that aspects of the discourse should be considered effectively hijacked (14). Their book *Free Speech and Koch Money:*

Manufacturing a Campus Culture War (2020) offers a "field guide" to "the integrated funding and political operation behind the so-called campus free speech crisis" (8), which involves sophisticated networks of well-funded ideologues, student groups, commentators, and provocateurs who all too often find their way onto college campuses. Focusing on the Koch donor network, Wilson and Kamola document the activity of figures and organizations who actively seek to capture not only campus progressive discourse, but broader discussions of free speech, academic freedom, and critical thinking as well: to manipulate these concepts and the language used to describe them, and to turn academics and especially campus progressives against themselves. The strategy involves "what some have called 'discourse sabotage,'" a method that involves "creating multiple, distinct-yet-overlapping organizations working together to manufacture the appearance of broad-based public opposition" (24–25). Wilson and Kamola report that these efforts have, unfortunately, been quite successful: "It turns out that the imposition of safe spaces, speech codes, and trigger warnings has been dramatically overstated. Most college students express strong support for free speech ...Far from suffering left-wing brainwashing, students rarely feel pressured to change their political views based on ideas expressed by their professors" (2–3). For Wilson and Kamola, in order to understand recent debate about free speech on college campuses, a debate that includes practices such as the trigger warning, it is necessary to "re-center" this debate "by following the money" (8). They argue, "what often appears as spontaneous local outrage is actually the product of a larger strategy" in which the Koch donor network funds not only campus student groups, but also the "provocative speakers" they invite to campus, as well as the media outlets, lawyers, politicians, and academic centers to exacerbate the perceived threat to free speech (4).

An encounter with Wilson and Kamola's "field guide" provides ample reason to rethink the extent to which the classroom trigger warning—the practice itself, and just as importantly the rhetoric surrounding it—may be shaped or even weaponized by well-funded political forces hostile to the supposed goals and ideals of pedagogical practice. When a well-funded right-wing provocateur such as Ben Shapiro lists the mantra "Facts don't care about your feelings" on his X (or, formerly, Twitter) profile—a statement that clearly evokes perceptions of the intentions of classroom trigger warning practices—he may not directly influence pedagogical praxis. As an utterance that is part of a broader rhetorical landscape, however, his comments nevertheless become part of the inertia fixing the discussion regarding trigger warnings on campuses. This includes the possibility of generating reflexive defensiveness against such rhetoric by some instructors.

Who is the trigger warning for? According to Grayson, trigger warnings can serve to uphold structures of racial injustice if not white supremacy itself. For Wilson and Kamola, trigger warnings, insofar as they can be flashpoints in broader campus conversations about free speech, may become entangled in a reactionary political agenda intending to disrupt organic campus discourse. Taken on their own, both of these reasons are sufficient to give teachers pause before automatically assuming trigger warnings are an inherent good to apply in classroom spaces. I propose both of these critiques also serve to further underscore the importance of, and in fact are a part of the question with which this account began: to what extent do trigger warnings serve the interests of the US security state, which has historically benefited from and promoted structural racism, as well as performed brazen discourse capture and sabotage?[5]

An especially revealing further clue occurs in the work of none other than Lukianoff and Haidt, the authors of the infamous "The Coddling of the American Mind" article, who briefly address security warnings and the post-9/11 security state in their theory of campus "safetyism," albeit only to offer an odd, premature dismissal of the topic. The moment occurs in the 2018 book by the same name as their *Atlantic* essay, which lays out the authors' conception of "safetyism" in detail. Not incidentally, Wilson and Kamola explicitly discuss Lukianoff and Haidt's work in *Free Speech and Koch Money,* arguing the "'coddled student' narrative" is neither representative of campus realities nor sophisticated (89). They see Lukianoff and Haidt and their theory as operating squarely within the plutocratic libertarian network their study documents, citing in particular Lukianoff's role as president of the extremely litigious campus free speech organization Foundation for Individual Rights in Education (FIRE) (87–89).

In a chapter of *Coddling* titled "The Bureaucracy of Safetyism," there is a brief subsection titled "See Something, Say Something," in which the authors lament one possible exigence for the regime of "coddling" they seek to identify: "It certainly did not help that today's college students were raised in the fearful years after the attacks of September 11, 2001. Ever since that awful day, the U.S. government has been telling us: 'If you see something, say something.' Even adults are told to follow their most anxious feelings" (Lukianoff and Haidt 203).[6] Lukianoff and Haidt then provide an image of a video sign that is an example of this campaign from a New Jersey train station, which provides the further advice, "If It Doesn't Feel Right, It Probably Isn't" (204). In response to this statement, Lukianoff and Haidt offer the following assessment:

> But that can't really be true. In all likelihood, there are millions of moments each year when some American somewhere thinks that something "doesn't feel right" and worries about an attack. However, there are only a few terrorist attacks of any kind each year in the United States, so in almost every case, the feeling is wrong. Of course, passengers on New Jersey Transit should alert someone if they see an abandoned backpack or suitcase, but that doesn't mean that their feelings are "probably" right. (204)

This is all that Lukianoff and Haidt have to say about the sign. They subsequently return to their discussion of campus culture, specifically to their outrage over a "Bias Response Line" at New York University (204). The post-9/11 security regime becomes but a further background context to help explain "safetyism." Yet strangely, the spirit of this particular species of safetyism—the brand promoted by the US Department of Homeland Security—is one with which they apparently concur, given their remark that "passengers...should alert someone if they see an abandoned backpack or suitcase" even though they would almost certainly be wrong to assume it actually presents a danger.

The contradictions of Lukianoff and Haidt's analysis of "See Something, Say Something" reveal several important features of the discussion surrounding security warnings, trigger warnings, and the politics of engaging with both as cultural forces. Significantly, these supposedly skeptical writers ultimately advocate consensus with the command conveyed by the New Jersey Transit sign, suggesting their support for (or possibly just their subconscious, personal benefit from) the assumptions and values of the security regime the sign represents (the most generous reading here may be an Althusserian one, imagining they have been "interpellated" or "hailed" by the sign (Althusser, 174)). Lukianoff and Haidt easily and mistakenly dismiss the instruction to question what "doesn't feel right" as part of a broader regime of state "coddling." For those of us observing the "See Something, Say Something" sign from a perspective that takes into account the larger system of the American security state, however, one cannot but say what "doesn't feel right" here is actually these authors' dismissal of the intentions of those who created this particular warning sign.

Who is this warning for? A security warning is not the same thing as a trigger warning. If Grayson's question about trigger warnings applies here too, however, then that may signal it is a related genre: a warning about potential danger or peril that does not necessarily execute the protective work that it claims to, and that in this case may perform rhetorical work participating in a logic of premediation. Although the transit warning may seem designed to promote safety and security, in reality—as Lukianoff and Haidt correctly point out—the sign exaggerates the potential danger likely posed by a randomly encountered unattended backpack or suitcase. The danger of terrorism is extraordinarily low, although paranoia about terrorism can surely lead to the undue suspicion, harassment, and persecution of bystanders who fit stereotypical, and very probably racist and/or xenophobic "terrorist" profiles. What the sign actually informs transit riders is how danger *could* lurk amid the supposedly quotidian, in the everyday suitcase left on a train platform by mistake.

One suspects the statistical odds of a trigger warning having a meaningful protective effect on student psychology and wellbeing (again, if such a metric were reliably obtainable) to be somewhat higher than the likelihood of Lukianoff and Haidt's wager that diligently reporting abandoned luggage to the authorities is a viable strategy for policing terrorism. What both practices have in common is nevertheless their shared status as genres of "warning" that have come to depend upon a logic of premediation: a set of interconnected cultural practices imagining permutations of possible dangers and traumas that afford an "affective prophylactic." They do so not to protect anyone in any realistic way, but in order to maintain a "low-level of anxiety" in the service of a broader security regime, which relies upon a culture of ever proliferating, abstract warnings. In this way, neither kind of warning is really much of a warning at all, at least not against the primary dangers they actually cite.

The recent work of Grayson as well as Wilson and Kamola make it clear that there are legitimate reasons to question the effectiveness of trigger warnings, and from progressive spaces. Despite their more conservative politics, Lukianoff and Haidt may appear to share with these scholars a spirit of skepticism. Yet their revealing dismissal in *Coddling* actually betrays their tacit allegiance to a US security state of hypervigilance against terrorism. It also provides an occasion for us to reconsider the inscription of trigger warnings—and indeed of all forms of safety warnings that have proliferated since 9/11—not as expressions of a campus culture of liberal or leftist "coddling" or "safetyism," but as manifestations of the logic of the security state itself. The specific, evolving agendas of that state are beyond the scope of the present chapter, although one would hope they remain under the control of democratic deliberation and oversight. But that such agendas *do* exist is an absolute certainty. Our obligation as teachers, and as theorists and observers of culture, remains one of questioning these agendas—including the proliferating, evolving "warning" genres by which they are conveyed and maintained—when something "doesn't feel right."

NOTES

1 This framework for approaching propaganda depends heavily upon Jonathan Auerbach and Russ Castronovo's "Thirteen Propositions about Propaganda."

2 Beginning in 2005, US President George W. Bush led a coordinated effort to fold pandemic preparedness into a US and global security agenda. For a detailed account of this history, see Thomas Abraham's "The Chronicle of a Disease Foretold: Pandemic H1N1 and the Construction of a Global Health Security Threat."

3 According to the *OED*, the earliest documented usage of the term "trigger warning" in this way occurred in 1993, on the Usenet newsgroup *alt.sexual.abuse.recovery*.

4 See also Grayson's book *Race Talk in the Age of the Trigger Warning: Recognizing and Challenging Classroom Cultures of Silence.*.

5 For example, one might look to the media debacle surrounding the so called "woke CIA recruitment ad" in May 2021, which outraged and confused critics on both the right and the left (Ongweso).

6 This is partially correct. The "See Something, Say Something" campaign was actually first deployed locally by the New York Metropolitan Transportation Authority, although similar messaging was used across the country. It wasn't until 2010 that the Department of Homeland Security obtained the rights to the slogan, where it became part of a national campaign and rolled out alongside the Nationwide Suspicious Reporting Initiative ("If You See Something, Say Something").

WORKS CITED

Abraham, Thomas. "The Chronicle of a Disease Foretold: Pandemic H1N1 and the Construction of a Global Health Security Threat." *Political Studies*, vol.59, no. 4, 2011, pp. 797–812.

Althusser, Louis. "Ideology and Ideological State Apparatuses (Notes toward an Investigation)." *Lenin and Philosopher and Other Essays*. Translated by Ben Brewster, Monthly Review P, 1971, pp. 127–86.

Auerbach, Jonathan and Russ Castronovo. "Thirteen Propositions about Propaganda." *Oxford Handbook of Propaganda Studies*, Oxford, Oxford University Press, 2013, pp. 1–16.

Contagion. Directed by Steven Soderbergh, Screenwriter Scott Z. Burns, Participant Media, 2011.

Cottom, Tressie McMillan. "Should There Be Trigger Warnings on Syllabi?" *The Society Pages,* 13 Mar. 2014.

Douglas, Edward. "CS Interview: Contagion Writer Scott Z. Burns." *ComingSoon.net*, 6 Sept. 2011.

Grayson, Mara Lee. *Race Talk in the Age of the Trigger Warning: Recognizing and Challenging Classroom Cultures of Silence*. Rowman and Littlefield, 2020.

Grayson, Mara Lee. "Who Is It Really For? Trigger Warnings and the Maintenance of the Racial Status Quo." *College Composition and Communication*, vol. 73, no. 4, 2022, pp. 693–721. https://doi.org/10.58680/ccc202232015.

Grusin, Richard. *Premediation: Affect and Mediality after 9/11.* Palgrave Macmillan, 2010.

Haidt, Jonathan and Greg Lukianoff. "The Coddling of the American Mind." *The Atlantic*, Sept 2015.

Haidt, Jonathan and Greg Lukianoff. *The Coddling of the American Mind: How Good Intentions and Bad Ideas Are Setting Up a Generation for Failure.* Penguin, 2018.

"If You See Something, Say Something: About the Campaign." *US Department of Homeland Security*, 21 Mar. 2023, https://www.dhs.gov/see-something-say-something/about-campaign.

Marcotte, Amanda. "The Year of the Trigger Warning." *Slate*, 30 Dec. 2014. Accessed 25 Aug. 2023.

Moore, Kevin C. "Readapting Pandemic Premediation and Propaganda: Soderbergh's *Contagion* amid COVID-19. *Arts*, vol. 9, no. 4, 2020, https://doi.org/10.3390/arts9040112.

Ongweso, E. "The CIA's 'Woke' Ad is an Absurd Psyop That's Melting People's Brains." *VICE: Motherboard,* 5 May 2021, https://www.vice.com/en/article/5dbbyd/the-cias-woke-ad-is-an-absurd-psyop-thats-melting-peoples-brains.

Wilson, Ralph and Isaac A. Kamola. *Free Speech and Koch Money: Manufacturing a Campus Culture War*. Pluto P, 2021.

PART FIVE

MEDIA ENGAGEMENTS

CHAPTER SEVENTEEN

"PLEASE LISTEN WITH CARE"

Learning from Podcast Content Warnings

Whitney Lew James

I listen to podcasts both to learn and to escape. At their best, podcasts—like all forms of media—help us understand the world around us. That world is often deeply troubling and upsetting. This means that my daily experiences, such as walking my dog, running errands, or cooking, are awash with warnings to "listen with care," a common refrain in podcast content warnings. Here are a few examples:

- "This show includes adult language and occasional descriptions of violence. Please keep that in mind when choosing when and where to listen."—Helen Molesworth, *Death of an Artist*
- "A quick note before we start: This episode includes a brief description of sexual assault that some listeners might find upsetting. If you'd rather skip it, I'll flag it again when we get there."—Sue Lin Wong, "Seeds of a Pomegranate," *The Prince*
- "So, we're going to be talking about calorie counts and weights today. You can't talk about fat camp without talking about those things. So, take care if those are going to be hard for you to hear. There will also be a couple of mentions of sexual assaults. We are

talking about some pretty distressing treatment of children throughout this episode. So, heads up there. I think it's generally pretty tough when it comes to this stuff. Like, I live in it a lot and I absolutely had to take some breaks to cry."—Aubrey Gordon, "Fat Camp," *Maintenance Phase*

Listening to podcasts can be a surprisingly intimate experience with hosts speaking directly to listeners about pressing and difficult topics. For me, the content warnings feel like respectful invitations to continue listening and engaging. Positioning podcast content warnings at the start of each episode both acknowledges that listeners have unknowable vulnerabilities and lived experiences, but also recognizes that we must face and explore these traumas to better understand the world around us and address oppression. After all, each of the above podcasts takes unflinching looks at things many of us want to turn away from: domestic violence, the rise of a brutal dictator, and fatphobia, respectively. Most listeners, including myself, come to these podcasts to be challenged, to be educated, and to reflect on the harsh realities that multiply marginalized people, ourselves included, face. Thus, the content warnings do not necessarily "warn off" listeners, as some critics argue, instead these introductory notices invite listeners to engage with difficult topics in ways that respect their needs and vulnerabilities. Importantly, these content warnings leave open what "listening with care" might mean for individuals. While the hosts suggest possibilities—choosing when and where to listen, skipping content, taking breaks to cry—listeners have agency to decide how best to care for themselves while listening.

More often than not, I am listening to podcasts during down times or breaks from my work as a university writing instructor. Like podcast hosts, as a professor of required writing courses, I invite students into a small classroom space and ask them to explore the world around them through deep research and thoughtful writing. Unlike podcast listeners, my students have little choice but to take my course, which makes the need to be attentive to the lived experiences of students and create space for student agency all the more pressing. Since 2020, beginning in the height of the COVID-19 global pandemic, podcasts and content warnings have become increasingly integrated into my teaching. The pandemic had and continues to expose our individual and social vulnerabilities. Although I was not conscious of it at the time, I understand now how the pandemic pushed me to be more open with and sensitive to my students. In this personal teaching narrative, I reflect on the ways podcasts and content warnings have become increasingly central to my teaching, even as I moved between institutions. While I offer no definitive guidelines for incorporating content or trigger warnings in the required writing or any other classroom, I do provide some insights into how I continue to develop my use of content warnings in light of student responses.

I use the term "content warning" in this narrative as an umbrella term for introductory notices about discussions or depictions of content that may be destabilizing to audience members. This draws on Kendell Gerdes' articulation of trigger warnings that emphasizes "the ability of words or representations to affect us without specifying a necessary outcome of this affection" (5). I reserve the term "trigger warnings" to denote what Disability Studies scholar Angela M. Carter describes as a specific physical and psychological response where individuals "mentally and physically re-experience a past trauma in such an embodied manner that one's affective response literally takes over the ability to be present in one's bodymind." While I do not want to remove my discussion of content warnings from Disability Studies or Feminist Disability Studies, I do want to recognize that students—and faculty—may be destabilized by texts without being explicitly triggered. As a woman of color, I understand all too well the pain of living in the United States, the country where I live and teach, as a multiply marginalized person, which can sometimes be triggering, but also destabilizing in other ways. For me, the term "content warnings" opens up the discussion to a range of different vulnerabilities and emotional responses, while respecting the specific experience of being mentally and physically triggered. Similarly, the concept of using "care" to engage with texts opens up a range of different approaches to being attentive to one's needs without dictating a specific response.

Part of the power of both content and trigger warnings is that they are evolving genres based in rhetorical sensitivity; that is, they are flexible and responsive to particular rhetorical contexts and the needs, expectations, and intentions of both rhetors and audiences. In her response to the public and scholarly debates surrounding the use of trigger warnings,

Amy E. Robillard argues that the use of content warnings in university spaces does not signify a rejection of the "real world" that students must inhabit, but instead is evidence that "we've played a part in shaping students who are sensitive to the workings of language, to the effects of trauma, to the workings of systemic oppression and injustice" (344). To me, the messiness of content warnings makes them a perfect fit for the required writing class where we foreground rhetorical sensitivity and audience awareness.

My personal journey with podcasts and content warnings began in fall 2020 when I incorporated true crime podcasts into my writing courses as a way of discussing how to conduct and present research. Given the ubiquity of content warnings in true crime podcasts, it seemed fitting to incorporate them in my course content, both in the syllabus and throughout homework assignments. For example, for two episodes of the podcast *Missing and Murdered: Who Killed Alberta Williams?* (Walker), which examines the missing and murdered Indigenous women and girls in Canada, I prefaced the homework "reading" assignment by noting that

> these episodes include discussions of systemic violence, including sexual assault, and systemic racism that might be upsetting and/or uncomfortable, but are necessary to understand the context of the crime depicted and to shed light on these historical and current issues. Please listen with care.

These content warnings served two related functions: (1) to alert students about the content and (2) to explain the purpose for listening to this content. The call to "listen with care" invites students to care for themselves when listening, while also suggesting that they "listen with care" for the subjects of these podcasts. Thus, I hoped to prompt students to take agency in their listening while developing empathy through learning. Stephanie Phillips and Mark Leahy write that if "[writing] instructors are asking students to risk, push boundaries, and thus construct more meaningful compositions, it is necessary that instructors consider how to create spaces that will best allow students to complete these kinds of assignments" (123). Although I did not ask students to create true crime podcasts, I required them to meaningfully engage with podcasts as required "reading" that pushed them to think about people and places that they might not otherwise. In keeping with Phillips and Leahy, I felt I had a responsibility to articulate the purpose for engaging with this content.

A year later in fall 2021, at my new institution, I began teaching a multimodal writing course that provides students with the options and encouragement to compose podcasts as well as content warnings. Although I still include a broad content warning in the course syllabus, I am no longer the one bringing in potentially triggering or destabilizing material into the course. Instead, students are now creating their own podcasts about research topics of their choosing. As you might expect, the range of topics is wide, from the fast fashion industry and racism in the criminal legal system to artificial intelligence and pay inequity. At the end of the semester, students create videos, podcasts, or websites developing arguments about their topic. Not infrequently, student research projects contain references to or discussions of destabilizing material, such as sexual assault, state violence, racial and gender oppression, and suicide.

Since fall 2021, I moved from raising content warnings as a possible genre convention of podcasts, to encouraging students to include content warnings with the drafts of multimodal projects at the end of the semester, to requesting that all students include content warnings on all drafts throughout the semester. This shift has been informed by increasing uptake of content warnings among students. Whereas I received little feedback or comments on the content warnings I provided with true crime podcasts, students seem to increasingly expect content warnings as part of their daily lives. In workshops, students began suggesting that their peers use content warnings within the videos and podcasts they created for especially sensitive material, such as discussions of sexual violence and suicide. Because students were expressing their expectations and need for content warnings without my prompting, I felt it was important to the culture of the classroom to make content warnings more central. The following semester, I began to require that students include content or trigger warnings on drafts that they shared for whole class workshops, where all students are required to review drafts of each peer's final podcast, video, or website. In the workshops, students continued to include content warnings for widely flagged material, but also suggested that content warnings could be used for graphic footage of head injuries sustained during football games and about discussions of Catholic ideals of masculinity and femininity. Providing content warnings for football and religious content reflects the local learning context: a Catholic institution with a deep football tradition and culture.

In the fall 2023 semester, during discussions about potential research topics, a student recognized immediately that to explore their proposed topic—work culture in Japan—they would need to include content warnings throughout their work in the course. Based on this early discussion about content warnings, I updated all peer workshop prompts to include language about the need to use content warnings as necessary, using the following language:

> If applicable, please also include a content warning for any potentially sensitive material in your [assignment] draft. Content warnings can help your peers more thoughtfully engage with your work and they are becoming an increasingly common genre convention across a range of mediums. For guidance on content warnings, see "An Introduction to Content Warnings and Trigger Warnings" from the University of Michigan.

While I do link to resources regarding content warnings, I generally leave the decisions about how to frame warnings and what content to warn about up to students. This requires students to think critically and thoughtfully both about the expectations of the evolving genres they are working in and the needs of their audiences, both the imagined audience for their projects and the addressed audience of their classroom peers.

During one peer workshop of visual arguments developed in the middle of the semester, students wondered aloud if a content warning was necessary for a cartoon-style depiction of blood in a visual about the practice of sportswashing, the use of sports by individuals, corporations, or governments to sanitize troubled reputations or histories. While the students laughed during this discussion, critically thinking about the effects that verbal and visual rhetoric might have on audiences is exactly the type of conversation that should be happening in writing classrooms.

Acknowledging vulnerability can "uniquely enable acts of empowerment and agency" especially for disabled and mentally ill students, writes Sarah Orem, and the use of trigger warnings by students "often serve as inventive devices, inviting authors to compose more expressive, visceral writing," Neil Simpkins argues (Orem and Simpkins). When instructors use content warnings, students can feel empowered and agential. When students use content warnings, they can more deeply and honestly explore the topics most important to them. Both uses of content warnings focus on developing rhetorical sensitivity and audience awareness, two of the most foundational elements of writing instruction.

In spring 2023, for the first time, a student included a content warning for their final project as a comment in our course learning management system (LMS). Including the content warning as a comment in the LMS, rather than only within the body of the project, emphasized that I, the instructor, was the primary audience for the content warning. At that moment, I thought of myself as an audience member not only as a professor completing the traditional work of assessment, but as a human being with a life, as a person who can be affected by language. The experience was profound. I can only imagine that some of my students experience this each semester when their peers include content warnings on the projects they share with one another.

WORKS CITED

"An Introduction to Content Warnings and Trigger Warnings." College of Literature, Sciences, and the Arts, University of Michigan, https://sites.lsa.umich.edu/inclusive-teaching/wp-content/uploads/sites/853/2022/04/An-Introduction-to-Content-Warnings-and-Trigger-Warnings.pdf.

Carter, Angela M. "Teaching with Trauma: Disability Pedagogy, Feminism, and the Trigger Warnings Debate." *Disability Studies Quarterly*, vol. 35, no. 2, May 2015, doi:10.18061/dsq.v35i2.4652.

Gerdes, Kendall. "Trauma, Trigger Warnings, and the Rhetoric of Sensitivity." *Rhetoric Society Quarterly*, vol. 49, no. 1, 2019, pp. 3–24.

Gordon, Aubrey and Michael Hobbes, hosts. "Fat Camp." *Maintenance Phase*, *Spotify* app, Jan. 2022.

Molesworth, Helen, host. *Death of an Artist*. Pushkin Industries, 2022, https://www.pushkin.fm/podcasts/death-of-an-artist.

Orem, Sarah, and Neil Simpkins. "Weepy Rhetoric, Trigger Warnings, and the Work of Making Mental Illness Visible in the Writing Classroom." *Enculturation*, 16 Dec. 2015, https://enculturation.net/weepy-rhetoric.

Phillips, Stephanie, and Mark Leahy. "Anticipating the Unknown: Postpedagogy and Accessibility." *Peitho Journal*, vol. 20, no. 1, 2017, pp. 122–43.

Robillard, Amy E. "Confronting the Real: The Trigger Warning Debate and the Rhetorical Space of the Classroom." *Pedagogy,* vol. 20, no. 2, April 2020, pp. 327–47.

Walker, Connie, host. *Missing and Murdered: Who Killed Alberta Williams?* CBC News, Season 1, 2016.

Wong, Sue Lin, host. "Seeds of a Pomegranate." *The Prince, The Economist, Spotify* app, 28 Sep. 2022.

CHAPTER EIGHTEEN

SPOILER

This May Contain Sensitive Content—Warnings, the Social Media of Books, and Colleen Hoover's It Ends with Us

Pauline Menchavez

A NOTE ON WARNINGS

Warning labels in media appear in a variety of contexts, often with varying degrees of meaning and specificity. For the purposes of this short chapter, it is therefore important to define their language and particular uses. Intended to caution the consumer that the material before them may contain disturbing information that could induce a traumatic response or uncomfortable experience, warnings play an integral role in how content is shared, produced, and perceived. The online platform *Language, Please* is a website created by Vox media in 2022 in collaboration with the Google News Initiative that consolidates information gathered by teams of DEI (diversity, equity, and inclusion) professionals and experts across academic disciplines, institutions, and organizations to provide a resource for writers, teachers, and creators to thoughtfully navigate the constantly changing social and cultural landscape of mental wellness and identity-related issues. They create a useful distinction between content warnings, advisory warnings, and trigger warnings: (1) content warnings "alert the audience to potentially sensitive material" on a more general scale and can be used as an umbrella term when discussing media warnings at large; (2) an advisory warning "signals to parents that the piece may contain content inappropriate for children or teens," like the Motion Picture Association's age ratings PG-13, R, or NC-17; (3) trigger warnings are "catered to individuals who have mental health symptoms that can be 'set off,'" and are used in specific situations ("Content, Advisory, and Trigger Warnings"). The main distinction between these three warnings is the audience they broadcast to. *Language, Please* gives the example that a veteran's counselor might use a trigger warning for gunshot sounds before playing a video about gun safety, but that warning would probably be generalized to "gun violence" for a broader audience. In this chapter, I use these definitions for clarity purposes. Take this also as a content warning for further sections as I discuss sensitive issues of domestic violence, rape, and suicide in the coming sections.

THE ONLINE BOOKSCAPE AND COLLEEN HOOVER

Most everyone can probably recall a time when a story surprised them: a character's untimely death, a second love interest, a friend's betrayal. These plot twists and turns make the reading, viewing, or listening experience entertaining. But what happens when these narrative elements deal with potentially harmful material like assault, rape, or suicide? For video or digital media, it's common for content, trigger, or advisory warnings to precede such sensitive information with the intention that audiences use these labels to make an informed decision on whether or not to engage with that content. Still, the use of these warnings is frequently and broadly contested by both academia and the general public. In recent years, collections like Jordana Greenblatt and Keja Valens' *Querying Consent: Beyond Permission and Refusal* or Emily J.M. Knox's *Trigger Warnings: History, Theory, Context* grapple with the complex and controversial implementation of content warnings in multiple sectors of culture and society. Journals such as *The Chronicle of Higher Education* or *Inside Higher Ed* routinely explore their use in the lives of students and university classrooms. Similarly, trigger and content warnings are a popular topic of discussion in outlets like *The New York Times* or *The Washington Post* and a topic of frequent debate in online forums or social media platforms like Reddit, Facebook, and Instagram. In both the academic and pop cultural spaces, opinions and conversations surrounding content and trigger warnings populate a vast range. From praise or condemnation to finding their appropriate rhetorical situation to the specific language used to warn, different institutions treat warnings differently.

Therefore, it is curious to notice in what spaces their use is more widely accepted—though there is currently no legal obligation to include them at all in the United States. As previously mentioned, new media platforms are more likely to come with a content or trigger warning. For example, Instagram has a "Sensitive Content Control" algorithm that sorts through posts and user-reported data that may go against their Community Guidelines and blurs the photo with a label stating, "Warning: This photo contains sensitive content which some people may find offensive or disturbing," alerting users before they can click "See Photo" (Instagram). For books, however, the implementation of these warnings is much less common. Similar to these widespread practices, in my experience as a student, instructors are much more likely to include a warning before showing a video or a photo than when beginning a novel. Perhaps a remnant of the outdated bifurcation of print vs. digital, it doesn't surprise me that instructors don't typically include warnings before reading and discussing the likes of Vladimir Nabokov's *Lolita* or Toni Morrison's *Beloved*—books themselves rarely come with warnings. In the case of the book, with limited cultural precedent and no institutional demand to implement content or trigger warnings in the classroom, it understandably follows that there's no sense of obligation to adopt this practice in the context of literature. In the introduction to *Trigger Warnings,* Emily Knox, an expert in information sciences, discusses the history of warning labels in books by tracking the evolution of the Library Bill of Rights' language and stance on such labels, as interpreted by the American Library Association (ALA). She notes that their "statement on labeling" in 1951 described that "libraries do not advocate the ideas found in their collections" and "no person should take the responsibility of labeling publication" (Knox xv). As of 2023, this statement now reads:

> Prejudicial labels are designed to restrict access, based on a value judgment that the content, language, or themes of the resource, or the background views of the creator(s) of the source, render it inappropriate or offensive for all or certain groups of users. The prejudicial label is used to warn, discourage, or prohibit users or certain groups of users from accessing the resource. Such labels sometimes are used to place materials in restricted locations where access depends on staff intervention... Prejudicial labeling systems assume that libraries have the institutional wisdom to determine what is appropriate or inappropriate for its users to access. The American Library Association opposes the use of prejudicial labeling systems and affirms the rights of individuals to form their own opinions about resources they choose to read, view, listen to, or otherwise access. (American Library Association)

For the ALA, warnings are an exclusionary act because they put a barrier between an individual and their right to access information. This statement takes a neutral stance in the value judgments of information and argues that both individual persons and institutions cannot assume responsibility for the content in the books they house, and therefore do not have the capability to implement warning labels—excluding illegal or banned content such as child pornography. This opposes how information is treated in the digital space, where the creator and platform regularly enforce content warnings. On one hand, the lack of warning labels increases access to information and reduces the dangers of confirmation bias, but also makes audiences privy to content that may be harmful without giving them the opportunity to opt out. On the other hand, warning labels deter certain groups from engaging with specific information and ensure that content is always mediated by an external source, but ideally would provide transparency that allows audiences to more effectively curate their content consumption based on their individual needs—though the efficacy of content moderators is flawed.

However, networks of online communities and fandoms on social media platforms emphasize a desire for consistency across both print and digital media. Should books and their industry be subject to the same level of transparency and warning labels as digital content? And if so, whose responsibility is it to disclose such information? The author's, publisher's, or reader's? With the growing popularity of Bookstagram, BookTok, and BookTube—niche names for book communities and literary discourse on Instagram, TikTok, and YouTube, respectively—the conversation around the use of trigger and content warnings in books intertwines with debates over what should or shouldn't be labeled as "triggering" or "sensitive" on social media and other digital platforms, demonstrating the increasing overlap of our physical and digital worlds.

These questions have especially taken the forefront in the controversial popularity of the best-selling author of 2022: romance writer Colleen Hoover. She infamously posed a series of questions in response to negative reviews of her 2016 novel, *It Ends with Us,* because of its lack of warnings. In a since-deleted article on her website, "My Thoughts on Trigger Warnings," she asks, "What if the writer doesn't want you to know that the book deals with rape? Or extramarital affairs? Or domestic abuse? Or cancer? Or the death of a child? What if the reading experience would be ruined if one of these issues was not meant to be revealed before reading the book?" (Hoover, "My Thoughts"). She goes on further to emphasize that "the majority of readers don't want to know a single thing about books before getting into it, so is it fair to lay out what might happen in the book before people read it?" (Hoover, "My Thoughts"). Here, she suggests that content and trigger warnings would spoil the plot and therefore ruin the integrity of the book. She urges readers to use third-party platforms like Goodreads and Amazon reviews to look for potential triggers instead. This aligns with the ALA's prerogative on warning labels in books: reading is first an internal, individual experience.

But Hoover's millions of Instagram and TikTok followers would probably disagree with this "fend-for-yourself" idea of readership. These online book spaces emphasize that individual reader response only accounts for a fraction of the experience, as users often look to their communities to decide what to read and consult book influencers and reviews to determine how their opinions fit in the larger group consensus. They also use these platforms to air grievances and keep creators accountable for the content they make—regardless if that content is print or digital. And although many of Hoover's readers agree with the sentiment that they like to be surprised when reading a book for the first time, a majority of them realize the importance of having some sort of warning in novels that depict sensitive issues, especially if the marketing of the novel does not accurately reflect the tone or content of its story. Evident in the criticism Hoover faces for marketing *It Ends with Us* as a romance novel, as many readers advocate that it unfairly and harmfully depicts domestic violence, such calls for content warnings push creators to be mindful about how to discuss sensitive topics with compassion. In the following sections, I use reader responses, including my own, to argue that the virality and controversy around Colleen Hoover and *It Ends with Us* demonstrates that warnings can be a multimedia mechanism of accountability when used appropriately: a rhetorical device to persuade users, instructors, readers, students, and consumers of media to practice inclusivity and empathy because they signify an acknowledgment of the needs of others.

GENRE AND PRAXIS

Made known by her social media presence and her no-holds-barred, visceral depictions of trauma and violence, Colleen Hoover used YouTube and Facebook to promote her self-published novels beginning in 2011 before being picked up by Atria publishing in 2016. Today, Hoover maintains her social media roots with newer platforms like TikTok and Instagram playing an integral role in her success. Although first published in 2016, *It Ends with Us* was the best-selling book of 2022. According to National Purchase Diary (NPD) Bookscan market research from Amazon and Barnes & Noble, 8.6 million copies were sold by October 2022—even outselling the Bible that year (Kaplan). In an interview with *Forbes,* NPD Bookscan executive director of business analytics, Kristin McLean, attributes this success to Hoover's inextricable link to these online book communities, stating that this resurgence in interest in *It Ends with Us* is "almost exclusively there because of BookTok" (Kaplan). And while readers are usually generous with their reviews—with the novel having a rating around four out of five stars across several platforms such as Google, Amazon, Goodreads, and Barnes & Noble—even those that enjoyed the novel critique it for the link it creates between romance and violence, with many reviews coming with trigger warnings of their own.

The novel in question is based on Hoover's mother's experience with domestic violence and tells the story of an abusive relationship between 23-year-old Lily and 30-year-old Ryle from its origin of questionable consent to the birth of their first child. In the author's note about *It Ends with Us*, Hoover details how the story of Lily and Ryle—and later their child, Dory—mirrors her own family situation. In the novel, Lily leaves Ryle but allows him unsupervised, shared custody of Dory, despite his recent history of domestic violence. Hoover's mother allowed a similar situation between Hoover and her father, who was an abusive alcoholic at the time. Hoover emphasizes the remorse her father feels for his violent past and states that through this story, she wants to highlight her mother's strength in forgiving her father, writing, "I fashioned Lily after my mother in many ways. They are both caring, intelligent, strong women who simply fell in love with men who didn't deserve to fall in love at all" (Hoover, *It Ends with Us*, 278). She also goes on to describe how personal a story this novel was for her and how seriously she took the subject matter, writing, "In the past I've always said I write for entertainment purposes only. I don't write to educate, persuade, or inform. This book is different. This was not entertainment for me" (Hoover, *It Ends with Us* 279).

This author's note suggests that Hoover understands the severity of the subject matter contained in her novel and views it as a narrative meant to "educate, persuade, and inform" her readers about the complicated nature of domestic violence; however, many of her readers argue that the marketing of the book as a romance novel, along with the deceptive language of the book cover and blurb do not reflect this sentiment. They urge her to use content warnings for this book to alert readers who may be sensitive to descriptions of such topics, as it's not apparent that *It Ends with Us* deals with graphic depictions of domestic abuse, rape, and suicidal ideation. Readers on Reddit write on the "*It Ends with Us* Colleen Hoover" forum, "My issue with the book is that it's marketed as a romance. IT'S NOT. The title comes from the victim telling her abuser that the cycle ends with him," and, "I actually think this book is harmful...the book is already labeled as a romance book and then for the ending to suggest that Ryle gets away with everything...It's targeted towards teens and young adults and it's just a shitty 'lesson' to give them" (Reddit). Similarly, the most upvoted review of *It Ends with Us* on Goodreads states, after a list of warnings, "Everyday I grow more and more concerned with the number of people who romanticize this book...[which] is marketed as a love triangle...Colleen Hoover employs the fact that Ryle is abusive as a plot-twist" (Community Reviews).

The main issue these readers have with the novel surrounds its genre and Hoover's choice to portray Ryle, an abuser and rapist, as a desirable, redeemable character and romantic leading man. In Table 1 I've put side-by-side the language of the book description and actual content from the book, which includes scenes of Lily's unstable mental health, Ryle punching Lily over a shattered dish and pushing Lily down a flight of stairs in a fit of rage, and him raping her out of jealousy and obsession.

The vague language of the book blurb leaves little indication of the true nature of the content of the novel, framing abusive and manipulative qualities as merely "stubborn" and "arrogant" and passing off a serious mental health issue as "hasn't always had it easy." In this description Hoover also suggests that readers should root for Lily and Ryle's relationship, as it is something they "built" together that is under threat. While back cover summaries are supposed to be succinct, they should also accurately reflect the nature of the content of the book. Another top-voted review from Goodreads summarizes the issue:

> Although I wholeheartedly respect the personal nature of this story, the author's note does not exempt this work of fiction from criticism, especially when it comes to a topic as serious as domestic abuse...This book is marketed as romance, and the synopsis makes it seem like a lighthearted love triangle instead of a woman's experience with spousal abuse...the tone of *It Ends With Us* feels acutely inappropriate. It reduces domestic abuse to a lovers quarrel and presents a tactless caricature of the realities of abuse. I can acknowledge this may not have been the intention, but the elaboration in the author's note does not absolve this book of its reckless and irresponsible marketing. (Community Reviews)

This reader notes that genre plays an important role in readership and audience expectation. The genre of a book communicates what literary tropes and themes it deals with and makes an argument as to how those narrative and rhetorical elements should be interpreted, suggesting

Table 1: Book Description versus Book Content

Book Description	**Book Content**
"Lily hasn't always had it easy, but that's never stopped her from working hard for the life she wants…	"As I sit here with one foot on either side of the ledge, looking down from twelve stories above the streets of Boston, I can't help but think about suicide" (1).
Ryle is assertive, stubborn, maybe even a little arrogant. He's also sensitive, brilliant, and has a total soft spot for Lily, but Ryle's complete aversion to relationships is disturbing…	"I'm instantly not laughing anymore. I'm on the floor, my hand pressed against the corner of my eye. In a matter of one second, Ryle's arm came out of nowhere and slammed against me, knocking me backward. There was enough force behind it to knock me off balance (139)."
As questions of her new relationship overwhelm her, so do her thoughts of Atlas Corrigan–her first love…	"My phone. Atlas's number. The stairwell. I grabbed his shirt. He pushed me away. *'You fell down the stairs.'* But I *didn't* fall. He pushed me. Again. That's twice. *You pushed me, Ryle*" (182).
When Atlas suddenly reappears, everything Lily has built with Ryle is threatened."	"His hand grips my ankle and he yanks me until I'm beneath him. 'I'm not angry, Lily,' he says, his voice disturbingly calm now. 'I just think I haven't proved to you how much I love you.' His body comes down against mine and he takes my wrists with one hand above my head, pressing them against the mattress. 'Ryle, please.' I'm sobbing, trying to push him off of me with any part of my body. 'Get off me. *Please*'" (200)

Hoover's use of the romance genre (1) obscures the graphic and sensitive subject matter, putting readers at risk; and (2) inadvertently leads her readers in romanticizing domestic violence. The front cover of the novel also adds to this deceptive narrative. This story about domestic abuse comes packaged in shades of light pink and floral accents, pictured in Figure 5. The original cover designed in 2016 and still currently in print also features a review from another author, Kami Garcia—a young adult romance and fantasy writer responsible for the famed *Beautiful Creatures* series that was adapted to film in 2013—a recognizable name for Hoover's target audience. The review states, "Everyone with a heartbeat should read this book," arguing for a universal reader to *It Ends with Us*. However, reader response indicates that while Hoover and her mother may have had a more positive experience in continuing to have a relationship with her abusive father, this may not be the case for every woman. It is because of this dishonest marketing that readers suggest adding warnings to the novel, a rhetorical device to signify that Hoover cares about the sensitive nature of her story even when the blurb and the cover are misleading—a disparity that readers argue betrays the cultural expectations of the romance genre and transforms Hoover's story into a sensationalization of trauma that dangerously associates domestic abuse with romance.

While the reviews excerpted here come from forums and comments posted after the novel's resurgence in 2022, criticism for Hoover's marketing goes back to its original publishing date in 2016, though Hoover has not commented on this issue since. In her only response to criticism about *It Ends with Us* (Hoover, "My Thoughts") she re-emphasizes the personal nature of the novel and attempts to establish ethos by framing herself as a woman telling an honest, personal story and a fellow reader who wants to preserve the integrity of the book by not spoiling the plot with warnings. She vehemently disagrees with the idea of trigger warnings in books, asking, "If the book deals with a sensitive subject that might be a trigger to a traumatic past event, a lot of readers like to know beforehand. However, what if that trigger is part of the plot?... Yes, as the author, I prefer my readers to go in blind" (Hoover, "My Thoughts"). Many readers took this as a morally questionable stance, especially as Hoover herself refers to these plot points as "triggers," suggesting that she is aware of their harmful capabilities, and because she equates triggers to spoilers.

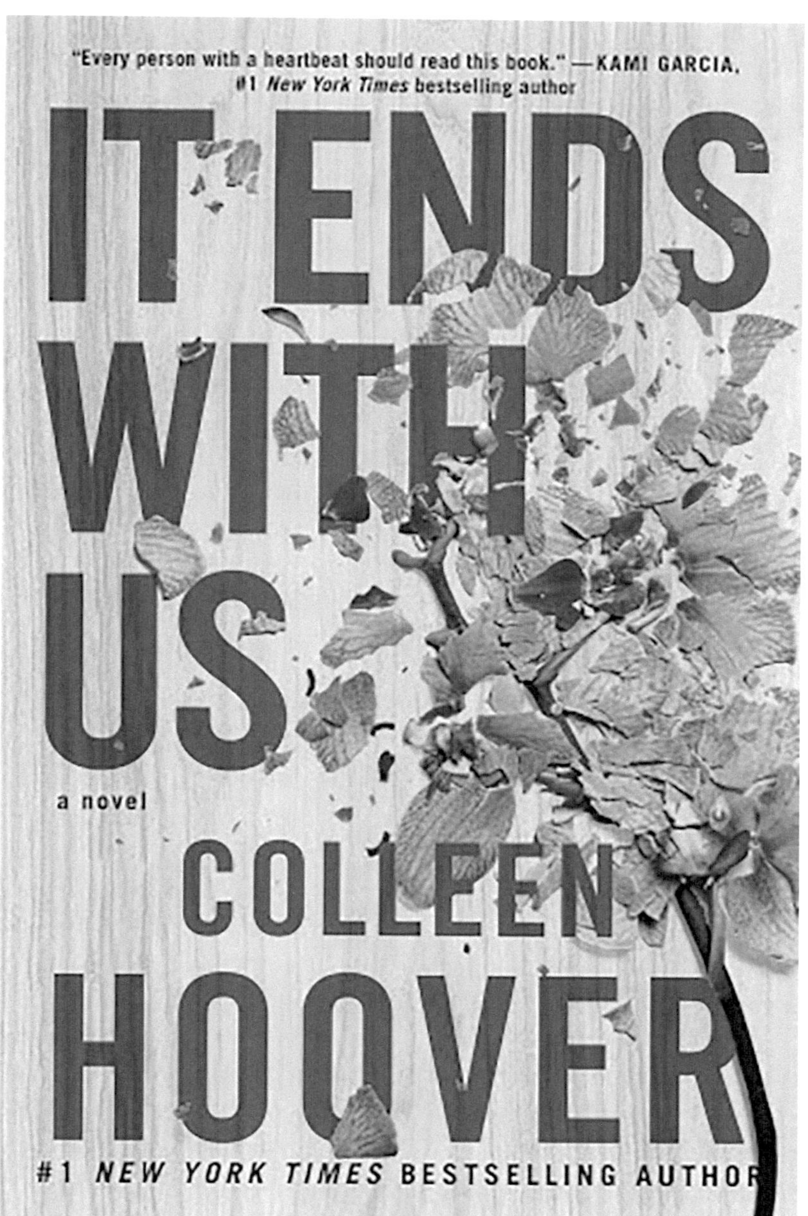

Figure 5. Original Edition Cover of *It Ends with Us* (2016)

She also assumes a stance of power by referring to herself as "the" author rather than "an" author, using a more direct article to emphasize that she is in control of the narrative surrounding her work.

And while she has every right to defend her story, especially one as personal to her as *It Ends with Us*, it gives this statement a placating tone rather than one of openness, a move in shutting down discourse instead of inviting feedback or collaboration, something she argues is a stylistic choice she takes in all her novels. She states, "I've received a lot of feedback, not only for *It Ends with Us*, but for every novel I've written...I've been faulted on this on more than one occasion and with more than one of my books" (Hoover, "My Thoughts"). She goes on to use this to defend her stance on why she chooses not to warn and "more than likely never will" (Hoover, "My Thoughts"). And although neither the book industry nor the institution of the author are democratic or participatory by tradition, the expansion of this field to include the social aspects of the internet—which Hoover utilized in both her self-publishing days and with her current social media presence via author-reader interactions and online book communities—makes these reader criticisms difficult to ignore without facing repercussions, whether that be economically or by risking reputation. Still, Hoover inconsistently claims that she values her readers' feedback and asserts that she has taken their criticisms into account, writing, "I completely understand the need for [warnings] which is why I'm writing this post...I feel this blanket trigger warning for all my future novels is a good balance" (Hoover, "My Thoughts"). However, this statement has since been deleted from her website and she has made no further comments explicitly addressing the criticisms of *It Ends with Us*, a notable choice considering the novel's 2024 film adaptation.

And although Hoover argues, "As a writer, I feel if I were to put in the blurb of a book that it specifically deals with cancer, or infant death, or abuse, then the reader will be waiting for that to happen as they read the book," netizens counter that warning is a common online practice that does not spoil the plot—Hoover herself acknowledges that "a lot of books have them" (Hoover, "My Thoughts"). Feminist writer Alexis Lothian, through her analysis of the language of warnings in fanfiction in her article "Choose Not to Warn: Trigger Warnings and Content

Notes from Fan Culture to Feminist Pedagogy," offers a way of including content warnings that addresses Hoover's claim that warnings spoil the story. For her, we must reimagine the "praxis of warning" as a mechanism of inclusivity rather than avoidance (Lothian 745). In alignment with Hoover's concern that warnings can be so specific to the point where they ruin the story, Lothian describes a method used by online fan forums to reimagine the system and language of warnings. She mentions the practice of "tagging" on the fanfiction website Archive of Our Own (AO3), which not only allows readers to know what sensitive elements the story might include, but also allows them to filter out stories that they don't want to read. It is the author's responsibility to attach the appropriate tags, and if they don't, they must select either the "Choose Not To Use Archive Warnings," signaling to the consumer that the story contains sensitive content but they chose not to tag, or "No Archive Warnings Apply," noting that no warnings were necessary. These labels include phrases like "Graphic Depictions of Violence," "Rape/Non-Con" (non-consensual), and "Major Character Death" (Lothian 747). Aside from these tags, authors can also choose to write their own, though these will not show up in the filtering system. But what is important about this practice of tagging is that it acknowledges that we operate in systems that reach audiences well beyond our intent. They account for the fact that not every author wants to warn while still giving users the freedom to decline to read without searching in third-party places, leaving little room for a situation where readers feel deceived or misled by the author.

Still, no tagging system or author or institution is perfect. Users could select "No Archive Warnings Apply" and intentionally obscure information. But the controversy surrounding Hoover and her novel reveals that audiences, to some extent, care about how stories are shared and represented, and their criticism over Hoover's lack of warnings suggests that this is one way to protect others from harmful information and to keep others accountable for how they depict sensitive topics. I don't blame Hoover for wanting to protect her authorial vision, and I do think uncomfortable stories like *It Ends with Us* deserve to be told. They allow survivors of trauma visibility and representation, but appropriate measures should be taken to ensure that audiences exercise the freedom to consume these sensitive stories at their own pace. By choosing to ignore her audience's call for content warnings for *It Ends with Us*, Hoover creates an argument rooted in the power of the author rather than an honest conversation with her readers under the guise of personal truth—a symptom of what I think is indicative of the growing pains of the publishing industry as it expands to include the impact and voices of readers and online book influencers as well as the further digitization of literary culture.

I work as a contract digital marketer and content creator for both traditional publishing houses and independent ones, primarily for debuting authors or writers of color in young adult and literary fiction. I receive an advance reader copy of a novel and create Instagram content to promote it to their target audiences and provide feedback on why I think certain stories sell well or why audiences tend to gravitate toward one author or the other. And while I think having a good story is the surest way to gain a loyal audience, in this age of online reviews and book influencers, readership has shifted to a more relational practice—a dialogue between other readers, authors, and publishers in which each party has a stake in choosing which pieces of information and entertainment enter popular culture. In my personal experience, the smaller publishing houses and independent authors tend to be the most concerned with trigger and content warnings—many of those I've worked with choose to warn in the pages preceding their book dedication—and making sure their marketing accurately reflects their book because of the closer relationship these authors have with their audiences. Although there are thousands of independent authors and publishers promoting their work online and connecting with others on the online bookscape, creators build a tight-knit community to share their work with. Some of my clients have become some of my closest friends. And while larger, more commercial publishing houses do not always have the resources or motivation to know their audiences in the same way, readers are now coming to expect some acknowledgment from them as a result of online book culture. As a product of the online indie publishing community, Hoover's choice not to warn her audience, not to take accountability for her morally questionable rhetoric, comes off, too, like a more personal betrayal.

MOVING FORWARD

Though I don't think any author or publisher releases a book with the explicit intention to deceive and harm readers, I do think that controversy surrounding Colleen Hoover's work signifies a need for more attention to be brought to how the social aspects of the internet are changing how readers, students, and consumers come to access information. Content and trigger warnings can be a way of combating the deceptive capabilities of rhetoric often found in the marketing and presentation of both print and digital media, something that signifies an empathetic acknowledgment of the audience in a changing and growing mediascape. I come from a generation of students and future educators who grew up embedded in the hidden literacies and social codes of the internet: a place where warnings are not only commonplace, but expected. Longer a participant in online fan culture and the digital forums, comments, and profiles of Bookstagram than I am a student of higher education, my interaction with literature and books has always had a digital component. And as future students enter classrooms even more accustomed to the online etiquette of warnings and tags, I expect the demand for warnings in the classroom to increase. While social media algorithms programmed to sort through content and determine potentially harmful information are far from perfect— with issues in racial, religious, gender, and political biases leading to unjust cases of shadowbanning—I do believe in their potential to promote more empathetic practices of sharing information.

WORKS CITED

American Library Association. "Labeling and Rating Systems: An Interpretation of the Library Bill of Rights," 2023, https://www.ala.org/advocacy/intfreedom/librarybill/interpretation/labeling-systems.

"Community Reviews." *Goodreads*, 13 May 2023, https://www.goodreads.com/book/show/27362503-it-ends-with-us#CommunityReviews.

"Content, Advisory, and Trigger Warnings." *Language, Please: Style Guide & Resources for Journalists and Storytellers*, Vox, 10 July 2022, https://languageplease.org/content-advisory-and-trigger-warnings/.

Greenblatt, Jordana, and Keja Valens, eds. *Querying Consent: Beyond Permission and Refusal*. Rutgers UP, 2018.

Hoover, Colleen. *It Ends with Us.* Atria Books, 2016.

Hoover, Colleen. "My Thoughts on Trigger Warnings," The Wayback Machine Internet Archive, 15 August 2016.

Instagram. "Introducing Sensitive Content Control." *Instagram Blog,* Meta, 20 July 2021, https://about.instagram.com/blog/announcements/introducing-sensitive-content-control.

"*It Ends with Us* – Colleen Hoover," *Reddit*, https://www.reddit.com/r/books/comments/wk04f8/it_ends_with_us_by_colleen_hoover/?rdt=52373.

Kaplan, Anna. "How TikTok Helped Fuel the Best-Selling Year for Print Books." *Forbes Magazine*, 1 Feb. 2022.

Knox, Emily J. M. "Introduction: On Trigger Warnings." *Trigger Warnings: History, Theory, Context*, edited by Emily J. M. Knox, Rowman & Littlefield, 2017, pp. xiii–xxi.

Lothian, Alexis. "Choose Not to Warn: Trigger Warnings and Content Notes from Fan Culture to Feminist Pedagogy." *Feminist Studies*, Vol. 42, No. 3, 2016, pp. 743–56.

CHAPTER NINETEEN

TEACHING "MEMORIES THAT SMELL LIKE GASOLINE"

Holding Space for Inner Rhetorics

Jessica Shumake

This chapter is a meditative essay that riffs on the contemplative writing studies scholar Paula Mathieu's concept of "inner rhetoric" or "the stories we tell ourselves about ourselves" in the context of teaching (178). While it is entirely possible that I have scrapped "perfectly good" assignment sequences and lesson plans due to "fears and doubts" (Mathieu 185) about them in connection to negative evaluations, it is also a fact that educators, specifically in the United States, are living and teaching in a political climate where fear of censorship is legitimate and educational gag orders are written into law. As the recent "CCCC Rights and Resources Document" makes apparent, building a sense of community within and beyond the classroom is more challenging than ever. As Mathieu acknowledges, place and time matter significantly, as do the material conditions of one's employment (178). As I discuss in this essay, the writing program where I teach first-year writing and rhetoric courses looks at "my teaching and teaching evaluations" as the main criteria for my continued employment (Rallin 16). Changing the material conditions in which one works and the process by which one is evaluated is an ongoing process that is beyond the scope of this chapter—I instead explore content and trigger warnings to follow Mathieu's suggestion of reorienting oneself by "focus[ing] on the sacred and important task of teaching" as opposed to reacting fearfully to negative student evaluations (184). Be forewarned that this essay twins with my inner rhetoric, and much of what I aim to communicate "does not seem expressible within the ordinary conventions of composition [...] I have been taught to construct" (Weathers 1). If you seek an argument here, it is implicit: I have experienced a chilling effect concerning what is possible in the writing classroom, and imaginative acts are required to explore what options exist beyond further investment in self-censorship and potentially self-defeating optimism; moreover, one cannot predict which course content might trigger trauma for students and suggesting students disengage for their well-being can look, variously, like students repeatedly changing seats, leaving the classroom, or performing disinterest and willful disconnection.

One of my most memorable experiences related to content warnings is the advice I received concerning my teaching philosophy from my dissertation adviser as I entered the job market a decade ago. I had written a draft of my statement of teaching philosophy in which I discussed implementing an anonymous Apgar system for student self-assessment during class meetings. I described how some students would disclose being unprepared for class discussions, often because they still needed to complete the assigned reading or viewing. This situation would result in an Apgar average symbolizing a lackluster discussion or the equivalent of a lifeless baby. My adviser noted that my statement of teaching philosophy could be a trigger for readers who experienced a stillbirth. Suffice it to say, no dead babies appeared in any version of my teaching philosophy after that conversation. With my adviser's feedback, I realized and corrected my mistake.

Before and after the birth of my daughter in 2023, I listened repeatedly to an audio meditation series authored and narrated by the Buddhist meditation teacher Kate Johnson. Johnson's meditations reliably brought up challenging memories, emotions, and sensations. Johnson's meditation, "Empowerment for Good Care," which can be found in her book *Radical Friendship*, resonated with me mainly because Johnson prompts her audience to think of someone who acted as an advocate, invoking a profound sense of care (*Radical Friendship* 69). Johnson further describes the meditation teacher Dipa Ma, whose name means "mother of light," as inspiring her—and many of her teachers—to engage in feeding one's child mindfully as a valid and equal path to solo meditation ("Feeding Baby, Nourishing Yourself"). I listen attentively to Johnson because these days, my life leaves me in awe of the time commitment and joy associated with human milk production and consumption. Caring for myself well is first and foremost in the season of life in which I find myself as I struggle to write, teach, and build community. I am forty-eight and a parent to two wanted children, a one-year-old and a four-year-old. My interest in writing about and understanding trigger warnings is connected to my vocation as a writing teacher, which is how I earn my living. Loving myself enough to write these words and share them is an act of resistance against inner rhetoric that suggests my silence—on the negative impact of being heavily pregnant and an outspoken feminist, among other identity markers and classroom content choices, can have on one's teaching evaluations—will protect me from being vulnerable to the inevitable criticism of colleagues, committees, deans, students, and others. If one believes, as I naively allowed myself to, that "promotion decisions" will be made mindfully with ethical consideration of the fact that "[s]tudents' judgments of professors are more than just an assessment of the professor's teaching abilities; what students learn about their professors as people, including their social roles, influences students' expectations and ultimately their evaluations," one should simultaneously steel themselves for the possibility that student evaluations may be leveraged against them as an outgrowth of the unequal gendered and other ideologies that are a fact of daily life (Baker and Copp 41–42).

When I call to mind people without whose support I would not have the career and educational credentials I do, one mentor stands out. I decided to withdraw from a PhD program in philosophy ABD in 2005–2006, and I taught my first writing course, "Writing: Process and Practice," at York University in Toronto. Aneil Rallin designed the course curriculum and assignments in the course I taught. Working with Rallin put me on a path that led to where I find myself today. I share this narrative because, when visualizing a standout mentor and teacher, I sometimes find myself overcome by tears and outrage when I think about the lack of basic respect Rallin experienced from administrators at Soka University of America (Morey 9). Soka is a private, Buddhist liberal arts college in California where Rallin taught for sixteen years and was tenured and recognized as "Professor of the Year" on three occasions—this is in addition to teaching for thirty-three years at eight other universities in the United States and Canada. Administrators at Soka cited complaints from students related to the alleged use of "triggering" course content and failing to create a "safe space" in the classroom as grounds for pursuing disciplinary action and dismissal (qtd. in Piro and Morey).

In the wake of Rallin's separation from Soka University, I, too, received feedback—by way of student midterm and end-of-course evaluations—that students perceived some of the content in my first-year writing classes as "triggering." Even though I teach at the University of Notre Dame, which is a private Catholic university in the Midwest, as I considered my students' feedback, Soka faculty member Ryan Ashley Caldwell's prescient observation that what happened to Rallin "could happen to me" resonated and continues to resonate with the stories I tell myself about teaching and its inherent risks (qtd. in Flaherty). Students' words have power, and accusations of failing to care well for the hurt or trauma they inevitably carry can cause more than reputational damage and potential loss of employment; it creates a chilling effect on one's willingness to teach difficult texts, to make space for students to write about risky topics, and to have meaningful conversations about what students write in response to risky topics and texts. Again, Johnson's wise words offer some perspective that helps me make sense of allegations of failing to demonstrate adequate care for students in the writing classroom: "I've frequently had encounters with whole groups of people who seem poised to struggle with me. It happens most often when I'm in a position of authority—teaching, facilitating, leading in some way—among people who have greater privilege than I do in society at large" (*Radical Friendship* 57). Those power struggles are compounded for me, as the median family income of the students I teach at Notre Dame is "$191,400, and 75% come from the top 20 percent" ("Economic Diversity and Student Outcomes at Notre Dame"). I hail from a blue-collar family where my father was the sole breadwinner and worked as a photocopier repair technician throughout his career. My mother has a disabling form of epilepsy. I attended public schools and universities my entire life and am the first person in my family to earn a college degree. Yet, as I marvel at how my path to being a faculty member at the University of Notre Dame does not look like most of my colleagues, it is not just class differences that make me a non-typical faculty member. Many of the students I work with hail from strict religious backgrounds and struggle when they choose to research topics, such as pornography addiction, on their own terms. I respect the struggle and approach students as whole people while seeking to embrace whatever tensions arise in the process. Since it is impossible to predict which content, research, or conversations may trigger students, I consistently encourage them to take the necessary time and space to process their reactions to the texts we study, including student-produced material, in a controlled environment outside the classroom. I include some variation of the following disclaimer on my syllabus:

> The topics we engage with in the course *may* be triggering. If this is the case, take care of yourself and know you can always disengage for your well-being. Your mental health and safety are of the utmost importance to me. When we discuss sensitive topics, student writing, and other content as a class, you are always invited to step outside class to take care of yourself. Trust that I take your mental health needs seriously and do not expect anyone to share personal information about past trauma. Additionally, I ask you all to please trust that I do not judge those who put their mental health first by disengaging when it comes to triggering content. I will never *require* you to engage with or write about images or content that is disorienting, distressing, or traumatizing. (Syllabus)

A question that looms large for me is what happens when content is excised preemptively from one's syllabi due to complaints—or the fear of complaints—that the content may be triggering to some. Additionally, I fear that some assignment sequences are so open-ended that students from strict religious backgrounds will embrace the opportunity to pursue risky research—out of personal interest—that could reflect negatively on me if a parent learns of "prurient" interests being given the space for inquiry.

In the writing program where I teach, all syllabi are available in a shared Google Drive archive for current and future instructors. As Michel Foucault contends, archives are "first the law of what can be said" (129). Further, Foucault explains that archives are "systems of statements (whether events or things)" with illocutionary force that serve an "enunciative function" (128–30). To say that an archive has illocutionary force means that current and future instructors' perceptions of risk, value, and meaning are maintained, altered, and reproduced by what goes into and is excluded from our writing program's syllabus archive. Syllabus archives serve as sites of enunciation that tacitly articulate institutional power structures that determine what is valued and taught. The notion that any instructor could refrain from teaching content and images that require a content warning is untenable because one cannot know what might trigger a traumatic reaction in another person. Trigger warnings are used in online spaces—in domains as diverse as fan fiction sites and YouTube videos—such that the following rangy list of triggers exists in the wild: "swearing, sex, male/male, pregnancy, addiction, spiders, bullying, suicide, sizeism, ableism, homosexuality, violence, abuse, transphobia, slut-shaming, victim-blaming, alcohol, blood, insects, small holes, hand job, and animals in wigs" (Brown 98). When I taught honors composition at the University of Arizona, I had a student who explained that seeing others' exposed toes triggered her to feel aversion and anxiety. Since Tucson is warm and many people on campus wear sandals year-round, I asked her to please feel free to move around the classroom as needed, and she told me this level of flexibility was beneficial to her learning. My current institution requires evidence of a faculty member's "salutary influence on colleagues and students," which means creating an environment that is holistically beneficial to all, to be eligible for promotion to or reappointment as an associate teaching professor (University Writing Program). Holding space for students to write about unsalutary or questionable topics of their choosing—especially when students may reach conclusions that are at odds with the Catholic Church—is risky at best.

In one of my recent first-year writing courses at the University of Notre Dame, a student-contributed photograph, which was part of a weekly collaborative photo activity, gave rise to an impromptu conversation about architecture, suicide-prevention measures, memorializing student suicides, and locations on college campuses where student suicide is an aspect of design history. In a subsequent anonymous midterm evaluation of the course, a student's most memorable moment of the semester was how I "carelessly" handled the discussion of the student-contributed photo of a vertigo-inducing stairwell on our campus, which the student who took the photo casually discussed captioning "downward spiral." Later that same semester, another student in the same class left a museum gallery viewing distraught after choosing to rhetorically analyze Dan Budnik's "Boy Peering Through the Berlin Wall," which is a black and white photograph from 1961 of a child grasping barbed wire and balancing on a pile of cinder blocks. The student, later, in an email to me, described traumatic memories of growing up in a war-torn border region and shared painful memories of witnessing murder and violence in Gaza. If our class felt like a space conducive to sharing her traumatic experience, that student may have stayed and shared with her peers. However, a white female student dominated the class and continuously distracted others by demonstratively reading messages on her smartwatch and actively signaling that she would rather be anywhere else. Perhaps the distracting student's behavior is an unintended consequence of my disclaimer that students should disengage when they feel triggered. Hence, her semester-long performance of Bartleby-esque "I would rather not" was part of her taking care of herself.

Given that the visual and rhetorical analysis of images has the potential to open and hold space for conversations about difficult topics—and the inevitable burdens, embodiments, and histories students carry with them into the writing classroom—that potential becomes challenging to realize when students choose to disconnect from one another or when student distress, tears, or emotional expression are interpreted as me being insensitive and "ignorant" to the affective needs of "international students."[1] Although I encouraged students to leave when they needed to care for themselves and process overwhelming emotions, I still faced criticism that I handled students' differing emotional responses to classroom content imperfectly. Such criticism leads me to wonder if the benefit of analyzing documentary photographs, which can easily elicit emotionally charged responses from students, is outweighed by the cost of needing to defend myself from accusations that I am, for example, gratuitously "showing photos of self-harm" and saying "triggering things about suicide" during class meetings. Student feedback in this vein hits home because my impact in no way aligns with my intentions for a mandatory general education course. Indeed, some students tell me they wish their Advanced Placement test scores exempted them from being required to take such a course in the first place.

I value marginalized, silenced, and excluded perspectives. However, I am also aware that what Augusto Boal and Susana Epstein have referred to as the "cop in the head" has become increasingly prominent in my mind due to student perceptions that I handled sensitive topics like mental health, student well-being, and suicide carelessly. This has led me to self-censor and seek refuge in silence, long pauses, closing my eyes, and indirect communication. As a non-tenure-eligible instructor, I am reviewed annually and never aim to accrue negative student evaluations. However, despite the risks to my continued employment and recent student criticism, I have continued to hold space for writing about topics such as mental health and psychiatric hospitalization. These topics are largely undiscussable at the University of Notre Dame except through photographs such as Mary Ellen Mark's 1976 "Brenda Sitting on Her Bed, Ward 81, Oregon State Hospital, Salem." It is arguably foolhardy to continue to curate and organize excursions to the campus art museum to view and discuss challenging documentary photographs. Yet, the alternative felt like capitulating to or collapsing under the weight of unearned criticism that I do not possess the teaching skills or dexterity required to accompany students well as they write and communicate about challenging topics without throwing them into what the writer Eli Clare describes as a "visceral tailspin" (xix).

I am who I am because of the good care I received from the teachers and mentors who believed in me, even though I needed wise counsel to remove references to dead babies from my job market materials. In what now feels like a lifetime ago, in a course titled "Sex, Health, and AIDS" in the Gender and Women's Studies Department at the University of Arizona, I taught the work of the multimedia artist, writer, and public intellectual, David Wojnarowicz—who is the antithesis of a milquetoast coward when he describes being raped, assaulted, and left for dead as a young, queer adolescent. Wojnarowicz sees his rapist exiting a screening of the movie *Stand by Me* in 1986 and finds himself frozen in a panic attack and flashback as he recalls the moment he thought his rapist was planning to burn him alive after brutalizing him and pouring what he thought was gasoline on him. What might students at the University of Notre Dame think, say, and write if I was brave enough to include Wojnarowicz's "Memories That Smell Like Gasoline" on a syllabus? I wish I could muster the courage to find myself arm-deep in a conversation about what one can learn about embodied writing from Wojnarowicz. I know that without first offering a content warning, I would altogether "lose access to conversations" such as the one Wojnarowicz's essay opens (Clare xix). I wish the worst-case scenario I can imagine in teaching Wojnarowicz's essay at the University of Notre Dame is reflecting upon unfavorable student evaluations of my inevitably imperfect efforts to facilitate challenging conversations. Yet, this line of thinking requires a flight of imagination and remains "a fantasy" (Rallin 96). I am chilled to the marrow—and not even the fires in the bellies of my beloved queer mentors and antecedents make me feel brave. But, still, the fire in my belly burns.

NOTE

1 This and all anonymous student end-of-semester Course Instructor Feedback (CIF) survey comments are quoted in their original form.

WORKS CITED

Baker, Phyllis, and Martha Copp. "Gender Matters Most: The Interaction of Gendered Expectations, Feminist Course Content, and Pregnancy in Student Course Evaluations." *Teaching Sociology*, 1997, pp. 29–43.

Boal, Augusto, and Susana Epstein. "The Cop in the Head: Three Hypotheses." *The Drama Review (TDR)*, vol. 34, no. 3, 1990, pp. 35–42.

Brown, Maury Elizabeth. "Pulling the Trigger on Player Agency." *The Wyrd Con Companion Book 2014*, vol. 1, no. 4, 2013, pp. 96–109.

Budnik, Dan. "Boy Peering Through the Berlin Wall (1961)." *Marble*, 30 Aug. 2023, https://marble.nd.edu/item/2015.056.

"CCCC Rights and Resources Document." *Rights and Resources for Anti-CRT, Anti-trans, Anti-2SLGBTQ+ Censorship and Workplace, Public, or Social Media Mobbing*. 30 Nov. 2023, https://cccc.ncte.org/wp-content/uploads/2023/09/Sept2023_CCCC_Resource.pdf.

Clare, Eli. *Brilliant Imperfection: Grappling with Cure*. Duke UP, 2017.

"Economic Diversity and Student Outcomes at Notre Dame." *The New York Times*, 18 Jan. 2017, https://www.nytimes.com/interactive/projects/college-mobility/notre-dame

Flaherty, Colleen. "'Faculty Should be Outraged.'" *Inside Higher Ed.*, 15 May 2022, https://www.insidehighered.com/news/2022/05/16/university-could-fire-writing-professor-over-deviant-pornography

Foucault, Michel. "Part III: The Statement and the Archive." *The Archaeology of Knowledge and The Discourse on Language*. Tavistock Publications, 1972, pp. 79–126.

Johnson, Kate. *Radical Friendship: Seven Ways to Love Yourself and Find Your People in an Unjust World*. Shambala, 2021.

Johnson, Kate. "Feeding Baby, Nourishing Yourself." *Calm* app, version 6.54. Calm.com, Inc. 2024.

Mark, Mary Ellen. "Brenda Sitting on Her Bed, Ward 81, Oregon State Hospital, Salem (1976)." Marble, 31 Aug. 2023, https://marble.nd.edu/item/2014.056.

Mathieu, Paula. "Excavating Indoor Voices: Inner Rhetoric and the Mindful Writing Teacher." *Journal of Advanced Composition (JAC)*, vol. 34, nos.1–2, 2014, pp. 173–90.

Morey, Alex. "Letter to Edward M. Feasel." *Foundation for Individual Rights and Expression (FIRE)*, 11 May 2022, https://www.thefire.org/research-learn/fire-letter-soka-university-america-may-11-2022.

Piro, Graham, and Alex Morey. "Soka Professor Unjustly Punished for 'Triggering' Students with Readings on 'Writing the Body' Gets Split Decision from Faculty Committee of Just Two." *Foundation for Individual Rights and Expression (FIRE)*, 9 June 2022, https://www.thefire.org/news/soka-professor-unjustly-punished-triggering-students-readings-writing-body-gets-split-decision.

Rallin, Aneil. *Dreads and Open Mouths*. Litwin Books, 2019.

Syllabus for Writing and Rhetoric 13100. Taught by Jessica Shumake, Fall 2024, U of Notre Dame, Notre Dame, Indiana.

University Writing Program. "Organization Plan for The Committee on Appointments and The Committee on Reappointments and Promotion." 22 Aug., 2024, https://facultyadministration.nd.edu/.

Weathers, Winston. *An Alternate Style: Options in Composition*. Hayden Book Company, 1980.

Wojnarowicz, David. "Memories that Smell Like Gasoline." *Memories that Smell Like Gasoline*. Artspace Books, 1992, pp.15–26.

AFTERWORD

Trigger Warnings, Trauma, and Their "Affects"

Anu Aneja

To offer an afterword for a book whose main subject serves as *fore*warning seems, at first, out of time. And yet, perhaps because trigger warnings, like cliffhangers of a precipitous teleology, always precede the unknown traumatic aftereffects they augur, they elicit a retrospection on this cause-and-effect temporality. In many ways, the diverse epistemic positions on trigger warnings, teaching, and trauma represented in this collection already suggest countercurrents to such a linear teleology. In defending, bolstering, questioning, dismantling, and even rejecting their importance for a progressive pedagogy, the voices gathered here call for a nuanced approach to our understanding, use, and relevance of trigger warnings in their relation to trauma. "Teaching through trauma," incorporated in the title, reminds us that whether we choose to acknowledge it or not, trauma may be an uninvited guest in our classrooms just as it is in the world outside. Through varied interventions, the contributors of this book ask how students and instructors might encounter/engage with/avoid "dangerous" content—words, images, sounds, and meanings that threaten to resuscitate trauma's memory, aggravate it, or even produce it for the first time among an unprepared audience. Exploring the many tensions lodged in the crevices between the "before" of trigger warnings and the "after" of trauma's effects, these diverse perspectives investigate the (in)appropriateness of trigger warnings in the interest of a democratic pedagogical contract. Such a progressive pedagogy, as Paulo Freire, bell hooks, and others have previously explored, embraces a view of students and teachers as whole, embodied human beings who bring to the classroom life experiences not confined to designated pedagogical spaces.[1]

This book evokes provocative questions: Are trigger warnings warranted in pedagogical contexts? How do understandings of trigger warnings and trauma determine how we view their interrelationships? Who is the intended audience of trigger warnings? Who gets left out? Who determines which content may be triggering, for whom, and on what basis? What is a "safe" classroom space? Do trigger warnings actually do the protective, caring work against trauma they are intended for, or can they be counter-therapeutic? When does "care" slide away from its intended purpose and prevent engagements with potentially transformative material? And a couple that strike me as particularly apropos at the moment in which we find ourselves: To what extent are the traumatic dangers foreshadowed by triggering content predetermined and constituted by the systemic nexuses of the heteropatriarchal, neoliberal, capitalist economies within which educational institutions function today? Relatedly, is it possible to conceive of trigger warnings in a way that does not reify the oppressive systemic forces that necessitate them in the first place, or that does not foreclose a "counter-hegemonic" resistance as argued in this book by Walter Lucken IV (Chapter 13)? Given the knotty nature of these questions, a forewarning for what follows may be fitting here: *This afterword offers no easy answers to these complex questions. Rather, it is very likely that it may only lead to other equally/more troubling questions.*

As reflected in the preceding chapters, it is clear that for many instructors and students, trigger warnings have come to signify critical measures of a pedagogy of care toward those who may be at risk of being re-traumatized in their encounters with triggering content. On this side of the debate, trigger warnings represent an effective tool in constructing the classroom (ideally) as a "safe space" that capacitates students to make agentic choices about their engagement with pedagogical materials.

They can serve the important function of preempting emotional risk among vulnerable students, allowing them time and space to consider and make decisions about their encounters with potentially disturbing content. Trigger warnings may also be relied upon by instructors as survival strategies against the precarity of tenure and employment security[2] in university systems, especially given recent cultural assaults from the Right on educational curricula. On the other side, many are plagued by serious doubt about their benefits, with some seeing trigger warnings as counter-therapeutic and signifying "the coddling of the American mind," as signaled by the title of a 2015 essay by Greg Lukianoff and Jonathan Haidt.[3] Among those troubled by their use, there is unease about the detrimental impact of trigger warnings on academic freedom, as was the case when students at Oberlin first proposed their implementation in college classrooms in 2013–14 (Flaherty). Given increasingly virulent attacks on subjects including critical race theory, gender identity, and trans rights, these concerns have become even more pressing. Perceiving trigger warnings as flagging a culture of censorship and/or auto-censorship, those opposed balk at any suggestions to make them mandatory. With escalating encroachments on academic freedom, it is not inconceivable that institutional pressures against faculty whose views are perceived as misaligned with those of the institution may only intensify. Unrestrained control over faculty employment conditions in a corporatized education industry can result in brazen misuse of the discourse of trauma, student safety, and wellness to target individual teachers. As reported by the Foundation for Individual Rights and Expression (FIRE) (Piro and Morey) in the 2022 case against Aneil Rallin mounted by a private liberal arts college, Soka University of America, trigger warnings may be no guarantee against employment precarity or academic freedom. The weaponization of trigger warnings on both sides of the debate, as alluded to in this volume by Wendy Hayden (Chapter 6) and Morgan Read-Davidson (Chapter 9), should arouse caution, just as their instrumentalization in accusations of "wokeness" warrants some scrutiny as discussed by Paolena Comouche (Chapter 14). Consequently, possible middle-of-the-road alternatives (especially given the association of the term "trigger warning" with weapons of violence) such as content notifications and advisories have merited consideration and their relative advantages are variously elucidated in preceding chapters by Rhyan Warmerdam (Chapter 5), Whitney Lew James (Chapter 17) and Pauline Menchavez (Chapter 18).

Is there a way out of this impasse and if so, where might we look for viable propositions? Considering that trigger warnings first emerged in the context of feminist responses to triggering online content[4] and given that the dilemmas they pose often revolve around the place of emotions in pedagogical praxis, one possibility, it seems to me, would be to turn to insights issuing from feminist scholarship, particularly on affect and emotions. In what follows, rather than rehearsing all aspects of this debate whose contours have been meticulously delineated by the authors and editors of this book, I attempt to situate in such a dialogue some of the salient issues they raise.

One of the central dilemmas related to the use of trigger warnings stems from the undecidability of what constitutes trauma and for whom, and of the relative merits/disadvantages of engaging with/avoiding disruptive encounters with pedagogical resources. A lack of clarity about the nature of trauma has only amplified dubiousness about the use of trigger warnings. The recurring conflation of trauma with post-traumatic stress disorder (PTSD) and other forms of psychological pain has led to hesitancy about its widespread and indiscriminate applicability, as pointed out by Greg Lukianoff as well as several contributors to this book. Despite trauma's visceral physiological impact, a vernacularizing of the term in current cultural contexts has given way to flattened definitions, blurriness, and confusion over its meanings. Jack Halberstam, in particular, famously raised significant concerns about the risks of oversimplified understandings of trauma that could lead to reductive responses to materials students might encounter in the classroom. For others, however, overfamiliarity with the term and its occasional trivialization does little to negate the fact that trauma's aftermaths continue to proliferate in the face of various forms of violence and precarity that we live in today, and that seem to have only exacerbated in post-COVID years. From such a perspective, an outright dismissal of trauma's perils may just as easily obscure the pain of those most at risk to be re-traumatized, raising serious concerns about student safety.

In this context, a recurring issue seems to be that although clinical definitions of trauma are tied to embodiment, it is often misidentified with more generalized experiences of emotional or intellectual discomfort, aspects of which are discussed by several of the authors.[5] These perspectives address the significant distinction between emotional trauma that threatens to arrest learning, and intellectual discomfort/unease that may manifest as reluctance to engage with unsettling ideas. Where a re-traumatization of emotional pain could *accidentally* foreclose learning, intellectual discomfort might *intentionally* foreclose it, occasioning dilemmas about the suitability of trigger warnings in situations where it may be impossible to anticipate the nature of responses. It is also possible that preventing encounters with certain materials may forestall the growth and transformation that comes with "new forms of knowing" as suggested by Kelli Fuery (Chapter 2). As many of us who include literary texts in our syllabi might have experienced, prose and poetry offer prime examples of materials that hold the promise of enriching transformative encounters evoked by devices including imagery, symbolism, and metaphor, but which could be read in reductive, literalist ways[6] (see preceding discussions about genre by Michele Parker Randall, Chapter 8 and Pauline Menchavez, Chapter 18). Moreover, the distinction between intellectual discomfort and emotional trauma is complicated as soon as its undergirding cognition/emotion dichotomy is contested. Since knowledge may be *simultaneously* encountered intellectually and emotionally, cognitive discomfort and embodied trauma could share fuzzy boundaries. If the lines between feeling and knowing are blurred both in the classroom and in the world outside, how does one decide if a film/image/text/poem has the capacity to provoke an affective trauma or intellectual reluctance, and whether trigger warnings will serve to avert the pain of re-traumatization or only prevent the joy of new learning, a de-traumatization that may suggest alternative conceptions of "care"?

Interrogating the inadequacy of the deeply rooted cognition/emotion binary in the west, affect theory has underscored the stratified privileging of reason/intellect over emotion/feeling to draw attention to the significance of embodied emotions. Building on work by Brian Massumi and other affect theorists, feminist scholarship has turned to issues such as the pervasiveness of the social surveillance of affect and its relationship to power and politics. For instance, Jasbir Puar asserts that "bodily processes (how things feel) must be irreducibly central to any notion of the political"

(151), emphasizing the significance of *both* embodiment and sociality in approaches to affect. Similarly, in referencing the work of affect theorists including Ahmed, Ngai, Berlant, Sedgwick, and Massumi, Anna Ioanes notes that "theories of affect emphasize both the embodied experience of feeling and the cultural politics of those feelings—how people use representation to harness and construct feeling and make things happen in the world" (58). Attending to a feminist lens on sociality and the cultural politics of emotions may offer insights for widening a narrow focus on fragmented measures for dealing with trauma. It may also allow us to readjust the tunnel vision often generated by the fetishization of embodied emotions in neoliberal economies.

It is no secret that subject to consumerist pressures, higher educational institutions in capitalist economies rely on corporatized, neoliberal frameworks of health and wellness within which emotions find their value in promoting a sense of wellbeing perceived as intrinsic to productivity. In a neoliberal ethos that thrives on atomization, personal wellbeing gets constructed as owned commodity, faculty as able workers, and students as clients. Health and wellness, of both instructors and students, are therefore crucial to sustaining ability and ensuring successful outcomes. Feminist disability scholars like Angela Carter have argued that the debate about trauma is itself located in a culture of ableism and call for an understanding of trauma as a state of disability, as also referenced in this book by Kristi M. Wilson (Chapter 1). Beyond helping us frame trauma as disability, feminist disability studies resists neoliberal formulations of capacity and debility by complicating our understandings of trauma through an affective politics that interrogates the privileging of certain traumas and the silencing of others. As Puar observes, "attachments to the difference of disabled bodies may reify an exceptionalism that only certain privileged disabled bodies can occupy" (153). If, as Puar asserts, "all bodies are being evaluated in relation to their success or failure in terms of health, wealth, progressive productivity, upward mobility, enhanced capacity" (155), and debility is a state to be anticipated by everyone (if not already experienced by all), it becomes incumbent to think of forms of trauma that remain unacknowledged in neoliberal capitalism. In this regard, the editors' suggestion in their introduction that the term trauma be employed "loosely" facilitates a conception of trauma as something that, for one reason or another, impacts us all and debilitates us in varying degrees.

Contra such a flexible approach, neoliberalism's sustained interest in individuated models of care may result in an implicit pecking order of susceptibilities to trauma in pedagogical spaces, both in terms of who is vulnerable, and which topics should be deemed as triggering. At a time when, according to Athanasiou et al., we are witnessing "the commodification and spectacularisation of global victimhood" (8), such hierarchizations may only aggravate suspicions about the susceptibility of trauma discourse to claims of privilege. After all, we are led to ask, whose trauma gets represented in an implicit prioritizing of who can be traumatized? And what about those pervasive systemic traumas that, as the editors point out, "*affect us all*" (Ian Barnard et al., Editors' Introduction) and may easily escape attention?

Among the most endemic traumas, undoubtedly, sexual violence, along with gender and racial violence, remains a burning issue in a renewed cultural pledge to toxic forms of hegemonic masculinity under Trumpism. Given its rampancy, trigger warnings may continue to offer one strategy for shielding students against re-traumatization risked in unprepared exposure to disturbing representations of violence. At the same time, it is worth recalling that since the need for trigger warnings first arose in feminist responses to triggering online content about sexual violence, feminist discourse has evolved nuanced understandings of violence that attend to intersectional formulations of identity and account for gender alongside sexuality, race, ethnicity, class, disability, religion, caste, age, and other aspects assailable by varying systemic oppressions. The traumas of racism, colorism, imperialism, ethnocentrism, homophobia, transphobia, Islamophobia, classism, ableism, and others within which we are all immersed may be invisibilized by adopting selective approaches to trauma's manifestations, as discussed by several contributors, including Ryan Ashley Caldwell (Chapter 10), Walter Lucken IV (Chapter 13), Kevin C. Moore (Chapter 16), and gestured at by the bulleted list of triggers offered at the end of Aneil Rallin's chapter (Chapter 11). When trauma discourse becomes the go to escape hatch for the loudest voices that might end up dominating the classroom, certain student demographics may get overlooked, casting doubts about the effectiveness of trigger warnings as guarantees of inclusivity. Among others, these demographics, as Corrine E. Hinton points out, may include student veterans and military affiliated learners (Chapter 15), or those subjected to neglected forms of structural racism such as linguistic hegemonies as discussed by Gregory Shafer (Chapter 12).

Neoliberalism's valuation of health and wellness in relation to productivity permeates institutional systems to pathologize approaches to learning, shifting at least some of the onus of sustaining wellness on to instructors. As support for mental health has increasingly become the responsibility of teachers,[7] employers may expect them to incorporate emotional care as an aspect of their pedagogy. While most teachers are not trained therapists, we may be inclined to offer emotional care in an effort to be kind to students and, as Morgan Read-Davidson reminds us, it "cannot hurt us to learn more" (Chapter 9). Still, the pathologization of pedagogy steeped in a medicalized ethos of care suggested by a vocabulary of diagnoses (trauma), inoculations, and prophylactics (trigger warnings/content notifications) and therapy (safe spaces), is primed to foster productivity, efficiency, and profit by promoting neoliberal ideals of individual wellness. In the process, it might squeeze out room for alternative models of collective wellbeing and spaces of mutual affective encounters, severing us from what Sophia Greco refers to as our "relational nature" (Chapter 3). The occlusion of a politics of mutual affective care by neoliberal agendas obliges us to ask what it means to "care" for the safety and success of students in instances when collective engagement may be precisely the recommended therapy, and when preventing pedagogical encounters through trigger warnings may, in fact, be counter-therapeutic as David J. Morris notes (Chapter 7). Given that we operate within violence-inured cultures that both generate traumatic encounters *and* require individualized preventive strategies to safeguard those at risk of re-traumatization, trigger warnings will most likely continue to be regarded as vital strategies by many. That said, the lone student, free to exit the classroom, turn off their camera, not read a certain novel, brush past a page, not see a sentence—encourages a conceptualization of re-traumatization primarily in the form of isolated encounters with troubling content. It returns us to the conundrum addressed by many of the authors in this book—some encouraging collective engagement with troubling content in the form of discussion, debate, and analysis, others urgently emphasizing the risks of underestimating the embodied dangers leveled by traumatizing materials on lone distressed bodies. It also leaves us to deal with trauma as a terminal end stop—an anticipated affliction for which trigger warnings serve as temporary preventive fixes—rather than as the symptom of a deeper cultural malaise whose roots are all pervasive.

Feminist interrogations of the appropriation of care work for financial gain may raise equally critical questions about approaches toward a pedagogy of care. Although pedagogical care work often aligns with progressive liberal views that tend to place such labor in opposition to capitalist economies, feminists have time and again demonstrated how capitalism continues to benefit from the exploitation of feminized emotional labor. Most recently, Nancy Fraser has drawn attention to the "romantic" (often anti-capitalist) view that imagines care work outside capitalism and as "intrinsically anti-capitalist" (22). This despite the fact that, according to Fraser, care is very much a part of the "enabling background conditions" that capitalism cannibalizes in order to sustain itself (23). In the context of corporatized educational economies built on the backs of capitalism, Fraser's work impels us to interrogate the feminized nature of pedagogical care work that often places higher expectations and greater burdens on certain instructors (such as women/of color and queer faculty) and on certain "soft" disciplines (which often include the liberal arts, gender studies, and other social justice-focused domains) to model best practices in pedagogies of care. Ultimately, Fraser's work provokes us to ask: when does the emotional labor of a pathologized pedagogy become the unwaged surplus component that the capitalist institution cannibalizes and whom does the freeriding benefit?[8]

This is not to suggest a turn away from attention to trauma and the care and prevention students rightly deserve in a liberatory pedagogy. Rather, calling upon feminist scholarship, I wonder if a resistance to the atomization of traumatized bodies could be envisioned through ways of thinking about emotions and feelings that deny their containment in unequally ranked bodies, severed from each other. Drawing upon Brian Massumi's work, renée hoogland emphasizes the distinction between emotions and affect. While emotions belong to psychological categories that "tend to personalize and depoliticize the operations of our current information," suggesting political inadequacy, affect is relational and neither pre-social nor reducible to personal psychology, leading hoogland to call for a "new vocabulary to theorize affect" (11). In a similar vein, Sara Ahmed's conceptualization of affective economies highlights the relational nature of emotions such that "feelings do not reside in subjects or objects, but are produced as effects of circulation" (8). Ahmed's perspective on the "sociality of emotion" contests the commonplace psychological interiority—"I have feelings, and they are mine" (8)—presumed in locating emotions as contained within discrete bodies, and may have particular resonances for thinking about how a pedagogy of care toward trauma may be differently imagined. Feminist affect theorists are not alone in aspiring to coalitional politics as a possible remedy to neoliberalism's focus on individualism, narrow identity politics, consumerism, and commodification. In contesting neoliberalism's atomistic individualism, Chris Beasley and Carol Bacchi propose the concept of "social flesh" as "a new ethico-political ideal" that highlights our "human *embodied* interdependence" (279). They see "social flesh" as a radical politics beyond a vocabulary of trust and care, of giver and taker, one that "presumes a role for theory in political praxis" and where "concepts are political interventions" (280). Further, "social flesh also marks our diversity, challenging the privileging of normative over 'other' bodies" and "puts into question the social privilege that produces inequitable vulnerability and the associated need for 'altruism'" (293).

These relational perspectives inspire a pedagogical praxis based on a coalitional politics that does not insist on atomizing and hierarchizing, so that none of us are left "alone" with our bad feelings. They also elicit a rethinking and redressal of trauma at the level of its embeddedness within larger systems that tend to normalize its systemic triggers, as for instance cisheteropatriarchy does for sexual/gender violence, and racism, ethnocentrism, and xenophobia do for various forms of racial violence and hate crimes. The classroom, by definition a place of collaborative learning where many bodies come together to forge collective encounters with knowledge (understood here as both ideational and experiential), is perhaps the ideal place for such a coalitional affective politics. While therapists are professionally trained to treat clinical forms of trauma and teachers are not, teachers are surely best placed to situate ideas and experiences in larger contexts, and to partner with students in identifying participatory opportunities for collective encounters, collaborations, and agentic decisions that make room for a concerted shift from self-care to mutual care, from safety and protection to agency and capacitation, from selection to inclusion.

How then do we imagine such a praxis? Given the exploratory nature of this afterword, I can only hazard a few tentative thoughts for collective strategies, and I am far from certain what concrete practices might emerge in specific classroom contexts even as many of us continue to rely on trigger warnings. Whether such strategies take the form of paired/small reading groups that explore shared reading/viewing activities, peer group conversations including about the pros and cons of tagging warnings onto a specific resource prior to assigning it, whole classroom discussions aimed at identifying structural causations of certain forms of trauma in the context of systemic conditions that have made them inevitable, or other suitable exercises devised in consultation by a classroom community would of course depend on individual instructional contexts. While it is possible that not all materials perceived to be potentially traumatic facilitate collective participation and immersion, a communal mulling over that engages with the debate about trigger warnings may function as its own kind of affective bulwark for mitigating trauma's effects in an environment that allows us to come together and acknowledge our "embodied interdependence." It might also enable us to collaboratively place in perspective the symptomatic nature of trauma and shift our gaze and our collective energies toward its root causes. For some of us, it is also conceivable that to prevent trigger warnings from arresting the engagement and dialogue that remains central to democratic teaching and learning, such warnings may need to come packaged with caveats about the potential losses that incur, a trigger warning with its own proviso! The delicate dance of warnings and mutual encounters that we all, as instructors and students, continue to partner in suggests neither that students are intentionally infantilized and "coddled," nor that all forms of warnings need to be disavowed outright. Rather, it is a reminder about the critical role that coalitional politics can play in a liberatory pedagogy.

These exploratory (after)thoughts are animated as much by insights proffered by feminist scholarship as by the nuanced approaches to the idea of the classroom as a safe space addressed by this book's contributors. These thoughtful approaches cast light on the classroom as contested space within which "care" is administered cautiously alongside the imparting of critical skills, and where safety and care must be carefully distinguished from policing. A refusal of neoliberal discourses of safety and security[9] hinging on protection and personal wellbeing calls for an expanded definition of the classroom as safe space. Even when trigger warnings are deemed necessary to keep trauma at bay, it may be productive to imagine how such a safe space could make room for disruptive "unsafe" ideas such as global war crimes and ethnic genocides whose horrors and traumas currently deserve our collective attention, and which may be pushed aside in the name of safety and "neutrality." A refusal to disavow resistance against the foreclosure of dialogue and the pressures of censorship might suggest inviting rather than precluding such "unsettling" ideas from the safe space of the classroom. If we are all subject to trauma, what better way to deal with our collective rage than to redirect it against the most common triggers of trauma—sexual violence, racism, xenophobia, transphobia, homophobia, cultural exceptionalism, imperialism, settler colonialism, classism, ableism, hetero-patriarchy, casteism—by grounding our pedagogy in a coalitional affective politics that enables a shift away from the atomized abjection that these reigning systems subject us to, to begin with? More questions than answers, as forewarned!

NOTES

1 See bell hooks' elaboration of "engaged pedagogy" in the context of Paulo Freire's concept of liberatory education that recognizes the humanity of all students.

2 See Jessica Shumake's (Chapter 19) discussion of concerns about employment precarity in relation to student feedback on potentially triggering material.

3 For a counter to the coddling argument, see Anna Klieber's 2021 essay listed in the Works Cited.

4 See Jennifer Medina, "Warning: The Literary Canon could Make Students Squirm."

5 Editors' Introduction; Kristi Wilson (Chapter 1); Megan Friess (Chapter 4); Rhyan Warmerdam (Chapter 5); Michele Parker Randall (Chapter 8); Morgan Read-Davidson (Chapter 9); Corrine E. Hinton (Chapter 15).

6 This is not to suggest that only metaphorical writing is liable to reductionism. Even spare, lyrical prose, as for instance, employed by Marguerite Duras in novels like *La Maladie de la Mort* and *Le ravissement de Lol V Stein*, which have the potential of powerful transformative encounters, may be susceptible to reductionist readings of sexuality and sexual violence.

7 See similar comments by Josalin J. Hunter cited by Corrine E. Hinton in Chapter 15.

8 See, especially, Chapter 3, "Care Guzzler: Why Social Reproduction is a Major Site of Capitalist Crisis" in Fraser's book, *Cannibal Capitalism* (53–74), for a discussion of capitalist freeriding on feminized labor.

9 For important insights, see Kevin Moore's discussion of "safetyism" in Chapter 16.

WORKS CITED

Ahmed, Sara. "Introduction: Feel Your Way." *The Cultural Politics of Emotion*. Routledge, 2004, pp. 1–19.

Athanasiou, Athena, Pothiti Hantzaroula, and Kostas Yannakopoulos. "Towards a New Epistemology: The 'Affective Turn.'" *Historein*, vol. 8, 2008, pp. 5–16.

Beasley, Chris, and Carol Bacchi. "Envisaging a New Politics for an Ethical Future: Beyond Trust, Care and Generosity—Towards an Ethic of 'Social Flesh.'" *Feminist Theory*, vol. 8, no. 3, 2007, pp. 279–98.

Carter, Angela M. "Teaching with Trauma: Disability Pedagogy, Feminism, and the Trigger Warnings Debate." *Disability Studies Quarterly*, vol. 35, no. 2, 2015.

Flaherty, Colleen. "Trigger Unhappy." *Inside Higher Ed.*, 13 April 2014, https://www.insidehighered.com/news/2014/04/14/oberlin-backs-down-trigger-warnings-professors-who-teach-sensitive-material.

Fraser, Nancy. *Cannibal Capitalism: How our System is Devouring Democracy, Care, and the Planet and What We Can Do About It*. Verso Books, 2023.

Halberstam, Jack. "Trigger Happy: From Content Warning to Censorship." *Signs: Journal of Women in Culture and Society*, vol. 42, no. 2, Jan. 2017, pp. 535–42.

Halberstam, Jack. "You Are Triggering Me! The Neo-Liberal Rhetoric of Harm, Danger and Trauma." *Bully Bloggers*, 2014.

hoogland, renée c. *Violent Embrace: Art and Aesthetics after Representation*. Dartmouth College P, 2014.

hooks, bell. "Engaged Pedagogy." *Teaching to Transgress*. Routledge, 1994, pp. 13–22.

Ioanes, Anna. "Feeling and Form." *the minnesota review*, no. 89, 2017, pp. 57–70.

Klieber, Anna. "On the Epistemology of Trigger Warnings: Or, Why the Coddling Argument Against Trigger Warnings Is Misguided." *Feminist Philosophy Quarterly*, vol. 7, no. 4, 2021.

Lukianoff, Greg, and Jonathan Haidt. "The Coddling of the American Mind." *The Atlantic*, Sept. 2015.

Lukianoff, Greg. "Trigger Warnings: A Gun to the Head of Academia." *Unsafe Space: The Crisis of Free Speech on Campus*. Palgrave Macmillan, 2016, pp. 58–67.

Massumi, Brian. "The Autonomy of Affect." *Cultural Critique*, no. 31, 1995, pp. 83–109.

Medina, Jennifer. "Warning: The Literary Canon Could Make Students Squirm." *The New York Times*, 17 May 2014.

Piro, Graham and Alex Morey. "Soka Professor Unjustly Punished for 'Triggering' Students with Readings on 'Writing the Body' Gets Split Decision from Faculty Committee of Just Two," *FIRE (Foundation for Individual Rights and Expression)*, 9 June 2022, https://www.thefire.org/news/soka-professor-unjustly-punished-triggering-students-readings-writing-body-gets-split-decision.

Puar, Jasbir K. "Coda: The Cost of Getting Better: Suicide, Sensation, Switchpoints." *GLQ*, vol. 18, no.1, 2012, pp. 149–58.

Notes on Editors and Contributors

Anu Aneja is Professor, Women and Gender Studies, at George Mason University. She has research interests in the areas of transnational feminist theory, affect and aesthetics and has explored their inventive crossings across South Asia and the west in *Feminist Theory and the Aesthetics Within: A perspective from South Asia* (2022). She is the editor of *Women's and Gender Studies in India: Crossings* (2019), a comprehensive anthology that maps the contemporary contours of the field, and coauthor of *Embodying Motherhood: Perspectives from Contemporary India* (2016, with Shubhangi Vaidya). She has also edited a focus volume on *Gender & Distance Education: Indian and International Contexts* (2019).

Ian Barnard (they/them/their) is Professor of Rhetoric and Composition at Chapman University, and the author of three monographs, including *Sex Panic Rhetorics, Queer Interventions* (U of Alabama P, 2020), winner of the 2021 Conference on College Composition and Communication Lavender Rhetorics Book Award for Excellence in Queer Scholarship.

Ryan Ashley Caldwell (they/them/their) is a philosopher-sociologist trained in critical cultural studies, applied ethics, and cultural theory. Ryan is a trans* gender queer/gender non-conforming (TGNC) nonbinary activist and professor-educator/learner, probably couldn't live without espresso, and has a Great Dane emotional support dog named Edwin. Dr. Caldwell's expertise is in gender and sexuality, narratives for body and embodiment, queer/queering archives, queer and transgender theory, and social epistemology. Their previous research focused on war crimes, where they were an expert witness at many of the courts-martial associated with Abu Ghraib and other military torture cases in Afghanistan and Iraq (see *Fallgirls*, 2013; *The Routledge Handbook of War and Society: Iraq and Afghanistan*, 2011). For the last decade, Ryan has engaged in public sociology as Sister Electra-Complex through drag-activism with the Los Angeles Sisters of Perpetual Indulgence, an international LGBTQIA2-S+ nonprofit. Ryan has most recently published about their service to the Sisters in *Imagined Bodies, Lived Ambiguities*, 2019.

Paolena Comouche received her bachelor's degree in journalism at California State University, Fullerton, and her master's degree in English at Chapman University. She is currently a PhD candidate in rhetoric and composition at the University of South Carolina, specializing in feminist rhetorics and new materialism.

Megan Friess is an avid, lifelong reader and writer who earned dual master's degrees in English and Creative Writing from Chapman University. She teaches English composition at Cypress, Saddleback, and Irvine Valley Colleges, public community colleges in California, and Creative Writing at the Orange County School of the Arts.

Kelli Fuery is Professor of Creative and Cultural Industries at Chapman University. Her research explores why we mediate the world around us in the ways that we do, examining how our inner worlds influence the social and cultural contexts which influence our choices. Focusing on various modes within visual culture, Fuery is interested in the positioning and mechanics of power and knowledge, the assembly and dismantling of structures, and the role ethics plays in the exchange of aesthesis. She is the author of six books and is a founding scholar for the British Psychoanalyst Council, an Editorial Board Member for *Film-Philosophy* journal, and Special Issues Editor for *Film Matters*.

Sophia Greco is a queer Chilean Californian writer, unschooler, language nerd, and fruit forager. They enjoy life most when collaborating with writers, abolitionists, radical educators, artists, and learners of all ages.

Wendy Hayden is Associate Professor of English and co-director of first-year composition at Hunter College, City University of New York. Her publications include *Evolutionary Rhetoric: Sex, Science, and Free Love in Nineteenth-Century Feminism*, articles in *CCC, College English, The Journal of Academic Librarianship,*

Rhetoric Review, and *Rhetoric Society Quarterly*, and a collection edited with Tarez Samra Graban, *Teaching through the Archives: Text, Collaboration, and Activism*.

Corrine E. Hinton is Dean of English and Humanities at Lincoln Land Community College and a veterans studies scholar who has been exploring the transitional experiences of post-9/11 veterans to higher education for over a decade. Her research has been published in *Composition Forum*, the *Journal of Veterans Studies*, and the collection, *Generation Vet: Composition, Veterans, and the Post-9/11 University* (Eds. Lisa Langstraat and Sue Doe, Utah State University, 2014). She has served as Junior and Senior Chair of *Writing with Current, Former, and Future Members of the Military*, a standing group of the Conference on College Composition and Communication (CCCC) and is currently Secretary of the Veterans Studies Association.

Whitney Lew James is an Assistant Teaching Professor at the University of Notre Dame whose teaching and research traverses digital cultural rhetorics, translingual and antiracist pedagogy, and disability rhetorics.

Walter Lucken IV is Assistant Professor of English at Queens College, where he teaches rhetoric and literature courses in the Search for Education, Elevation, and Knowledge (SEEK) program. His writing has appeared in *Michigan Quarterly Review*, *Community Literacy Journal*, *Art & the Public Sphere*, and *Refractions Journal*.

Pauline Menchavez is a graduate student in English Rhetoric and Composition and a First-Year Composition (FYC) instructor at California State University, Long Beach. Her research concerns the impact of digital rhetoric and participatory cultures on the teaching of writing and composition, as well as how these networked communities shape identity and ontology.

Kevin C. Moore is an Advanced Lecturer in the Program in Writing and Rhetoric at Stanford University, and the Coordinator of Stanford's Notation in Science Communication. He holds a PhD in English from UCLA. His current research interests include propaganda studies and scientific communication.

David J. Morris is a former Marine and the author of *The Evil Hours: A Biography of Post-traumatic Stress Disorder* (Mariner, 2016). From 2004 to 2007, he worked as a reporter in Iraq. He teaches creative writing at University of Nevada, Las Vegas.

Jada Patchigondla has been teaching writing at the university level for the past twelve years and is passionate about demystifying writing and the writing process for students, especially those from disadvantaged backgrounds. She is currently a lecturer in the Writing Programs at UCLA.

Aneil Rallin (they/them/their) is a recovering academic who has survived working at nine universities in the United States and Canada (including Soka University of America, York University, California State University, San Marcos, and University of Southern California), author of *Dreads and Open Mouths: Living/Teaching/Writing Queerly* (Litwin Books), coeditor of a special issue "Queer and Now" of *The Writing Instructor*, and convener of the special issue "Rhet/Comp for Palestine: A Gathering of Spirit" of *The Journal of Multimodal Rhetorics*.

Michele Parker Randall is a Sullivan Visiting Lecturer at Stetson University, and teaches Poetry, Fairy Tales, and the Literature of Mental Health (Neurodivergent Lit). Author of *Museum of Everyday Life* (Kelsay Books 2015) and *A Future Unmappable*, chapbook (Finishing Line Press 2021).

Morgan Read-Davidson is an Associate Professor at Chapman University, where he directs the Rhetoric and Composition program. He teaches both rhetoric and creative writing, with a focus on composition pedagogy, posthuman rhetorics, ludonarratology and game writing, screenwriting, and fiction.

Gregory Shafer has graduate degrees from Michigan State University and the University of Michigan. He has taught at Mott Community College in Flint, Michigan for almost thirty years and has published articles in *English Journal* and *Community College Journal of Research and Practice* and many other publications. He was the editor of *Language Arts Journal of Michigan* from 2016 to 2019.

Jessica Shumake (she/they) is an assistant teaching professor of writing and rhetoric at the University of Notre Dame. Their research draws from community-engaged writing, archives and public memory, and gender and sexuality studies.

Ethan Trejo is a doctoral student at the University of Southern California, working toward a PhD in English with a graduate certificate in Gender and Sexuality Studies. He holds an MA in English from Chapman University and a BA in English and Political Science from Whittier College. His scholarship is largely situated in the fields of Queer Studies and Latinx Studies. His major interests lie in Joto Studies, Affect Theory, Performance Studies, Biopolitics, Television Studies, HIV/AIDS Studies, Drag Studies, and Contemporary Queer and Latinx Literature.

Rhyan Warmerdam received his MA in English from Chapman University in 2025. He currently teaches college composition at Northern Virginia Community College.

Kristi M. Wilson is a Professor of Rhetoric and Composition at Soka University of America. She is an editorial collective member at the journal *Latin American Perspectives*, and the coeditor of three anthologies on film and visual culture.